영어로 읽는 **먼나라 이웃나라** 12

United States of America

영어로 읽는 먼나라 이웃나라 제12권 미국 3
이원복 글·그림 | 은정 옮김

1판 1쇄 인쇄 2008. 12. 04. | 1판 1쇄 발행 2008. 12. 11. | 발행처 김영사 | 발행인 박은주 | 등록번호 제406-2003-036호 | 등록일자 1979. 5. 17. | 경기도 파주시 교하읍 문발리 출판단지 515-1 우편번호 413-756 | 마케팅부 031)955-3100, 편집부 031)955-3250, 팩시밀리 031)955-3111 | 저작권자 ⓒ 2008, 이원복 | 이 책의 저작권은 저자에게 있습니다. 서면에 의한 저자와 출판사의 허락없이 내용의 일부를 인용하거나 발췌하는 것을 금합니다. | COPYRIGHT ⓒ 2008 by Rhie, Won-Bok All rights reserved including the rights of reproduction in whole or in part in any form. Printed in KOREA | 값은 표지에 있습니다. | ISBN 978-89-349-3237-6 77940 | 좋은 독자가 좋은 책을 만듭니다. | 김영사는 독자 여러분의 의견에 항상 귀 기울이고 있습니다. | 독자의견 전화 031)955-3200 | 홈페이지 www.gimmyoung.com, 이메일 bestbook@gimmyoung.com

영어로 읽는 **먼나라 이웃나라**

United States of America

이원복 글·그림 | 은정 옮김

Won-bok RHIE

③

12

C O N T E N T S

As the person holding the highest office in the world's only superpower, the President of the United States is the most powerful person in the world. What kinds of persons have reached this office? To date, there have been 42 Presidents* over a period of 200-plus years. They have come from diverse backgrounds, as some were lawyers, soldiers, engineers and even tailors. But these persons all had one thing in common in that they were elected by the people as the best person to serve in the presidency and that they used their best efforts to serve the nation and the people. Among them, there were remarkably capable Presidents who nevertheless failed due to the difficulties of their times, while there were not so capable Presidents who still succeeded. All of these 42 Presidents did their best and have left their legacies in history.

Ever since the founding of the Republic of Korea, our nation has adopted the U.S.-style presidency. For the first time in history, the United States adopted a system by which the people elected the nation's leaders. Korea, which has emulated the United States, has also adopted such a presidential system. As such, in Korea too, the presidency is a most important office that steers the direction and determines the destiny of the nation. In this regard, as for these 42 U.S. Presidents, it is important for Koreans to know what kinds of persons have become President, which Presidents have succeeded and what were the reasons of their successes. This is why I have added this volume on U.S. Presidents as the third part of the *Monnara* series on the United States.

Whether we like it or not, we encounter reports on the U.S. President on a daily basis in newspapers and broadcast media. But we are only familiar with such well-known Presidents as Washington, Lincoln and Roosevelt and other Presidents who served in the late twentieth century. There are more Presidents with whom we are unfamiliar. If

---

* To date, although the U.S. has had 43 Presidents, only 42 persons have actually served in the office because Grover Cleveland served non-consecutive terms as the twenty-second and twenty-fourth Presidents.

we were to only look at achievements or historical significance, perhaps it would be sufficient to only look at a few major Presidents while disregarding the rest. But whether it's a stormy day or a warm breezy day, each day is recorded as just another day in the calendar. Likewise, each of the 42 Presidents has had his own share of both stormy and breezy days throughout his term.

Thus, there is no one President who can be written off as an unimportant President in U.S. history. This is why I have equally allocated six pages to each of the 42 Presidents in this book. I believe that this approach will help the reader to objectively evaluate each President, independently from the existing evaluations generally available on each President. Besides, there are many biographies and critical examinations of the lives of well-known Presidents. If I were to ignore the many other not so well known Presidents, Korean readers may never have the opportunity to become acquainted with those other Presidents. The purpose of this book is not to discuss the achievements of the U.S. Presidents, but to focus on the individual characteristics and the human sides of those persons who were elected by the American people as the best persons of the times to serve in the presidency.

After studying and writing about the Presidents, I have come to the conclusion that all "successful Presidents" have had one thing in common: They were "helped by their times" and were men of "vision." Some Presidents failed because they did not see that a crisis had dawned upon them, while other Presidents succeeded by using a "crisis" as an "opportunity." Clearly, all successful Presidents were men of keen insight who understood their times; they were also men who possessed the "vision" to clearly steer the nation in the right direction during their times.

I am grateful to President Eun-Ju Park and the employees of Gimm-Young Publishers for their support, and I also extend my sincere gratitude to my beloved students with the Grimmté Illustrator Group.

Won-bok Rhie

The *Monnara* series was first published and introduced to readers in book format in 1987. The series was subsequently revamped and supplemented and republished as the *New Monnara* series in 1998. Since then, the world has changed so much, and we now live in a new century. The 20th century has ended, and we now have entered the 21st century. Every five years, I revamp or revise the *Monnara* series so that I can provide information that does not lag behind the times to my readers. Due to the ever-increasing pace by which the world is changing, this work will probably have to be performed more frequently in the future.

The *21st Century Monnara* series is different from the previous edition in two major aspects. First, the black-and-white format has been changed to an all-color format, and the series has been supplemented with much more vivid illustrations of historical materials. I believe that the more elegant but subtle all-color edition will provide a more lively and interesting reading experience to the newer generation of my readers raised in the age of visuality and color. Second, since historical materials are graphically illustrated next to the relevant content, I am confident that my readers will come away with a more vivid experience of history and culture and deeper understanding of the persons who have moved history of mankind.

My beloved students with the Grimmté Illustrator Group have participated in the computer coloring works with much devotion. This was a huge endeavor that involved the coloring of almost 3,000 pages of manuscript. I convey my sincere gratitude and affection to them. Also, I could not have completed the *21st Century Monnara* series without the strong support and cooperation of President Eun-Ju Park and the entire staff of Gimm-Young Publishers. I convey my sincere gratitude to them as well.

The *Monnara* series, which is in its sixteenth year of publication, is rare in that not many works of comic have had the unflagging support of readers that I enjoyed over such a long period. This has been a source of both pride and responsibility for me, and I promise to continue to make every effort to improve the *Monnara* series for my readers in the future.

Won-bok Rhie

George Washington 1789~1797

America's Founding Father who Laid the Foundation of Democracy

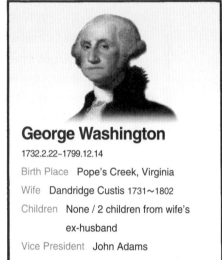

George Washington

1732.2.22~1799.12.14

Birth Place   Pope's Creek, Virginia

Wife   Dandridge Custis 1731~1802

Children   None / 2 children from wife's ex-husband

Vice President   John Adams

George Washington, a great man, is most respected by Americans as their national father and even as a sage.

His name lives on as the names of the capital city of the United States and a state.

Most significantly, Washington served as the first President of the United States.

The 1st President of the USA

He was elected to the presidency, an office that did not exist in any other country.

As an elected leader, which was unprecedented,

he laid the foundation of a new nation by admirably overcoming obstacle after obstacle where there was no precedent to follow.

Born as the son of a wealthy plantation owner in Virginia,

Washington left school at the age of 15.

He wasn't as knowledgeable in history as Thomas Jefferson* or resourceful as James Madison,**

*3rd President **4th President

but he was a great leader who could inspire people with his clear judgment and prominent leadership.

His half-brother Lawrence was a great influence on the young Washington.

Attracted by Lawrence's stories on military life, he tried to enlist in the British Navy.

However, his widowed mother persuaded him otherwise, so instead of joining the navy, he worked as a land surveyor for six years from the age of 15.

*Washington the surveyor (right)

When he was 21 (1753), he joined the Virginia militia,

and later on was detached to the regular British army to fight in the French and Indian War.

French and Indian War

1754~1763

France — alliance — Indians — Britain

After the war, Washington returned to the Mount Vernon plantation he had inherited from his parents.

*Washington's Mount Vernon residence.

At that time, he met his wife-to-be Martha Dandridge Custis,

the widow of Daniel Park Custis, once the richest man in Virginia.

Martha Dandridge Custis

1731 Born
1749 Married to Custis
1757 Widowed
1759 Remarried to Washington

Through his marriage to Custis in 1759, Washington came to own more than 3,000 slaves and 17,000 acres of land.

He eventually became one of the wealthiest men in Virginia, with his land holdings alone reaching 22,000 acres (about 34 million pyong).

After Washington became President, his slaves outnumbered the civil servants employed by the U.S. federal government.

Perhaps this is why he refused to serve a third term as President.

Anyway, when the Revolutionary War started, Washington emerged from his quiet life at Mount Vernon and became commander of the colonial forces.

*Washington crossing the Delaware River

He overcame all sorts of hardship and finally won victory, achieving independence for America.

After winning the Revolutionary War, Washington returned to his hometown without any lingering attachments.

However, in 1787, he became the representative of Virginia,

and finally, in 1789, he was elected as the first President of the United States.

Number of Votes per Candidate	
G. Washington	69
J. Adams	34
J. Jay	9
R. Harrison	6
J. Rutledge	6
J. Hancock	4
G. Clinton	3

Standing tall at 185cms, George Washington was a physically imposing man.

Although he was a war hero who had achieved victory in the Revolutionary War, Washington's reputation as a soldier was no match for his reputation as a man with impeccable character.

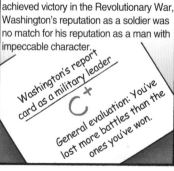

Instead, what earned him immortal fame was his decision, as the first President, to leave office on his own initiative.

When America was born as a country and Washington became inaugurated as its first President,

*Washington taking the presidential oath of office.

the American people didn't understand the concept of the presidency.

President? Democracy?

It's supposed to exist only in America.

Most people thought the President was an 'elected king.'

So kings can be elected too?

Well, since there's no king in America, I suppose the first one has to be elected.

Washington conducted himself in such fashion.

Social classes will not disappear.

Ruled class

Ruling class

Initially, he liked the title 'Your Highness.'

Your Highness!

His attitude bore an air of regalia, and he desired to be treated like a king.

Like the kings of other nations who referred to themselves in the third person,

He said you are welcome to this country...

I guess a king couldn't refer to himself as 'I,' like his subject.

Washington also referred to himself in the third person.

He wishes to be served dinner!

Yes, Sire!

He held numerous receptions and parties modeled after those held by European royalty,

and traveled throughout America like the British Queen.

The people received him with splendid welcoming ceremonies as if he were a king.

Long Live Washington!

HURRAY

HURRAH

Long Live His Majesty!

He probably dreamed that America, one day, would become stronger than Britain or France, perhaps as a much more powerful empire.

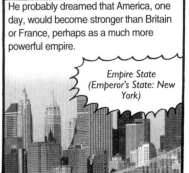

Empire State (Emperor's State: New York)

*Empire State Building

Washington's regal manner

He must think he's a real king!

strengthened the newly created U.S. presidency in the new nation known as America from the very beginning.

Washington was instrumental in empowering the Office of President!

*White House Logo

More than anyone else, Washington helped shape the U.S. presidency, where there was no precedent to follow.

President

The 10-year period that followed Washington's inaugural year of 1789 was marked by division and political infighting more than any time in U.S. history.

Federalists

Anti-federalists

GRRR

Federalists who wanted to create an even stronger federal government

We can create a strong nation

only if a strong federal government rules over and directs the states!

Federal Gov't

State State State State State

severely clashed with Anti-federalists who wanted to retain independence and autonomy of the states.

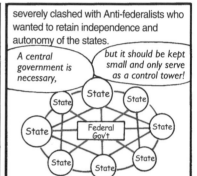

A central government is necessary,

but it should be kept small and only serve as a control tower!

State State State
State Federal Gov't State
State State State

Washington evenly appointed cabinet members from both sides to balance

Federalists

Anti-federalists

and mediate the situation that could have led to a bloody confrontation.

Wait!

When the Whiskey Rebellion, an uprising of thousands of farmers who opposed a tax on whiskey, occurred,

If you suddenly raise the tax on whiskey just because of the lack of budget funds,

you'll reduce the demand for whiskey! Are we to starve to death?

ROAR ROAR

he used force to put it down, and in doing so preserved the dignity of the government.

Whoomp!

By using both carrot and stick, Washington showed virtuoso leadership skills.

When his second term ended in 1797, the people requested that he continue to serve as President.

President forever!

No, You should be king!

Washington, however, firmly turned down that request.

If I were to serve a third term as President,

in the future, there will be dreadful political fighting to hold onto power on a long-term basis.

Re-election, 3rd term, 4th term... Forever!

As he left the presidency, Washington issued his famous Farewell Address, which lives on to this day as a sacred historical statement of American values.

With this address, I bid you farewell my dear citizens...

Farewell Address

In the Farewell Address, he emphasized the importance of unity above all,

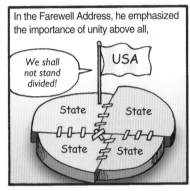

We shall not stand divided!

USA

State   State

State   State

and warned Americans of the dangers of extreme partisan confrontation.

Hey, cut it out!

He also warned against excessive dependence and antagonism in America's external relationship with foreign powers.

Whatever you do, do it in moderation!

After finishing his term, without any lingering attachments to the presidency, he returned to his private residence at Mount Vernon, where he passed away two years later

*Washington on his deathbed

in 1799. The two-term tradition that he established

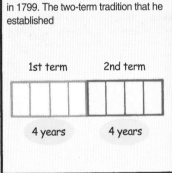

1st term	2nd term
4 years	4 years

operated as a hard-and-fast rule and was seen as a virtue of moderation until it was broken by Franklin D. Roosevelt in 1940.

After Roosevelt, Amendment 22 to the Constitution

barred Presidents from running for President more than twice.

4th term

Washington, as the founding father of America and its first President, showed how a leader should conduct himself when his time is up.

Bye   Bye

Washington supported patrician politics and acted regally. By doing so, even though he did not popularize politics,

Power isn't for everyone.

Power

Danger

he still played a great role in creating mass democracy in the United States.

George Washington,

a remarkable man, enabled the rule of the common ordinary man.

John Adams 1797~1801

Man of Self-sacrifice who Put Country before Ambition

John Adams

Conviction for my country

No! No!

John Adams

Federalist Party, 1735.10.30~1826.7.4

Birth Place Braintree, Massachusetts

Wife Abigail Smith Adams 1744~1818

Children Abigail, John Quincy, Susannah, Charles, Thomas

Vice President Thomas Jefferson

John Adams, who succeeded Washington as the second President, wasn't really presidential material.

He was wise and well studied, and made many contributions to the founding of the United States.

But his picky, irritable and hot temper made him many political enemies that led him to fail as President.

Re-election

Adams was more deeply and widely educated than any other man during his times.

John Adams

Thomas Jefferson

Benjamin Franklin

He was born into a wealthy family in Braintree*, Massachusetts,

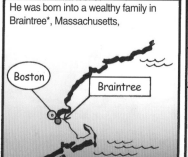

Boston

Braintree

and became a lawyer at the early age of 23 in 1758 after graduating from Harvard University.

Wow~ A genius! How'd you do it at so young an age...

It was the norm during those days.

*Braintree: Nowadays known as Quincy

He was especially very knowledgeable about British law and history.

In colonial America, we, of course, studied the law and history of Britain, our home country.

After he left the presidency and until his death, he authored many books in these fields.

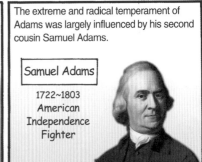

The extreme and radical temperament of Adams was largely influenced by his second cousin Samuel Adams.

Samuel Adams

1722~1803
American Independence Fighter

Adams entered politics through the opposition movement against the Stamp Act of 1765.

All colonial goods must bear revenue stamps to show that taxes have been paid.

No way!

Britain

America

Surprisingly, five years later, he defended a British officer who was involved in the Boston Massacre.

How could he defend a Briton!

Well, isn't that his job as a lawyer?

Adams drafted the Declaration of Independence with Thomas Jefferson.

THE DECLARATION OF INDEPENDENCE

Adams and Jefferson, once comrades, later on confronted each other as Jefferson became the most significant political adversary of Adams.

Federalist!

Anti-federalist!

In 1780, Adams drafted the Constitution of Massachusetts, his home state.

These skills came in handy

when I later on drafted the Federal Constitution.

Toward the end of the Revolutionary War, when the Americans conducted negotiations for independence with Britain in Paris,

Adams joined Benjamin Franklin and John Jay as America's representatives.

B. Franklin   J. Jay   J. Adams

He took the lead in obtaining Britain's recognition of America's independence in 1783,

Independence shall be recognized as long as America does not meddle with Canada!

and became the first Vice President of the United States.

Bam ba bam!

John Adams, who became the second President in 1797,

I shall adhere to the Constitution...

received Thomas Jefferson as his Vice President due to the now-repealed system under which the presidential candidate with the second most electoral votes became Vice President.

This is going to be a major headache.

Instead of assisting Adams during his four-year term, Jefferson became a thorn in his side by opposing his policies to the end.

Hey, cut it out right now!

This was because Jefferson was a central leader of the Anti-federalist camp,

If the federal government increases in size, it will repress freedom and independence of the states!

Jefferson faction

whereas Adams was an ardent Federalist. The two men held diametrically opposite political ideologies.

Without a strong central government, America will remain as a third-rate country!

Adams faction

Naturally, discord and bad feelings only deepened between the President and the Vice President.

Rrrrip!

Amer ica

The most serious problem confronting Adams as President was the conflict between Britain and France.

France   Britain

America

As a newborn nation, America was insignificant and weak.

I'm powerless...

Britain and France competed with each other to exert influence on the American continent.

America

They fought with each other to bring America to its knees to control the newborn nation.

I'll give you a hard time if you don't join my camp!

In particular, Britain seized American ships and forced American seamen to serve in the British military.

All of this reached a point that could no longer be tolerated by America.

Even though we're a weak nation, this is too much!

So Adams sent three emissaries to France, which was at war with Britain.

Let's get France involved to check Britain's hostilities.

Control a heathen with another heathen.

This dispatch of emissaries became known as the so-called 'XYZ Affair.'

*XYZ referred to the emissaries.

When the emissaries went to France and explained America's position, the French Minister of Foreign Affairs Talleyrand demanded a huge bribe.

*Caricature that depicts France demanding a bribe

This episode outraged the American public.

The President sent emissaries without even asking Congress?!

And they returned after receiving many insults?

The pro-British, anti-French faction led by Hamilton demanded that strong measures be taken against France,

Aren't we going to take action against the arrogant French?

Declare war right away!!

Roarrr!!

thereby forcing Adams to enter an undeclared war with France.

Tung

Hey!

At the same time, anti-French sentiments greatly increased.

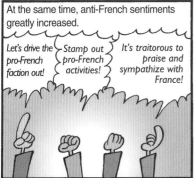

Let's drive the pro-French faction out!

Stamp out pro-French activities!

It's traitorous to praise and sympathize with France!

Adams signed the Alien and Sedition Act that could penalize anyone who cooperated with France and other foreign countries.

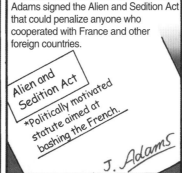

Alien and Sedition Act

*Politically motivated statute aimed at bashing the French.

J. Adams

The pretext of this statute was to prevent instigation, espionage and traitorous acts,

Fr...

Anyone praising France is a traitor!

---

but, in essence, it was a very undemocratic statute that silenced and blocked the ears of the people.

In the name of national security...

Naturally, opposition by Jefferson and other Anti-federalists friendly to France became stronger,

To support France is nothing more than a movement to overthrow the government!

That's just a conspiracy to silence the people!

leading to a more fierce fight with the Federalists.

Anti-British!

Thump

Plump

Anti-French!

Adams, who was waging a war without any particular justification or benefit,

Why are we in this war?

Beats me...

eventually entered into a truce with France.

Let's stop this useless war of attrition!

Ok, we're already pretty busy fighting the British.

This time, the pro-British Federalists became enraged and turned their backs on Adams.

As a Federalist yourself, how dare you betray your comrades?

ROAR
ROAR

For the American national interest, Adams had sent the emissaries to France and later on entered into the truce.

One side is crying out for war,

while the other side is demanding a truce.

Don't you know all this partisan fighting only hurts our country?

However, he ended up becoming estranged not only from his political enemies the Anti-federalists (led by Jefferson),

Undemocratic!

Oppressor of the people!

Hard core pro-British

Fickle as a weed!

but also his comrades the Federalists (led by Hamilton).

Turncoat

Traitor

President without a backbone

Incompetent!

Both his enemies and allies disregarded his foreign policies and his administration, which were based on his conviction.

CHILL

As a result, Adams lost the 1800 presidential election to Jefferson.

#1	Thomas Jefferson	73
#2	Aaron Burr	73
#3	John Adams	65
#4	C. Pinckney	64

After all, for his country, he had set aside his personal ambition of becoming re-elected as President.

I won't bend my conviction just to become re-elected as President again!

I really hate the way my opponents sway public opinion!

His irritable and hot-tempered personality was revealed again at the end of his term. He didn't even attend Jefferson's inauguration.

I can't stand the sight of Jefferson!

Inauguration ceremony →

On the eve of his last day in office, he appointed John Marshall as Chief Justice of the United States, which selection Jefferson had opposed.

Give Jefferson a hard time forever.

Of course!

He also appointed many persons—who became known as the 'midnight cabinet'—from his faction to important government posts.

Jefferson, it ain't going to be easy!

Public Notice

Secretary of ✕✕
Secretary of △△
Secretary of ✕△   All from Adams' faction
Secretary of △✕
Secretary of ○○   Federalists
Secretary of △○

His appointment of Marshall as Chief Justice was an important step toward establishing the judicial branch's independence from presidential powers,

which led to the separation of powers among the legislative, executive and judicial branches.

After losing the presidential election, John Adams returned to his hometown Braintree,

and spent much of his time writing books for the next 25 years until his death.

Toward the end of his life, Adams reconciled

with Jefferson, his long-time comrade and enemy.

On July 4, 1826, which was the fiftieth anniversary of American independence,

John Adams passed away.

His last words are quoted as...

But that wasn't true. Jefferson had died a few hours earlier than Adams.

John Adams sacrificed his personal ambition for his country.

From Adams, we discover that political failures are irrelevant when evaluating a true leader.

Thomas Jefferson 1801~1809

Author of the Declaration of American Independence, of the Statute of Virginia for Religious Freedom and Father of the University of Virginia*

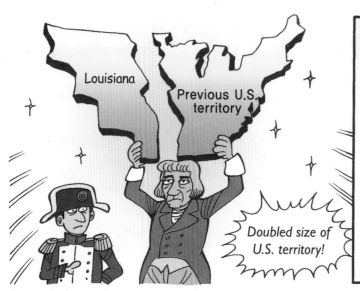

Louisiana

Previous U.S. territory

Doubled size of U.S. territory!

Thomas Jefferson

Anti-federalist Party (Democratic-Republican Party), 1743.4.13~1826.7.4

Birth Place   Goochland County, Virginia

Wife   Martha Wayles Skelton Jefferson
1748~1782

Children   Martha, Jane, stillborn son, Mary, Woodson, Beverly Hemings, Madison Hemings, Easton Hemings

Vice Presidents   A. Burr, 1801
G. Clinton 1805

*Jefferson's epitaph

Among all U.S. Presidents, Thomas Jefferson was the most well-educated and talented man.

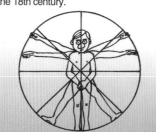

With Benjamin Franklin, he is regarded as the foremost Renaissance Man* of the 18th century.

America was clearly lucky to have had such a President as its leader.

What advantage does a presidential system have over a monarchy system?

The best person of the times can be selected as the leader!

*A person with encyclopedic knowledge whose thinking is based on humanism

At 190cms, Jefferson boasted a big frame that was larger than Washington's,

I'm pretty tall myself...

but due to his informal and shy personality, he didn't enjoy appearing in public.

Sir, everyone's waiting for your speech.

No way!

During his eight-year term, he only gave two public speeches.

The first time was when I gave my first inaugural speech.

The second time was when I gave my second inaugural speech.

He was a plantation owner and lawyer, diplomat and architect and scientist and philosopher.

He was also an inventor, hobby musician, founder of a university and President of the United States.

Jefferson was born as the son of a famous and wealthy plantation owner in Albemarle County, Virginia.

Young Master Thomas.

After graduating from the College of William & Mary, he started his career as a lawyer.

Named after William III and Queen Mary II

who ascended to the British throne through the Glorious Revolution.

The College of William & Mary

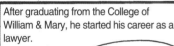

Heavily influenced by the Enlightenment and the human rights movement in Europe,

Break the chains of class!

No human being is more or less than another!

Jefferson joined the fight against Britain from 1769.

I hate Britain and love France.

In 1776, he drafted the famous American Declaration of Independence.

I'm from the 386 generation!

In my 30s, I joined the independence movement. In the 1780s, I became a legislator. In my 60s, I served as President.

Declaration of Independence

During the Revolutionary War, he served as Governor of Virginia

I was behind the battle lines since I wasn't a soldier.

Bang bang!

and commenced the procedures to repeal slavery in Virginia.

One day...

Although he criticized slavery, he was one of the many American slave owners during the early years of the nation.

Slavery is a really shameful and inhumane institution.

But to be without it would be very inconvenient!

Amazingly, Jefferson accurately predicted that a civil war would break out over slavery.

One day, there will be terrible bloodshed as a result of slavery.

Although he supported the American central government, he placed more importance on each state's freedom and independence.

State freedom and independence

Central gov't

...nsidered America as an ...ation for which industrialization ...irable.

That vast plain...! America must go in the direction of a peaceful agrarian nation...

Naturally, as a key member of the Anti-federalists,

Pro-farmer, Anti-federalist, Pro-French.

Jeffersonian

he collided with Alexander Hamilton, himself a key member of the Federalists.

Metropolitan, patrician, Federalist, pro-British, pro-commerce and industry.

Hamiltonian

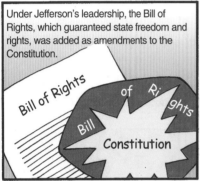
Under Jefferson's leadership, the Bill of Rights, which guaranteed state freedom and rights, was added as amendments to the Constitution.

Bill of Rights

Bill of Rights

Constitution

Jefferson became Vice President in 1797. For the next four years, instead of cooperating with President Adams, he continued to confront him.

How can you call yourself Vice President?

In particular, Jefferson worked very hard to repeal the Alien and Sedition Act, which contained unconsti-tutional elements.

Alien and Sedition Act

In the 1800 presidential election, Jefferson defeated Adams' bid for re-election and was elected as President.

President

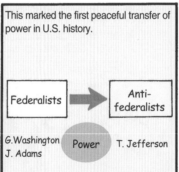
This marked the first peaceful transfer of power in U.S. history.

Federalists → Anti-federalists

G. Washington
J. Adams

Power

T. Jefferson

Based on this victory, the Anti-federalists founded the Democratic-Republican Party, giving birth to the very first political party in America.

Democratic Republican Party

Jefferson also sent U.S. troops to Tripoli to assist in the suppression of pirates there.

This is recorded as the first overseas dispatch of the American military in U.S. history.

Meanwhile, Jefferson's greatest achievement was the purchase of Louisiana.

Real estate sale at rock bottom price Louisiana -Napoleon-

*U.S. troops suppressing pirates

With the purchase of Louisiana, the U.S. doubled the size of its territory.

The vast uncharted territory was the decisive factor that prompted the development of the United States.

In response to criticism that so much money went to the purchase of 'useless' land,

What was he thinking?!

We don't even have enough money to construct the capital!

Jefferson responded:

Doesn't it bring you happiness just to look at the endless Western skyline?

However, the Louisiana Purchase entailed the issue of whether or not to adopt slavery in new states from the Louisiana Territory.

Will we permit or restrict slavery

in new states joining the Union?

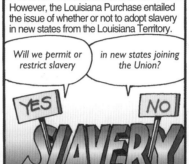

For the Louisiana Territory, the U.S. paid a severe price in the form of the Civil War, 50 years after the end of Jefferson's term.

From its founding to the Civil War,

U.S. history was marked by conflict over slavery.

Although U.S. territory suddenly expanded twofold, no one had been to this territory.

Did Napoleon know anything about it?

Neither the seller nor the buyer knew anything about it.

It was an unknown land where people had trouble distinguishing between the Mississippi River and the Colorado River.

Jefferson sent Lewis and Clark to explore the new territory up to the Pacific Ocean.

*Arrowsmith's map that served as Jefferson's reference (1802, London)

The information they brought back prompted Western expansion.

Hmm... so these things were

found south of the Mississippi!

Lewis & Clark Report

In the 1804 presidential election, Jefferson easily won re-election.

Results of 1884 Election

Democratic-Republican	Federalist
Thomas Jefferson	Charles C. Pinckney
George Clinton	Rufus King
162	14

Electoral votes

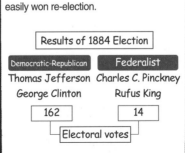

However, during his second term, Jefferson suffered from an ever-decreasing approval rating and attacks from his political enemies.

Boy, this ain't an easy job!

Jefferson's approval rating

His progressive thinking was fiercely attacked by Christians.

There was serious conflict with Marshall, the Chief Justice, who was appointed by Jefferson's adversary and predecessor John Adams.

But Jefferson's biggest mistake was the Embargo Act that he signed into law in 1807.

While Britain and France fought in the Napoleonic Wars, America declared its neutrality.

But the British and French navies accused the U.S. of making exports to the enemy and routinely seized U.S. merchant ships and their goods.

The British even went as far as 'impressing' (conscripting) U.S. sailors to fight in its military, inflicting serious losses on the U.S.

In response, Jefferson enforced the statute that closed all U.S. ports to foreign merchant ships.

However, this statute dealt a fatal blow to U.S. trade, wreaking havoc on the U.S. economy.

Jefferson's approval rating plummeted as the resentment of the people grew.

In 1809, Jefferson left office at a time when his approval rating was at rock bottom,

and returned to his residence in Monticello.

During his later years, he established the University of Virginia and focused on academic pursuits such as serving as the president of the American Philosophy Association.

Commending his achievements, future Americans extolled Jefferson as the 'Sage of Monticello.'

Jefferson was an enlightenment thinker and pioneer who advocated for human equality and thought ahead of his time,

but he had certain limitations because he was an owner of a plantation who possessed 200 slaves throughout his life.

Also, although Jefferson advocated for democracy, he held the view that power should not be conferred on the people.

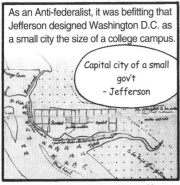

He was undemocratically inclined to the belief that a privileged minority should govern as a matter of birthright.

He also persecuted Indians. These were his negative traits.

As an Anti-federalist, it was befitting that Jefferson designed Washington D.C. as a small city the size of a college campus.

*Washington D.C. as designed by Jefferson

But the capital city was designed as a city with a grand scale at the wish of Washington who dreamed of an empire.

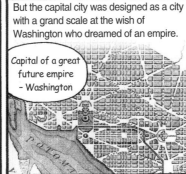

*Capital city as envisioned by Washington

By the time he became President, Jefferson had been a bachelor for nearly 20 years. He was the first President to serve without a First Lady.

Jefferson and Adams both died on the same day on July 4, 1826, America's Independence Day.

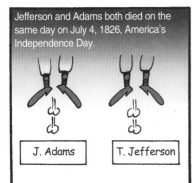

He is synonymous with the progressive man of inquiry, contemplation and action.

Even Jefferson's residence at Monticello was designed by himself.

James Madison 1809~1817

Father of the Constitution that Established Separation of Powers and Checks and Balances

WAR OF 1812
AGAINST BRITAIN
1812 - 1814

James Madison
Democratic-Republican Party,
1751.3.16~1836.6.28

Birth Place   Port Conway, Virginia

Wife   Dolley Payne Todd Madison 1768~1849

Children   None

Vice Presidents   G. Clinton 1809
E. Gerry 1813

James Madison was the first President to fight another war against Britain after the American Revolutionary War.

Revolutionary War		Battle of pride	
Bang!			Bang!
1st Wash-ington	2nd Adams	3rd Jef-ferson	4th Mad-ison

At that time, America was an insignificant third-rate nation that had been in existence for only about 20 years.

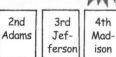

USA

How cute!

To Britain and France, which held sway over the world, America was just an infant who had started toddling.

I'm not being taken seriously!

USA

In an effort to bring the North American continent under its influence, Napoleon's France and its nemesis Britain

Need to put it under control now...

It'll be a major headache if America sides with France!

---

waged a fierce contest. America itself was divided between pro-British and pro-French factions.

I ♥ France

We still originate from Britain.

Eventually, the pro-French faction prevailed, and America started a war in which it ultimately prevailed against Britain, thereby confirming that it was a genuinely independent nation.

You won't poke your nose into our affairs again, right?

James Madison was born as the son of a wealthy plantation owner in Virginia.

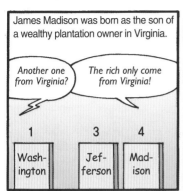

Another one from Virginia?

The rich only come from Virginia!

1	3	4
Wash-ington	Jef-ferson	Mad-ison

He graduated from College of New Jersey (later to become Princeton University) and became a lawyer.

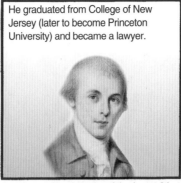

*Madison in his young days (Charles W. Pilgrim)

Remembered as the 'Father of the Constitution,' Madison shines in U.S. history.

I'm an expert in the law.

He played a leading role in the drafting of the Constitution.

Hmm, what kind of nation do we want to create?

He came up with the concept of separation of powers, which up to that time was never even imagined in other nations.

If power is concentrated,

we would be no different from a European monarchy.

The separation of powers among legislative, judicial and executive branches.

Legislative   Judicial   Executive

The basic principle of checks and balances among these three branches

CHECK & BALANCE

was conceived by James Madison.

I took into account the British parliamentary system,

but replaced the 'king-parliament' concept with separation of powers between the three branches.

This basic principle governs not only the U.S. Constitution but also the state constitutions of all U.S. states. It's the bedrock of democracy.

Hope you don't mind my plagiarism...

U.S. Constitution

Together with his friend and comrade Thomas Jefferson, Madison was a key member of the Anti-federalist faction.

We do need a central (federal) gov't,

but it should be limited to a coordinating role, without infringing upon state freedom and rights.

Anti-federalism

After Jefferson became President, Madison served as his Secretary of State,

and with Jefferson founded the Democratic-Republican Party, which later on became the Democratic Party. Their efforts made way for Jeffersonian Democracy.

Jeffersonian Democracy

Despite his capabilities and achievements, Madison as President is recorded as having left serious historical stains.

During his first term, he failed to adequately control the struggle between pro-British and pro-French factions within his government.

In 1812, he eventually started a war against Britain without any particular justification.

Why couldn't he have prevented the war?

That calls into question his qualifications as a leader!

During his second term, although he ultimately won the war against Britain,

I'm out of breath!

Victory

the official residence of the President* and the Capitol were burned, while Washington D.C., the capital city, was occupied and trampled by British forces.

Washington D.C.

*Later on became the White House

The entire country fell into chaos over the enormous losses from the war.

War has left us in shambles!

Ruined economy!

Destruction of homes and infra-structure...

USA

Fortunately, Madison was able to maintain a certain level of approval rating (which was still terribly low) due to the popularity of his ebullient and sociable wife Dolley Todd.

We love you Dolley!

She's the best First Lady!

In particular, it is well known that when British forces burned the White House,

Dolley Todd escaped with Washington's portrait in her arms.

I can't allow the enemy to trample on the national father's portrait!

With the war victory, Madison's approval rating recovered a bit,

*What was left of the burned White House

but he was overshadowed by the general who became an American hero for annihilating the British forces at the Battle of New Orleans in January 1815.

NEW ORLEANS

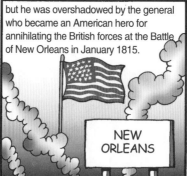

That man was Andrew Jackson.

As for the Alien and Sedition Act that Adams signed and promulgated into law,

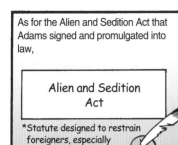

Alien and Sedition Act

*Statute designed to restrain foreigners, especially the French.

Adams

Madison fiercely attacked this statute as undemocratic and oppressive of the press. He stood at the forefront of the movement to repeal it.

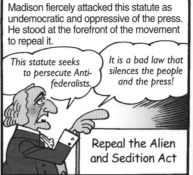

This statute seeks to persecute Anti-federalists.

It is a bad law that silences the people and the press!

Repeal the Alien and Sedition Act

He made dangerous assertions.

A bad law, even if it were a federal law, can be disobeyed!!

America as a nation could maintain unity only if all of the states unconditionally respected and complied with federal law.

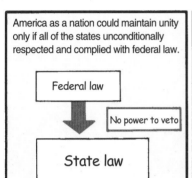

Federal law

No power to veto

State law

If the states were to have the right to veto a federal law because it was a bad law,

No!

Federal law

State

We cannot accept a bad law!

then that could serve as a basis for the states to reject and secede from the Union based on their own interests.

Independence

State

State

State

State

State

Union

So later on when the Civil War actually broke out,

1861 Civil War

as the Southern states formed the Confederacy and seceded from the Union,

Secession and independence!

USA

they cited Madison's precedent as their justification.

Madison said that we are entitled to refuse a bad law!

Madison's bad and good reputation both stem from the War of 1812 against Britain.

Madison and Jefferson shared the perspective that Britain was the most significant threat to America.

Britain has still not given up on America!

Britain is still upset over the loss of America, its former colony.

Britain's a strong economic power that resorts to looting.

We can become a genuinely independent nation only if we can somehow manage to emerge from Britain's shadow!

Britain decided to take strong action against the unfriendly American government.

So it permitted the British Navy to seize and plunder American ships.

The Madison administration reached a conclusion that America should strike first against Britain if war could not be avoided.

Its strategy was to secure an advantage in the war by attacking Canada before British reinforcement troops arrived.

But America possessed only a small military with no qualified officers, not to mention the lack of rations and weapons. Eventually, America's initial Canadian campaign failed.

*Battle between U.S. and British warships

Just at the right time for Britain, Napoleon's Russian campaign failed, and he was ousted from power.

Britain was thus able to commit a large number of troops, and it started trampling all over America.

In August 1814, Britain defeated the U.S. in the Bladensburg Battle and occupied Washington D.C., the American capital.

Madison, who witnessed the battlefield, is the only incumbent President to have personally experienced a brutal loss at battle.

If it had the will, Britain could have completely destroyed the U.S.

However, it was too tired of the war with France that had continued for so long. Thus, without going to extremes, Britain ended the War of 1812 with the Treaty of Ghent.

Although the War of 1812 was horrible, America in any event prevailed.

Nationalism engulfed the Americans, who had completely freed themselves from British influence.

We are a great nation! We won!

Through this war, it became clear that America was no longer an easy match, even for Britain, the world's most powerful nation.

They're now beyond our control...

Even though the war was criticized and resented,

Madison was prideful of his philosophy as a leader.

Popularity doesn't mean a thing to me.

I carried out a consistent policy for this nation and its people.

I waged an inevitable war and won that war. The war increased America's prestige, and America secured complete independence.

The American national anthem, which contains nationalistic lyrics, is based on Francis Scott Key's poem written during the War of 1812.

Oh, Say can you see by the dawn's···

After the inauguration of his successor James Monroe as the fifth President,

James Monroe

James Madison returned to his hometown Montpelier in March 1817.

Montpelier

Before he passed away, he served as the president of the University of Virginia an institution established by Jefferson, for nearly 10 years (1826 – 1836).

Thomas Jefferson

The Federalist Papers, in which he advocated for the ratification of the Constitution, remains as an American classic in political science.

The Federalist Papers

J. Madison

The name of James Madison, the fourth U.S. President and the 'Father of the Constitution,' lives on as the capital city of Wisconsin.

Madison Capital City of Wisconsin

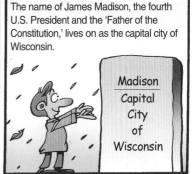

James Monroe 1817~1825

Defender of the New World from European Interference

James Monroe

America

Europe

Monroe Doctrine (1823)

Europe better not cross this line!

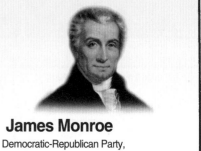

James Monroe

Democratic-Republican Party,

1758.4.28.~1831.7.4.

Birth Place   Westmoreland County, Virginia

Wife   Elizabeth Kortright Monroe 1768~1830

Children   Eliza, son with unknown name, Maria

Vice President   D. D. Tompkins

James Monroe was one of the last remaining members of the Revolution Generation.

I'm from the generation that fought against Britain for independence,

the generation that founded America.

He was the last President from among the four Presidents from Virginia who served two consecutive terms.

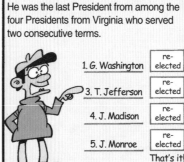

1. G. Washington	re-elected
3. T. Jefferson	re-elected
4. J. Madison	re-elected
5. J. Monroe	re-elected

That's it!

He was also the third President from among the five Presidents who died on Independence Day.

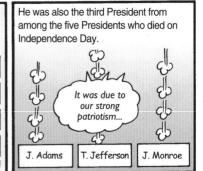

It was due to our strong patriotism...

| J. Adams | T. Jefferson | J. Monroe |

Although he was not a thinker or philosopher like Jefferson or Madison,

Philosophy

Ideology

Logic

Don't know much about those things...

---

he outstandingly led the country based on his wealth of experience and conviction.

Conviction

Insight

Experience

Monroe left an important legacy in American history with the Monroe Doctrine, which blocked European interference in the Americas.

MONROE DOCTRINE

As with his predecessors, James Monroe was born as the son of a wealthy plantation owner in Westmoreland County, Virginia.

Another one from Virginia?

Don't worry. There won't be another one for a long time.

President

He studied at the College of William and Mary for a while,

College of W&M

and then after the Revolutionary War broke out, left college at the age of 17 to fight under General Washington.

*Washington and Monroe

Monroe was severely wounded during the Battle of Trenton when Washington carried out an attack on Christmas Eve,

but he emerged as a hero from this battle and returned to Virginia two years later.

Under Jefferson's guidance, he studied law in Virginia, and subsequently entered public life with his election to the Virginia House of Delegates.

I also soon became a U.S. Senator!

Washington D.C.

In 1794, when he was 36, Monroe was appointed minister to France. Charmed by France, he became pro-French.

Monsieur!

Bonjour, Madame!

This conflicted with the Washington administration's strong policy to maintain neutrality between France and Britain.

USA Neutrality

Eventually, Monroe was summoned back to America, and became estranged for good from Washington, Adams and other Federalists.

If you're not with us, you're against us!

Washington administration

After returning to Virginia, Monroe was elected governor.

I'm not finished yet!

Governor of Virginia

In 1803, President Jefferson asked him

COME! Marilyn, no, James Monroe!

Yes, Sir!

Vroom~

to assist James Madison and Robert Livingston in the negotiations for the Louisiana Purchase with Napoleon.

I hope this land will benefit America.

In 1808, Monroe and Madison collided in the presidential primaries.

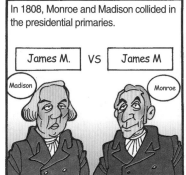

James M. vs James M
Madison   Monroe

Madison prevailed, and his victory had the effect of chilling the relationship between the two men who were once allies.

But they soon patched things up due to the strong intervention of Jefferson.

What're you guys doing?

Make up right now!

Madison, who became President, appointed Monroe as his Secretary of State.

Secretary of State

Looks good on you.

When the War of 1812 against Britain started, Madison also appointed Monroe as Secretary of War.

The incumbent secretary's not doing a good job, so it's all yours.

Secretary of War

In such fashion, Monroe built a diverse career as a soldier, lawyer, governor, senator, diplomat, negotiator and cabinet member.

Wow... This guy's CV is so impressive!

J. Monroe

In 1816, Monroe was finally nominated as the presidential candidate to succeed Madison.

I told you, one day it would be your turn.

See that your day has come?

HURRAY

YAY

He defeated Rufus King, the Federalist Party candidate, and was elected as the fifth U.S. President.

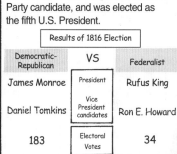

Results of 1816 Election		
Democratic-Republican	VS	Federalist
James Monroe	President	Rufus King
Daniel Tomkins	Vice President candidates	Ron E. Howard
183	Electoral Votes	34

At the time of his election, American nationalism was at its height after the U.S. war victory against Britain.

America is great!

The American people realized that as a united nation, they could defeat Britain, the most powerful nation in the world.

Boom Boom Boom

There was a mood to come together under a 'United States.'
Based on this trend,

Americans!

Let's unite!

Monroe became re-elected in a landslide victory in the 1820 election.

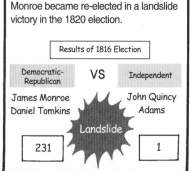

Results of 1816 Election		
Democratic-Republican	VS	Independent
James Monroe		John Quincy
Daniel Tomkins	Landslide	Adams
231		1

In the 1820s, independence movements engulfed the South American continent that was under Spanish control.

Uprisings demanding independence occurred here and there.

Spain responded by sending a large number of troops to suppress the independence movements.

This development made America very uneasy and apprehensive,

while it must have looked as an opportunity to Britain, which was salivating over South America.

Britain subsequently approached America.

Rejecting Britain's proposal, Monroe announced the so-called 'Monroe Doctrine,' which he delivered in his New Year's message to Congress in December 1823.

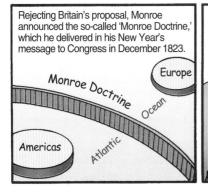

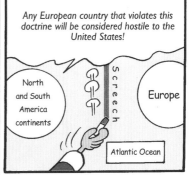

The Monroe Doctrine served as the basis for U.S. expansionism toward the end of the 19th century.

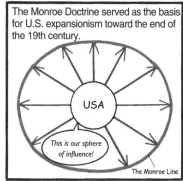

and served as a foundation for American policy to hold sway over the entire world in the 20th century.

It also helped America oust European powers and take the initiative,

As the size of U.S. territory continued to expand, the question of whether to maintain or repeal slavery became an increasingly serious problem.

This was not just a controversy as to whether to maintain or repeal slavery. In essence, it was a power struggle over which side would take political control.

So the question of slavery was a critical issue to politicians and the Northern and Southern states. Concession was out of the question.

This was because back in the Monroe era, slave states and free states were maintaining a 50:50 equilibrium in Congress.

If a new state were to join the Union, that would break the balance,

and allow one side to take the initiative in U.S. politics.

It was at that time that Missouri petitioned for statehood.

Since Missouri was a slave state, its admittance would adversely affect the abolitionist movement.

Eventually, Congress agreed to the so-called Missouri Compromise of 1820, which only temporarily solved this problem.

In exchange for admitting Missouri, a slave state, to the Union,

Maine would be separated from Massachusetts, a free state, and added as a free state,

Hereafter, slavery would not be allowed north of the parallel 36°30' north.

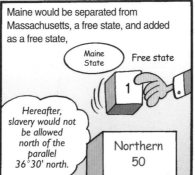

thereby retaining the 50:50 balance.

However, new states would continue to petition for statehood.

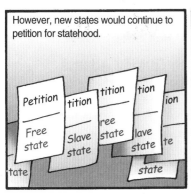

The issue of slavery was by no means a problem that could be resolved by temporary solutions forever.

A blood civil war seemed inevitable...

From Washington to Lincoln, U.S. history

was marked with conflict between the Northern and Southern states over slavery!

In 1825, Monroe finished his term and left the White House with the respect and affection of the people,

Clap clap clap

Good job!

Clap clap clap

We love you James!

WHITE HOUSE

and moved to his daughter's house in New York.

Welcome home!

Hi, Eliza...

When he left the White House, all that was left was $75,000 in debt,

Daddy, how'd you rack up so much debt?

It takes a lot of money to be President!

even though his annual pension was $25,000, a significant amount at that time.

Daddy, you have bad credit!

Oh my

"Monroe was the highest paid President in the history of the United States,

Did you spend money on a mistress?

Of course not!

but at the age of 72, he faces death as a meager and poor man,"

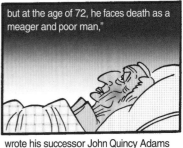

wrote his successor John Quincy Adams in 1831.

John Quincy Adams 1825~1829

Intellectual Leader with Top Educational Background

J. Q. Adams

During war times, even though an ordinary leader can shine,

during peace times, an ordinary leader is bound to lose his luster...

PEACE · STABILITY

I don't see the President these days.

What's he up to these days?

I guess it's better to be unseen than to be seen talking too much!

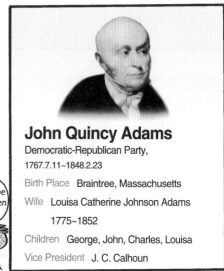

John Quincy Adams

Democratic-Republican Party,
1767.7.11~1848.2.23

Birth Place   Braintree, Massachusetts

Wife   Louisa Catherine Johnson Adams
          1775~1852

Children   George, John, Charles, Louisa

Vice President   J. C. Calhoun

JQA (John Quincy Adams) was the son of the second President John Adams.

Men from the East Coast seem to have monopolized the presidency!

Don't worry, that tradition will be soon broken.

The 6th President

J. Q. Adams
Virginia

It was the first time both father and son had become President.

The second time was when father-and-son Bush became President...

41st
G.B.

43rd
G.W.B.

Father-and-son Adams also became the first and second Presidents to fail in their bids for re-election.

He failed just like his father!

Re-election

Nevertheless, JQA was a 'prepared President' and the recipient of a 'presidential education' from his childhood days.

Son, a son must follow in the footsteps of his father.

Of course, father, a President's son has to become President.

He was one of the most well educated Presidents in U.S. history,

Wow, an impressive academic background!

---

who sought dignity as an intellectual, not popularity with the people. For this reason, he became the last leader from high society to fail in his bid for re-election.

Politics shouldn't be at the mercy of the whim of the shallow people!

JQA was more of a distinguished scholar than a politician. He was fluent in seven languages.

A speech he made in his fluent French even impressed the famous French historian Tocqueville.

JQA accompanied his father (who was a diplomat) to France when he was 10 years old.

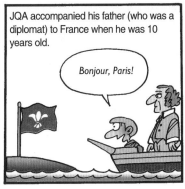

Except for a brief return to America when he was 12, he spent the next seven years studying and widening his horizons in Prussia, Russia, Sweden, Britain, the Netherlands and France, among other nations.

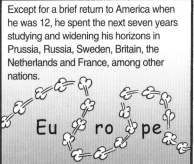

At the age of 17 (1785), JQA returned to Massachusetts to study law at Harvard, and eventually became a lawyer.

During the Washington administration, he served as minister to the Netherlands.

During his father John Adams's administration, JQA served as minister to Prussia, among other nations, and accumulated a wealth of diplomatic and administrative experience.

Afterwards, when he was 35 (1802), he was elected to the Massachusetts Senate and the next year to the U.S. Senate,

thereby taking his steps to the presidency in an orderly fashion.

During the Monroe administration, JQA was appointed as Secretary of State based on his great experience.

The Monroe Doctrine that was announced in 1823 was conceived by JQA.

It was a product of his insightful outlook on the changes taking place in the world, an outlook that was sharpened by his long diplomatic career.

As Secretary of State, JQA gained a reputation for his great ability.

The 'Monroe Doctrine' was first conceived and promoted by JQA,

but his greatest achievement was the acquisition of Florida and the Pacific Northwest from Spain.

Florida was Spanish territory located right below U.S. territory.

The Pacific Northwest was also Spanish territory.

Using his expert diplomatic skills, JQA got a good bargain for these territories,

and expanded U.S. territory from the Atlantic Ocean all the way up to the Pacific Ocean.

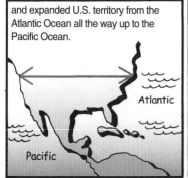

By making the Spanish withdraw from all territories in the Caribbean Bay,

JQA helped pave the way for America to greatly expend its territory to its present day size.

This achievement by JQA is recorded as the greatest diplomatic victory in U.S. history

because the U.S. was able to acquire so large a land without shedding a drop of blood.

Oregon, Washington... all of this golden land became U.S. territory thanks to JQA.

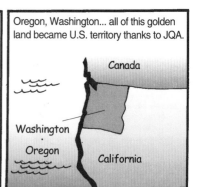

JQA, who displayed remarkable ability and much knowledge and insight as Secretary of State,

was naturally considered as a presidential candidate to succeed Monroe.

But Andrew Jackson, who had emerged as a national hero from the war with Britain, also had ambitions to become President.

JQA and Jackson ran against each other during the 1824 presidential election, but an unprecedented event unfolded.

Jackson surpassed JQA in the number of popular votes,

Results of 1824 Election

Candidate	Popular Votes	Electoral Votes
Andrew Jackson	151,271	99
JQA	113,122	84
William Crawford	40,856	41
Henry Clay	47,531	37

but no candidate won a majority of the electoral votes.

So, for the first time in history, the presidential election was thrown to Congress,

and the House of Representatives declared JQA the winner on February 9, 1825.

However, JQA's victory was the result of his bargain to win the support of Henry Clay, one of the candidates.

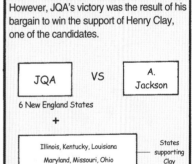

After the results were announced, JQA announced that he was appointing Henry Clay as Secretary of State.

This outraged Jackson and his supporters,

and JQA and Jackson became each other's greatest political adversary and fought each other for the next four years.

Unfortunately, JQA didn't leave a significant legacy as President.

Legacy of JQA as President

The End

Perhaps it is more accurate to say that there was not much to leave because he governed during a time of peace and prosperity

and there were no significant events that required him to display his leadership skills.

A captain doesn't have the opportunity to shine if his ship sails on a calm sea.

At times of war and crisis, even an ordinary leader shines,

Attack!

but easygoing and stable times do not produce great Presidents.

Who cares about politics!

Even though the people desire peace and prosperity,

Peace!

I pray for prosperity for this nation and a thriving economy!

they do not give high marks to politicians who lead during comfortable times.

Did he actually do anything?

I know, he was a really incompetent leader.

JQA was such a person. There are some who even see him as a 'failed President.'

JQA failed...

Why do you have to bring that up everyday? How do you think the people would feel?

Meanwhile, as the 1828 presidential election approached, Andrew Jackson—loser of the last election—vowed revenge.

There ain't going to be any corrupt bargain this time!

The Democratic-Republican Party became split between JQA supporters and Jackson supporters.

Democratic-Republican

National Republicans JQA

CRACK

Jacksonian Democrats

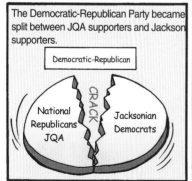

At that time, the phrase 'one man can write, while the other can fight' was used to describe the two men.

Intellectual
JQA

Soldier
A. Jackson

JQA, a high intellectual from an aristocratic family, clashed with Jackson, a soldier and commoner from Tennessee.

Demagogue, Populist out to sway public opinion!

East Coast conservative idiot!

Jackson was highly critical of JQA.

JQA, the son of a President, pursues patrician policies!

He's the running dog of vested interests who dreams of establishing a monarchy!

He runs an immoral administration that supplies women to the Russian Czar!

Not to mention that he also runs a corrupt administration that installed a billiards table in the White House with public funds!

Let us drive out this aristocratic President, who only supports the interests of the wealthy, upper class and vested interests, and establish a progressive and reformist government of the people!

JQA didn't defend himself against those attacks from the Jacksonian Democrats.

Whatever they say, it would be degrading to stand against them.

Roar
Roar

To respond to such a low class crowd would only demean politics.

NO TO POPULISM!

Even if I were to lose my bid for re-election to the presidency, I will not instigate the people with shallow populism. I will not bow to the people to stay in power!

So he lost to Jackson, just like his father.

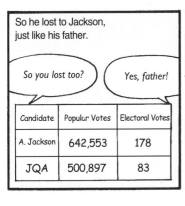

So you lost too?

Yes, father!

Candidate	Popular Votes	Electoral Votes
A. Jackson	642,553	178
JQA	500,897	83

JQA, a small and bald man with a cold stare,

enjoyed reading classics in Latin and Greek and had a particular interest in science.

AVE VERUM CORPUS
BESAME MUCHO
GAUDEA MUS
IGITUR

Instead of following public opinion, he sought to lead public opinion.

Follow me!

Above all, he valued unwavering conviction and faithfulness.

Wow, no one...

As both a philosopher and an educator, he was a rare President.

If that's the case, then my time is up.

White House

Andrew Jackson 1829~1837

Pioneer of the Era of Mass Democracy

Andrew Jackson

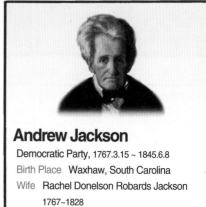

Andrew Jackson

Democratic Party, 1767.3.15 ~ 1845.6.8

Birth Place **Waxhaw, South Carolina**

Wife **Rachel Donelson Robards Jackson**
1767~1828

Children **None**

Vice Presidens **J. Calhoun 1829**
Martin Van Buren 1833

Andrew Jackson was totally different from his predecessors.

Eligibility Requirements to Become President
- Upper class
- East Coast background
- Strong educational background
- High net worth
- Strong personal connections
- WASP

First of all, he was the first President to not come from an upper class family in Virginia.

Don't eye ball me! First time you've seen a country boy?

Jackson received almost no school education. He studied law on his own and became a lawyer.

Dad, I want to go to law school.

What? You can become President only by becoming a lawyer on your own!

A. Jackson

Moreover, he was the son of an Irish, not English, immigrant.

Boy, how can an ignorant and uncouth Irish man become President?

America has gone to extremes...

From a lawyer, he turned into a soldier and delivered a crushing defeat to the British military, for which he became a beloved hero of the American people.

*Commander Jackson

Jackson opened the era of populism and mass democracy, so that even a commoner could become President.

Jacksonian Democracy

Even though Jackson did not have the scholarship and qualifications of his predecessors, ability doesn't seem to necessarily stem from one's education.

Of course not! Ability has nothing to do with educational background!

As a general and President, he commanded armies with strong charisma and leadership.

OK! So you want a fight? I won't pull rank on you!

No, Sir!

A popular politician, he probably enjoyed more respect and affection of Americans than any other President.

We love you Andrew!

Jackson!

The Jackson Guards!

Jackson's nickname was 'Old Hickory.'

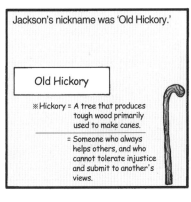

Old Hickory

※Hickory = A tree that produces tough wood primarily used to make canes.

= Someone who always helps others, and who cannot tolerate injustice and submit to another's views.

Like his nickname, Jackson lived a life full of difficulties and obstacles as a result of his stubbornness, conviction and struggles.

There are many who were

destroyed by crossing me!

Jackson was born the son of Irish immigrants Andrew and Elizabeth Jackson at a settlement village in South Carolina.

Wah ~

His father passed away before he was born, so he was a posthumous child who didn't have a chance to see his father.

Poor thing...

Without receiving a school education, he became a lawyer through self-study, and at the age of 21, came to Nashville, Tennessee for an apprenticeship.

I will learn about life in the big city.

Nashville

In Nashville, the 24-year old Jackson met and married Rachel Donelson Robards, at that time still a married woman.

Rachel then was not formally divorced from her husband,

What? She's not divorced yet?

They didn't formally divorce, so legally she's still a married woman.

so Jackson was criticized over this matter again and again from the then conservative American society.

He ran off with a married woman.

How filthy...

He's an immoral man.

Eventually, such criticism led him to fight duels, and even to kill one man in a duel. A bullet lodged in his body from that duel remained in his body for the rest of his life.

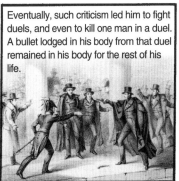

Jackson entered politics with his election to the U.S. House of Representatives from Tennessee.

Legitimate road to the presidency!

U.S. Senate

U.S. House of Representatives

State House of Representatives

After serving as a U.S. Senator, Jackson worked as a federal judge in Nashville for seven years (1797~1804).

Washington D.C.

Nashville

He is said to have been respected by the people for his clear and fair decisions.

He's a hot judge!

He's not an intellectual, but his decisions are very fair.

After finishing his term as a judge, Jackson retired and disappeared for the next eight years.

Jackson's missing!

Where'd he go?

But he returned as the leader of the 'Old Hickory' unit when the War of 1812 broke out between America and Britain.

Old Hickory

Jackson put down the Creek Indians, who had allied themselves with the British,

---

and, on January 8, 1815, he won the largest military victory in U.S. history at the Battle of New Orleans,

British troops killed: 2,037
American troops killed: 21

---

becoming the most highly regarded hero ever since Washington, and a strong contender for the next presidency.

JACKSON!

Roar~ Jackson!

Hurray!

Roar!

However, Jackson lost the 1824 election to John Quincy Adams who had made a bargain with Henry Clay.

Hey, politics isn't a career. It's an art!

Thereafter, Jackson gathered his supporters from the Democratic-Republican Party and formed his own Democratic Party.

Democratic-Republican Party

Anti-Jackson faction

Jackson faction

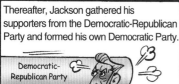

In the 1828 election, Jackson defeated JQA to become finally elected President.

Hey, politics is about having tenacity and guts!

A non-Virginian and uneducated lawyer from the frontier had become the new President of the United States.

Upper class from south of the river (Virginians living south of the Potomac River) Highly educated, personal connections

Jackson lowered the curtain on elitism in American politics,

The most significant implication of Jackson's election as President

was that he opened an era in which it became possible for anyone to become President!

and declared the opening of the era of mass democracy.

Sovereign power resides with the people,

not elite plantation aristocrats from Virginia!

The term 'Jacksonian Democracy' was coined after Jackson's election.

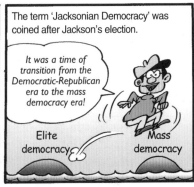

It was a time of transition from the Democratic-Republican era to the mass democracy era!

Elite democracy

Mass democracy

Jackson, however, left a disturbing legacy in the form of 'clique politics,' which became deeply rooted in American politics.

You're either with me

or against me!

He rewarded clique members or his election supporters with public offices,

Leader of the I ♥ Jackson

Trumpet Boy of the Jackson Guard

Aristocrat-cursing shaman

I ♥ Jackson

starting the abusive practice known as the 'spoils system.'

Allegiance to Mr. Jackson!

Minister

Secretarial staff

Minister

Jackson filled posts around him with his followers,

Your favors are immeasurable!

and, in handling state affairs, engaged in closed-door and clique politics with these persons aligned with him.

Whisper...

Kitchen of the President

Meeting in Progress
No Entry

Opponents sarcastically referred to such clique politics as the 'kitchen cabinet.'

All they do is eat and whisper among themselves everyday!

It's the extreme of closed-door and clique politics.

It's a kitchen cabinet.

Jackson argued that he himself did not belong to any particular party, but it was an undeniable fact that he was a member

I represent all American people!

of the Democratic Party, which was formed by his supporters who separated from the Democratic-Republican Party.

Jackson's Democratic Party

How could he say he doesn't belong to a party when he was the very person who created that party?

At that time, the Whig Party was formed in opposition to Jackson's Democratic Party, and America thus re-entered a two-party system era.

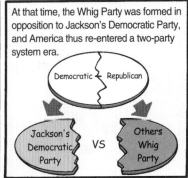

Democratic ← Republican

Jackson's Democratic Party

VS

Others Whig Party

The Whig Party was a new party with a conservative bent whose name was borrowed from the British Whig Party.

Anti-Jackson faction of Democratic-Republican Party (including JQA)	Southern Anti-federalist faction	Former Federalist Party members

Rallied into

Whig Party

The Whig Party was formed to oppose Jackson's progressive and popular Democratic Party,

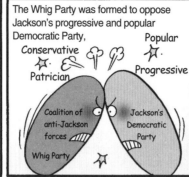

and consisted of a coalition of the former Federalist Party, Liberal Democratic Party and other conservative politicians.

The Whig Party is a bunch of misfits who've come under one roof!

Strengthened by his high approval rating, Jackson constantly battled with Congress throughout his eight-year term.

Congressmen and senators only represent their districts, whereas I'm a representative elected to represent the entire American people. Why should I yield to Congress?

There is probably no other President who so frequently exercised his veto power under the Constitution.

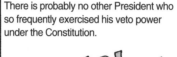

NO! VETO! NO! NO! NO!

Congress — White House

Also, there is probably no other President in U.S. history who had such a bad relationship with Congress. Jackson had even risked becoming impeached.

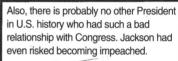

IMPEACHMENT!

Go ahead! I'm not afraid!

Congress — White House

In 1837, at the age of 70, Old Hickory left office at the height of his popularity.

For the next eight years, he lived vigorously and, in 1845, died at the age of 78 and was buried next to his wife at his residence.

Poor Rachel... You died just after seeing me become elected President.

Rachel D. R. 1767~1828 — Jackson 1767~1845

Article 1, Section 1 of the U.S. Constitution begins with the following declaration:

"All legislative Powers herein granted shall be vested in a Congress of the United States..."

Without submitting to such a powerful Congress, Andrew Jackson pushed forward with unshakeable conviction.

Congress

He vetoed more legislative bills than the sum of all bills vetoed by his predecessors.

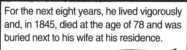

Law Law Law

NO! NO! NO NO! NO!

Jackson was clearly a giant who marked the beginning of a new age.

Early political culture

New political culture

Unfortunately, however, Jackson also cast the most disgraceful shadow on U.S. history during his term.

Jackson, who disliked Indians, stood at the forefront in their suppression.

During his presidency, he removed the Indians to wasteland called 'Indian Reservations.'

He was the very man responsible for making hundreds of thousands of Indians walk and spew blood and die on the Trail of Tears.

Ever since Jackson, American politics greatly changed,

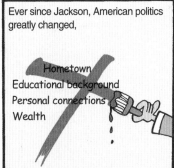

and patrician politicians like the 'Founding Fathers' largely disappeared.

Power became entrusted in the hands of the people.

Democracy became genuinely established, with America advancing forward

to become a nation with opportunities open to all. This advancement was clearly made during the Jackson era.

Nevertheless, while his predecessors tread the right path of making the right decisions without unduly falling under the influence of voters,

Jackson at times even manipulated the public opinion of voters, and sowed the seeds of populism to achieve his objectives as if they were the 'will of the people.'

It was once said of him that

Martin Van Buren 1837~1841

First Career Politician to Become President

Establishment of Two-party System

Introduction of Machine Politics

This is my masterpiece!

You fox! You schemer!

Van Buren always gets the last laugh, no matter how strong his opponent is...

Martin Van Buren

Democratic Party, 1782.12.5~1862.7.24

Birth Place   Kinderhook, New York

Wife   Hanna Hoes Van Buren 1783~1819

Children   Abraham, John, Martin, Smith Thompson

Vice President   R.M. Johnson

Martin Van Buren is peculiar in that his political skills and the political significance of his work command more weight than his political achievements.

Achievements

M. Van Buren

Political significance

As a career politician, his impact was greater in U.S. politics than in overall U.S. history.

U.S. History

M. Van Buren

U.S. Political History

M. Van Buren

He firmly fixed machine politics in America,

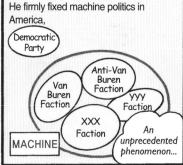

Democratic Party

Van Buren Faction

Anti-Van Buren Faction

yyy Faction

XXX Faction

An unprecedented phenomenon...

MACHINE

---

and also established the two-party system that was seen as an irregularity up to that time,

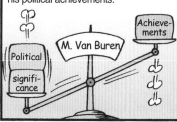

Why must there be only two parties?

Shouldn't we have more?

Two-Party System
Democratic Party
Whig Party

Van Buren's political senses were more developed than his policies or vision for the future.

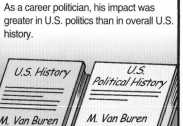

Sniff   sniff   sniff

As a 'power maker,' he skillfully put together people and effectively used them to achieve his objectives.

Even though I have no vision for tomorrow,

I can accurately look through power today!

Van Buren was born as the son of a farmer and tavern master in Kinderhook, New York.

As you can tell by his name, he was the descendant of a Dutch immigrant.

you're a real 'Yankee.'

As a Dutch immigrant from New York,

Van Buren married Hannah Hoes, a childhood friend and distant relative.

There are almost no records on her.

Van Buren didn't even mention her in his 800-page autobiography.

Even though he didn't receive further school education after the age of 14,

School is not for me...

he became a lawyer through self-study in 1803 at the age of 21 and opened a law office in his hometown.

Fastest track to success for someone without money and personal connections...

Thereafter, he entered politics and quickly moved up.

1812
New York State Senator

1821 U.S. Senator

1828
New York Governor

As an ardent supporter of Andrew Jackson,

Like myself, Mr. Jackson didn't receive a school education, but he has ambitions to become President...

Van Buren served as Jackson's campaign manager in the 1828 presidential election.

Only victory matters in an election!

Van Buren's election strategy for victory was to build up a friendly power base, *i.e.,* a systematic organization.

An election is an organizational war!

A party is a large organization comprising smaller organizations!

Van Buren rallied together Jackson's extensive supporters and formed various factions,

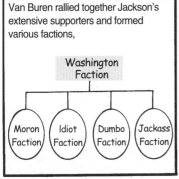

which became known collectively as a 'machine.'

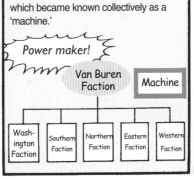

The 'Van Buren Faction' at the apex of the machine commanded great power.

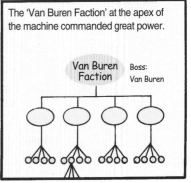

People referred to the Van Buren Faction as the 'Albany Regency.'

A regent exerts real power by controlling the ruler behind the scenes.

This name was attributable to Albany, the capital of New York State that was Van Buren's home state. Thus, 'Albany' referred to no one other than Van Buren himself.

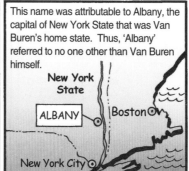

He was viewed as a regent controlling Jackson at will behind the scenes.

*Jackson (right) and Van Buren (left)

In fact, although he was the boss of the factions supporting Jackson, Van Buren didn't reveal himself.

Sir, this is what you have to say next!

Van Buren organized the victorious 1828 presidential election by putting Jackson at the forefront.

Hurray

Roar
Hurray

He was most instrumental to Jackson's election as President.

You made the most contributions.

I owe you much for your help!

Van Buren unified the various factions that supported Jackson and formed the Democratic Party,

Democratic Party

We love Jackson!

in response to which the anti-Jackson factions rallied together to form the Whig Party.

We hate Jackson!

Whig Party

From then on, the two-party system became firmly established in America.

Democratic Party

Whig Party

Hmph~

The introduction of machine politics and the establishment of the two-party system

Machine Politics

Establishment of Two-Party System

Unprecedented

gave birth to a new political system in America.

What are the characteristics of American politics?

Aren't they machine politics

and the two-party system?

Martin Van Buren is said to have made a great impact on U.S. political history because he played a leading role in that process.

See how a career politician is different?

Van Buren always achieved political victory by using his outstanding political skills.

His political adversaries called him the 'Red Fox of Kinderhook (his hometown),'

The Red Fox of Kinderhook!

whereas his supporters called him the 'Little Magician.' These were enduring nicknames that stuck with him throughout his career.

The Little Magician!

Van Buren always wins no matter how strong his opponent is!

When Jackson was elected as President in 1828, he appointed Van Buren to Secretary of State, an important office,

Hop!

Secretary of State

and made him his Vice President in the 1832 presidential election.

Hop!!

Vice President

In 1836, Van Buren entered the presidential election as Jackson's successor and was finally elected as the eighth President of the United States.

Hop!!!

President

However, this career politician, a genius in political maneuvering under the shadow of Jackson,

Jackson

didn't seem to be cut out for the presidency, which required leadership. Or perhaps it was just bad luck.

Hmm, this is different from being No. 2...

Martin Van Buren's achievements during his four-year term weren't very impressive.

Is that all you're going to cook during your term?

bubble bubble~

Befitting his personality as a career politician calculating and analyzing whatever came his way, Van Buren was overly cautious in whatever he did.

Hmm...

Should I do it?

To do or not to do, that is the question

As a result, he was unable to decisively implement policies. He always failed to make a move at the right time.

Let's do it!

Too late.

After his inauguration, the U.S. economy fell deeper and deeper into a recession.

H·E·L·P·

RECESSION

No less than 618 banks went bankrupt in just one year,

as the economy just kept getting worse.

Meanwhile, even though the discord from slavery was worsening day by day, Van Buren insisted on maintaining an ambiguous neutrality.

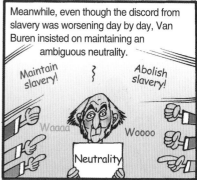

Also, an uprising of the Seminole Indians occurred in Florida that was acquired from Spain. It was as if a war had broken out.

U.S. forces were slow to deal with the crisis, and Van Buren failed to take appropriate action.

He also opposed Texas's petition to join the Union.

The indecisive and wait-and-see attitude of the Van Buren government caused its approval rating to plunge to rock bottom.

Against such a backdrop, Van Buren foolishly started large-scale repair works of the White House. His timing was really bad.

For this, he came under fierce attack from his political adversaries, not to mention the people.

The people turned their backs on him and ridiculed him by punning his name.

Even his aristocratic demeanor and taste became the target of mockery

because his parents weren't aristocrats but owners of a local tavern in New York State.

Van Buren's opponent in the 1840 presidential election was General William Harrison.

Harrison had lost to Van Buren in the 1836 presidential election.

Van Buren!

You shall pay for this...

Van Buren's enemies created and spread a song that ridiculed him.

Van, Van's a used-up man!

Van, Van's a used-up man!

Van Buren lost the presidential election. He became the third President to lose the bid for re-election.

I lost...

From Van Buren, without exception, the eight Presidents preceding Lincoln

8th President | Van Buren

Failed to win re-election

either died in office or failed to win re-election.

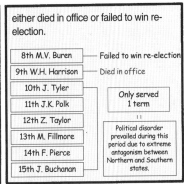

8th M.V. Buren	— Failed to win re-election
9th W.H. Harrison	— Died in office
10th J. Tyler	
11th J.K. Polk	Only served 1 term
12th Z. Taylor	
13th M. Fillmore	Political disorder prevailed during this period due to extreme antagonism between Northern and Southern states.
14th F. Pierce	
15th J. Buchanan	

Van Buren returned to his hometown and died 20 years later on July 24, 1862.

Back then, if you lived up to 80, that was pretty old...

On his deathbed, he is said to have whispered:

Slavery will bring forth the end...

in the form of a terrible upheaval...

I am afraid of what will come. But that time will inevitably come...

As a skillful politician, Van Buren tactfully evaded the issue of slavery during his term,

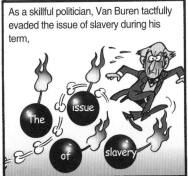

The issue of slavery

but he already forebode the Civil War based on his animal instincts as a career politician.

The fight over slavery

will someday ruin America!

Van Buren was unable to stop the realization of his foreboding of war. That was his limitation as a career politician.

You should've taken decisive action...

Hey, there aren't any 'decisive' career politicians. The priority was to preserve my position.

✝ Van Buren

William Henry Harrison 1841

First 'Image Politician'

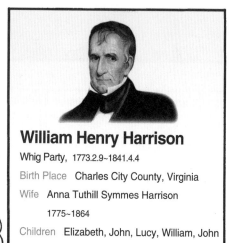

William Henry Harrison

Whig Party, 1773.2.9~1841.4.4

Birth Place   Charles City County, Virginia

Wife   Anna Tuthill Symmes Harrison
          1775~1864

Children   Elizabeth, John, Lucy, William, John Scott, Benjamin, Mary, Carter, Anna, James

Vice President   John Tyler

Harrison opened a new chapter in U.S. history for three things.

First, he was the first President to die in office. He passed away from an illness within less than one month of his inauguration.

Second, he was one of the most distinguished soldiers in U.S. history.

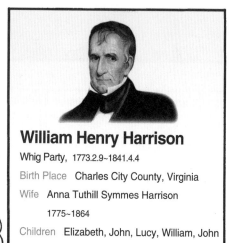

Third, he didn't fight over policies and ideologies in his presidential election.

Instead, whether it was muckraking or mudslinging, he used whatever means possible to win the election. Such 'image tactics'

turned the presidential election itself into a huge show. It was the beginning of the modern election campaign.

Born into a wealthy and aristocratic political family on the Berkeley Plantation in Virginia, Harrison received a fine education

Another one from Virginia?

Those descendants of Virginian families live grandly from generation to generation!

Harrison

and then joined the military. He became known for his fierce bravery and quickly moved up the ranks.

Strong backing from the family!

Family

In particular, he was famous for mercilessly suppressing the Indians. At the age of 28 (1801), he was named the first Governor of the Indian Territory and governed for 12 years.

I'm the Indian killer!

After threatening several Indian tribes, he seized 2,500 acres (about 10,000km²) of land from them. The white man's excessive oppression

prompted the Indians to form a confederation and rise up against the white man under Tecumseh, the leader of the Shawnee Tribe.

Harrison led the force that was called in to suppress the Indian confederation.

In November 1811, Harrison fought the Indian confederation at the Tippecanoe River.

Even though this was not a decisive victory, Harrison became famous nationwide over this battle.

Military achievement

Victory for the American people

Image

When the War of 1812 broke out against Britain, Harrison was named commander of the U.S. Northern Army.

He led the American forces to victory at the Battle of Thames in Ontario.*

At this battle, the American forces killed Tecumseh, the leader of the Indian confederation greatly feared by the white man. This battle turned Harrison into a national hero.

General Harrison quickly took advantage of his military reputation and successfully entered the U.S. House of Representatives based on his anti-Indian policies (1816).

We must drive out the Indians and expand the territory of the white man.

*Canadian territory.

*Tecumseh, rebel leader

In 1825, he was elected to the U.S. Senate. After his term ended, he retired and didn't resurface in the political world for a few years.

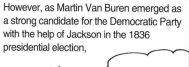

Harrison's not here!

Washington Politics

However, as Martin Van Buren emerged as a strong candidate for the Democratic Party with the help of Jackson in the 1836 presidential election,

YEAH

This is my true successor!

Hurray

the Whig Party, at pains to find a suitable candidate to compete against Van Buren, nominated the national hero Harrison as its candidate.

Andrew Jackson's a military hero,

but so is Harrison! This will be a great match!

But Van Buren, as Andrew Jackson's successor, was able to easily beat Harrison because Jackson was finishing his term amid great popularity.

Hey, a soldier doesn't always win!

V.BUREN

K.O.!!

After losing the election, the Whig Party promptly started preparing for the next presidential election with Harrison as its candidate.

Jab Jab Jab

This is my revenge match!

Harrison and the Whig Party completely changed their election strategy.

All that matters is that I end up in Washington!

Power will come my way only if I win the election, no matter what!

The shrewd Harrison selected John Tyler, a Southerner, as his running mate and vice presidential candidate.

I want you to win the Southern votes for me.

As his most important election strategy, Harrison focused on building an image of himself as a common man.

Post-Jackson elections can only be won with votes of the common people. I can't win an election based on an aristocratic image.

Because I was born into a wealthy and aristocratic family, I need to turn myself into a common man to approach the people.

Aristo-crats	Common people
Not many votes	A lot of votes

Image Change

The campaign slogan he used? 'I am a common man.'

Log Cabin
&
Hard Cider

Reference was made to a log cabin to show that Harrison was not an aristocrat living in a luxurious house,

HARD CIDER
AND
LOG CABIN
ALMANAC
18   41

but a common man living in a rough log cabin.

Isn't that a 'disguised transfer?'

When did you transfer your resident registration?

Also, reference was made to hard cider to show that instead of expensive high class wine and whiskey,

he enjoyed hard cider primarily consumed by the common people.

This ain't imported. It's locally brewed and raw!

Whatever his true background was, the point was to build an image that Harrison shared in the happiness and sadness of the common people.

The voters are naïve. The key is to appeal to their sensibility...

Hee

hee

hee

Also, he produced a campaign logo song that was popularized throughout the country. It was the first campaign logo song in election history.

Change Change Change Everything!

The logo song was named after the nickname 'Old Tippecanoe & Tyler, Too!' that followed him ever since his Indian campaigns.

Old Tippecanoe & Tyler, Too!

It was a ploy to remind the people of his military exploits.

From Indian war hero to President!

That's too much of an exaggeration!

Campaign slogans,

Harri~ Harri~ Harrison~

hats, balloons and banners and the like engulfed the country.

Yeah

Hurray

Roar

HARRISON

HARRISON

HARRISON

Harrison to the White House!

Log cabin models and rough cider cases were also utilized in the election campaign.

*Log cabin and cider case badge used in the election campaign

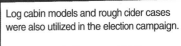

The 1840 presidential election was a battle between two well-organized national parties, marking the beginning of the modern political movement.

Party

Party

It was the first election in which candidates roamed the country to give speeches.

HARRISON TYLER

I gave more than 24 speeches attended by more than 50,000 people...

The election was clouded by muckraking, mudslinging and bantering.

Van, Van's a used-up man!

Van, Van's a used-up man!

The 1840 presidential election left a very bad precedent in U.S. history.

Quality of politics

Instead of battles over policy issues, elections became dominated by muck-raking, mudslinging and false propaganda.

He committed adultery!

He embezzled public funds!

He drank booze and partied on the job!

Wow... That really stinks!

Image took precedence over substance. Image politics and populism prevailed, with approval ratings dictating what policies would be implemented.

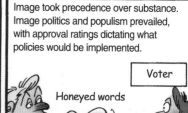

Voter

Honeyed words

Populism began to surface in even more extreme forms during elections and served as the basis for obscurantist policies that clouded the judgment of voters.

How about tax cuts?

I'll move the capital near your town!

Don't worry about subsidies!

Harrison won the 1840 presidential election in a landslide.

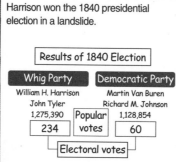

Results of 1840 Election

Whig Party		Democratic Party
William H. Harrison		Martin Van Buren
John Tyler		Richard M. Johnson
1,275,390	Popular votes	1,128,854
234	Electoral votes	60

Because the election took place amid a very weak economy, voters disappointed with Van Buren hoped for change,

Uh huh

We can't stand this anymore! Let's change!

Harrison's the choice!

so they chose a strong war hero over the indecisive and passive Van Buren.

Well, you know how aggressively I put down the Indians with much success.

That's how I will approach the economy...

After the election was over, Harrison confronted a serious problem.

Didn't know before I went,

but it really stinks...

W.C.

During his election campaign, people came to perceive him as a common man, who enjoyed cider and befriended common people living in log cabins.

LOG CABIN

HARD CIDER

However, having been born as an aristocrat who particularly enjoyed such lifestyle, Harrison intensely disliked his new image.

Me, a common man? No way...

I need a new image. People need to know that I'm not an ordinary and common man, but President. Otherwise, they'll start challenging my authority...

I'm a Virginian gentleman in the same league as Washington, Jefferson and Madison!

William Henry Harrison's inauguration as the ninth President of the United States was held on March 4, 1841.

Originally, the inauguration was always held on March 4.

March 4

He was 68 years old, the oldest President in U.S. history (as was Reagan who was inaugurated in 1981).

*Harrison's inauguration

His inauguration day is said to have been a very cold and dismal day in late winter, with even rain pouring on.

As a war hero and the oldest President, it seems Harrison wanted to show the people that he was still young and capable.

Mr. President, why did you take your coat off?

It's not stylish for a strong solider like myself to put on a coat in this sissy weather!

Without a coat, he read his inaugural address for a whopping one hour and forty minutes.

I will change America into such and such a country.

Unfortunately, he was unable to realize his ambitious plans and his dream for a grand future for America, which were put forth in his speech.

Looks like his speech will last forever.

He dedicated his entire life for this moment...

Harrison caught acute pneumonia for driving himself too hard at the inauguration,

AHCHOO

Did I emphasize style too much at the inauguration?

and died on April 4, 1841, one month after his inauguration.

Ist President to die in office during his term.

It's a pity that all that intense campaigning was for nothing.

May 14 was declared as a day of mourning for the deceased President.

Harrison, the political soldier, had crossed a river of blood and tears and sighs of countless Indians

and driven himself with so much focus to become President.

Power... Power...

White House

Although he realized his dream, his death showed the vanity of that dream.

Unrivaled war hero, died of a cold...

† William Henry Harrison

John Tyler 1841~1845

First Vice President to Ascend to the Presidency via Succession

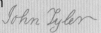

John Tyler

Whig Party, 1790.3.29~1862.1.18

Birth Place   Charles City County, Virginia

Wives   1. Letitia Christian Tyler 1790~1842

2. Julia Gardiner Tyler 1820~1889

Children   Mary, Robert, John, Letitia, Elizabeth, Ann, Alice, Teswell, David, John Alexander, Julia Gardner, Locklan, Ryan, Robert, Pearl

Vice President   No Vice President due to Tyler's succession to presidency

Without any allies, I face enemies everywhere!

Ninth President Harrison, who passed away one month after his inauguration,

Boy, I feel sorry for you...

So much effort for nothing...

---

created an unprecedented situation for the American people, even though such a situation was contemplated under the Constitution.

So, what happens now?

We do have a Vice President...

The Vice President were to succeed to the Office of President.

If the office of President became vacant, or the President became unable to discharge the powers and duties of the office, the Same shall devolve upon the Vice President.

At issue was the word 'Same.' If the word 'Same' were to be interpreted as the Vice President succeeding to only the 'same' powers and duties of the President,

Powers

Duties

President

---

then Vice President Tyler would have to remain for the next four years in the 'same' position as Vice President, merely serving as an acting President.

Vacant

President

Acting President

Vice President

Otherwise, if the word 'Same' were to be interpeted as the Office of the President itself 'devolving' on the Vice President, then he would become President.

Hum!

President

Vacant

Vice President

This was the very problem that Vice President John Tyler first confronted right after the death of Harrison.

Is he the President?

Or the Vice President serving as an acting President...

From his plantation, John Tyler was quickly summoned back to Washington D.C. after receiving an urgent message on the President's death.

Oh my...

President has died. Hurry up and return to D.C.!

Wasington D.C

When he returned, his colleagues referred to him as the Vice President.

Mr. Vice President, you're now to assume a heavy responsibility!

What? Vice President?

His first reaction was to take a firm stance.

From now on, I will not open any letters addressed to 'Acting President Tyler' or 'Vice President Tyler!'

He then immediately convened a cabinet meeting and made the following declaration.

I am happy that capable men like yourselves are members of the cabinet.

But I am the President of the United States!

whisper

whisper

murmur

If any of you do not accept me as President, your letters of resignation will be immediately accepted right here, right now.

Vice President John Tyler firmly took a stance to clarify the ambiguous provision of the Constitution.

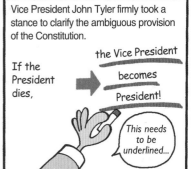

If the President dies,

the Vice President

becomes

President!

This needs to be underlined...

Under the U.S. presidential system, the President stands at the center of all aspects of politics; thus, the Vice President is but a mere shadow of the President.

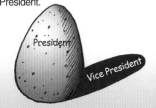

President

Vice President

The Vice President was perceived as someone to fill in for the President if the President were to become unable to discharge his duties.

President

Vice President

In this case, by making it clear that the Vice President succeeds to the Office of the President, Tyler could become President without undergoing a difficult and painful election.

I guess that's also one way to become President...

White House

John Tyler was born in Charles City County next to the James River as the son of a large plantation owner in Virginia.

Virginia again?

You can't be in politics without money.

Virginia
Charles City County

Due to his father's close relationship with prominent politicians such as Jefferson,

Son, in order to move ahead, there's nothing more important than personal connections.

Yes, father...

Tyler was able to easily and quickly establish himself in the political world of Washington D.C.

Mr. Tyler, you look just like your father.

Mr. President pro tempore, my father sends his best regards.

After graduating from the College of William and Mary, Tyler became a lawyer and, in 1811, at the age of 21, was elected to the Virginia House of Delegates as a candidate from the Jeffersonian Democratic Party.

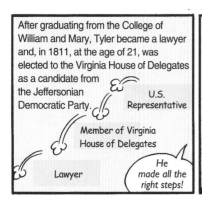

U.S. Representative

Member of Virginia House of Delegates

Lawyer

He made all the right steps!

Thereafter, his political career blossomed, as he became a U.S. Representative and then a U.S. Senator and matured into a leading politician. Originally, Tyler was

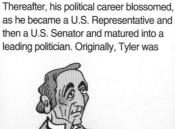

an Anti-Jacksonian, but because he didn't like John Quincy Adams, he joined the Jackson faction and became a member of the Democratic Party.

JQA

A. Jackson

VS

However, due to his upright personality, Tyler couldn't stand Jackson's stubbornness and self-righteousness.

Everything's white and black to him... He drives me crazy!

Tyler became famous for resigning from the House of Representatives for his opposition to the 1820 Missouri Compromise.

I'd rather just quit than make such a compromise!

U.S. Representative

Later on, repulsed by the vote on whether to delete the Senate's decision to withdraw the impeachment of Jackson from its minutes,

Let's delete it!

No, let's leave it in!

No, let's put it to a vote!

These guys are pathetic!

ROAR
ROAR

Tyler just resigned from the Senate, and, by doing so, really became the talk of the town.

Boy, Tyler's a really defiant guy... He just won't listen!

He's even more stubborn than Jackson!

Eventually, he turned his back on the Jackson faction and joined the Whig Party,

Traitor!

Fickle-minded politician!

Jacksonian Democratic Party

Whig Party

and ran as Harrison's running mate in the 1836 presidential election, which they overwhelmingly lost.

I still hate those sidekicks of Jackson!

They're too shallow!

Harrison and Tyler were from the same hometown.

Big bro!

Hey bro!

Both of their fathers were big-shot politicians and former governors of Virginia.

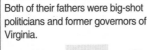

Father

Governor of Virginia

Father

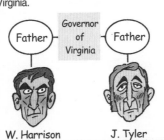

W. Harrison

J. Tyler

With such a solid family background, the two men were also alike in that they quickly and smoothly rose up the ranks in the political world.

Family

In the 1840 presidential election, Harrison ran as President and Tyler as Vice President,

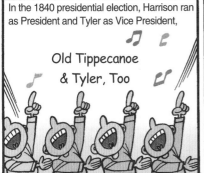

Old Tippecanoe & Tyler, Too

---

and finally defeated the Democratic Party and won the election.

Tyler, who succeeded to the Office of the President as a result of Harrison's sudden death,

Harrison did all the work, but Tyler reaps the fruits of Harrison's efforts...

---

preserved his authority by immediately establishing discipline and asserting himself as President.

Anyone challenging my authority will get the ax!

Within just a month, the American public, who had received the oldest President (68 years old), entrusted the government into the hands of the youngest President (50 years old).

68

50

In order to ride the wave of imperialism that prevailed back then,

Strong country

Weak country

Tyler overhauled the U.S. Navy.

America advanced to China and concluded the Treaty of Wanghsia in 1844 for the commencement of diplomatic and trade relations.

Already at that time, Britain had started its aggression in earnest against China through the Opium War.

CHINA

Because the U.S. was unable to move against China due to its complicated domestic situation,

its relationship with China was considerably more amicable than the relationship China had with other world powers.

Europeans are bad!

Americans are good!

Meanwhile, domestically, Tyler constantly clashed with his Whig Party.

Are you really a Whig President?

What can I do if Congress is always so uncooperative...

When he vetoed bills that were submitted by the party and the cabinet,

the cabinet resigned en masse, while the party declared the severing of its relationship with the President.

Let's see how you do by yourself!

This resulted in an odd situation where the incumbent President was without any party affiliation.

The party continued to demand his resignation and refused to cooperate with the President's policies.

How dare you disregard the party! Who do you think got you to be President?

Resign from office!

Likewise, Congress wasn't too friendly to Tyler's administration either.

This situation led to the failure of the economy, which caused Tyler's approval rating to plunge.

Eventually, both the Whig and Democratic Parties turned their backs on Tyler, who gave up on running for election and left the White House after his term.

It's such a shame that I'll never run again!

Before he left the White House, a crowd that saw him standing by a White House window cheered for him.

Yeah Yeah Tyler!

Seeing this, it is said that Tyler threw one of the few jokes he ever made during his lifetime.

Who will now say that I am a man without a party?*

Sniff

*In other words, he meant the people were on his side.

After returning to his hometown in 1845, Tyler rejoined the Democratic Party in 1852.

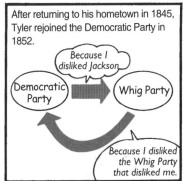

During the 1860 presidential election, the North and the South started undergoing a noisy split after the election of Lincoln as President.

Over slavery, division and war between the North and the South became imminent.

A supporter of slavery, Tyler was elected as chair of the Richmond Peace Convention in February 1861.

He delivered the resolution adopted by the Convention to President-elect Lincoln.

This is the unanimous opinion of the South.

The resolution made a demand for more extensive permission and expansion of slavery.

Slavery is clearly a state right, so the Union should keep out of state affairs,

and leave it up to the states newly joining the Union to decide...

Lincoln, of course, refused that proposition.

Any attempt to secede or separate from the Union over the issue of slavery

will not be tolerated on any account!

Tyler supported the secession of the South from the Union.

My words aren't getting through to Lincoln.

The only thing that remains now is separation of the South and the North!

Even though the threat of war looms, there is no longer any need to remain with the Union that seeks to revoke slavery and other state freedom and rights!

In November 1861, Tyler was elected as the Speaker of the newly created House of Representatives of the Confederate Congress,

but he died before he could assume office.

Tyler was the first President to remarry while he was in office. As a father of 15 children, he was also the President with the most children.

James K. Polk 1845~1849

Fierce Leader of the Era of Territorial Expansion

James Knox Polk

Democratic Party, 1795.11.2~1849.6.15

Birth Place   Mecklenburg County, North Carolina

Wife   Sarah Childress Polk 1803~1891

Children   None

Vice President   G.M. Dallas

Andrew Jackson was the political mentor of James Polk. Polk greatly respected Jackson.

Sir!

Boss!

One day, Polk asked Jackson for helpful advice on his political career.

Let me tell you this.

You need the help of a good wife to succeed in politics.

*So why don't you stop chasing women and get married.
Make a family.*

Taking Jackson's advice, in 1822, the 27-year old Polk proposed to Sarah Childress. She was 19 years old.

I'm politically ambitious just as much as you are.

If you become a state representative, I'll accept your proposal.

The next year, Polk was elected as a state representative, and the two were married in January 1824.

It's not easy getting married...

As the eleventh U.S. President, James Polk led America during a period of territorial expansion.

*Polk (second from right in front row) and his cabinet

He was a typical expansionist fully devoted to the expansion of U.S. territory.

Land!

And more land!

Land!

At that time, the theory that God had selected and granted to America control over the North American continent,

It's God's will. Go West!

That's a pretty self-seeking view.

i.e., Manifest Destiny, prevailed in America.

Manifest Destiny

It is God's order for America to rule!

Based on this belief, the U.S. mercilessly suppressed the Indians and took their land,

Out!

and also waged war against Mexico and Spain and seized huge territories.

Give it up!

At that time, America was busy with imperialistic territorial expansion.

USA

Going along with the times, Polk got elected by making a campaign pledge for 'territorial expansion' based on 'Manifest Destiny.'

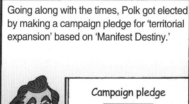

Campaign pledge

U.S. territorial expansion based on Divine Providence
∞

In order to 'faithfully' keep that pledge during his term, Polk used his best efforts and stood at the forefront of asserting 'U.S. supremacy.'

Take that land!

Buy that land!

White House

Is he in the realty business?

Born on November 2, 1795 in Mecklenburg County, North Carolina, Polk was raised in Tennessee.

KY   VA

Tennessee   North Carolina

South Carolina

AL   Georgia

Later on, he graduated from the University of North Carolina and became a lawyer in 1820, at the age of 25.

The system back then wasn't perfect,

so it wasn't difficult becoming a lawyer at so young an age.

Lawyer in 20s?

He then joined the Jacksonian Democratic Party and started his political career after winning election as a state representative.

· 1824   State Representative

U.S. Representative

· 1834~1839   Speaker of the House
(39~44 years old)

Governor of Tennessee

Polk twice failed to win re-election as governor after his first term.

Given such a background, it was a surprise that Polk emerged as a presidential candidate.

Polk? The guy who lost the gubernatorial election?

Unbelievable... The Democratic Party must be lacking for people.

Behind that decision was Andrew Jackson, the boss and leader of the Democratic Party.

I support Polk!

In the 1844 presidential election, Polk collided with Henry Clay*, the leader of the Whig Party and a senior member of Congress.

*1777~1852

Polk made two campaign pledges, both of which promised territorial expansion.

Pledge 1
Territorial expansion

Pledge 2
Territorial expansion

First, America would annex the huge territory of Texas.

691,201km²
(3 times the size of the Korean peninsula)

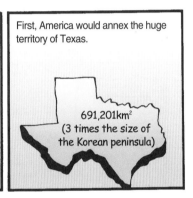

Second, America would push its northern border up to the 54°40'N latitude, and would not hesitate to go to war against Britain to achieve such objective.

Russian Alaska

Canada

54° 40′

Move up north to this point

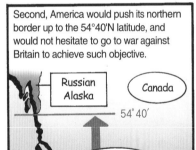

This was the campaign slogan of the Democratic Party!

Fifty-Four Forty or Fight!

54°40'N referred to the boundary of Alaska, which was then owned by Russia, meaning that America would take over the entire western coastline of the North American continent.

What about us...?

Canada

Pacific Ocean

United States

Britain, which ruled over Canada, was taken aghast by this American assertion.

This must be a joke...

If they say 54°40'N, doesn't that mean the entire western coastline of Canada would completely disappear?

The issue of America's northern boundary, i.e., the 'Oregon' question,

The Americans are so audacious. They're just going to take someone else's land?

was resolved without war after negotiations with Britain. The boundary was determined at 49th parallel north, the current boundary between Canada and America.

Alaska

Canada

Vancouver   49°

Victoria

United States

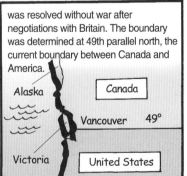

As he pledged, in 1845, Polk also annexed Texas as the twenty-eighth state of the United States.

Helped by such aggressive and expansionist campaign pledges, Polk narrowly won the election.

Results of 1844 Election			
Democratic Party		Whig Party	
James K. Polk			Henry Clay
1,339,494	Popular votes		1,300,004
170			105
	Electoral votes		

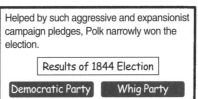

After he became President, Polk requested that Mexico sell its territory to America.

I'd like to buy some land from Mexico.

At what price?

I'll pay Mexico $30 million for both New Mexico and California. Let's throw Texas into that package.

I'm giving you guys a good deal in this depressed real estate market.

This guy's out to rob us...

Why don't you just take it from us!

I ain't selling!

As war became imminent between America and Mexico,

Stop poking your nose this way!

Polk issued a secret order to General Zachary Taylor, commander of U.S. forces.

I want you to keep provoking the Mexican Army

to induce them to attack first!

Only if Mexico attacks will America have the justification to go to war.

Provoked by the U.S. Army, in 1846, the Mexican Army clashed with the Americans at the Rio Grande and killed 16 American soldiers.

That was just what America had wanted. War finally broke out!

BOOM

But the 7,000 American troops were outnumbered by the 32,000 Mexican troops.

*Mexican War (1846~1848)

When the war broke out, American public opinion was divided.

Territorial expansion is a good thing! But...

We're opposed to doing it with military force!

Hey, how can you acquire new territory without a war?

NO WAR

ONLY WAR

Intellectuals like Henry David Thoreau* protested the war by choosing time in prison over payment of war taxes.

I dislike civilization

and the greed of man!

Walden Pond

*Author of 'Walden'

Ralph Waldo Emerson* was embarassed by America's display of brute force.

Wait and see, Mexico will continue to remain a thorn in America's side!

*American poet and thinker

A century and a half later, America is seeing the realization of his prediction.

Sharp increase in Hispanic population in the U.S.

Explosive illegal immigrants from Mexico!

U.S.

Mexico

Later on, General Ulysses S. Grant, the Civil War hero, is also said to have lamented what America did to Mexico.

America did things that were truly embarassing!

In any event, the U.S. Army defeated the numerically superior Mexican Army,

and brought the two-year war to an end.

· May 13, 1846
U.S. declaration of war
· September 14, 1847
U.S. occupation of Mexico City
· February 2, 1848
Conclusion of peace treaty

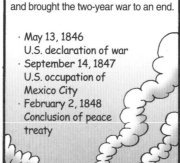

In 1848, America and Mexico concluded the Treaty of Guadalupe Hidalgo.

Sign here!

By this treaty, America acquired California, Nevada, Utah, significant portions of New Mexico and Arizona (including portions of Wyoming and Colorado),

Territory ceded to America by Mexico

and also acquired Texas with a border at the Rio Grande, for which America paid to Mexico only $18,250,000.

This is barefaced robbery...

In one stroke, America acquired 1,280,000km^2 in new territory that is six times the size of the Korean peninsula.

POP!

Despite the acquisition of this new territory, Polk's political adversaries fiercely attacked him.

What's wrong? Didn't I win the war?

The opposition Whig Party cited an ethical issue,

Wasn't the war intended to boost your approval rating by expanding territory without regard to principle?

while New England states cited the slavery issue.

The newly acquired territory is all in the Southern region!

It's clear they will become slave states. Polk seeks to preserve slavery!

Despite the war victory, Polk's approval rating plunged.

Approval rating

How could this happen when I won the war...

Although he kept his promise and achieved his objectives as a 'strong President,'

They complain whether or not I keep my promises...

It ain't easy being President!

He failed to win confidence with his military exploits, nor did he have the charisma to overcome the public opinion against him.

Polk is incompetent!

ROAR ROAR

In particular, General Zachary Taylor, a Mexican War hero,

was nominated as the presidential candidate of the Whig Party,

Yeah

WHIG VICTOR

Hurray

ZACHARY

and spread all kinds of criticism and vicious rumors that dealt a decisive blow to Polk.

He's a war fanatic who sacrifices American soldiers!

Territorial expansion was intended to satisfy his personal ambitions.

His father evaded fighting in the Revolutionary War.

Polk failed in his bid to obtain nomination as the presidential candidate for the Democratic Party. He gave up his dream

You didn't make the cut. Your prospect for election is nil.

Democratic Party

of re-election and returned to his hometown, where his health rapidly deteriorated.

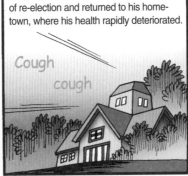

Cough cough

He died three months after leaving the White House.

If Andrew Jackson was old hickory, Polk was young hickory.

JAMES KNOX POLK

Zachary Taylor 1849~1850

Career Soldier who Went Straight to the White House

A war breeds heros!

Mexico

General

President

Zachary Taylor

Whig Party, 1784.11.24 ~ 1850.7.9

Birth Place Orange County, Virginia
Wife Margaret Mackall Smith Taylor
1788~1852
Children Ann, Sarah Knox, Octavia, Margaret, Mary, Elizabeth, Richard
Vice President Millard Fillmore

Zachary Taylor wasn't a politician.

Don't know much about that...

Politics

Even though he became President based on his distinguished military service as a soldier—just like Washington, Jackson and Harrison—

---

he had never held elected office, nor had he ever voted in a presidential election other than in his own election.

A soldier should not poke his nose into politics!

He became President only because he was a Mexican War hero.

Voters turned their backs on Polk, the actual victor in the war, and selected Taylor who had fought in the war at Polk's orders.

Taylor! Taylor!

Hey... I was the producer and director of the war...

This showed that American politics had already become heavily influenced by candidate popularity, populism and image politics.

You go to the playhouse to see the actor, not the director.

The American public saw Taylor catapult to hero status through the victory in the Mexican War.

The Whig Party, which was hardpressed to find a candidate who could defeat the Democratic Party's President Polk,

Wow, Taylor's a really popular guy!

ROAR ROAR

The WHIGS

nominated Taylor as its presidential candidate over Daniel Webster and Henry Clay, political bigshots in their own right back then.

Sir, please accept our party's nomination!

Candidate

Even though Taylor had no experience in any election let alone politics itself,

This isn't my style...

Candidate

the Democratic Party was divided as a result of Martin Van Buren, who was seeking to run for President again.

Democratic Party

Free Soil Party

Thus, Taylor was able to win the election by playing off this situation.

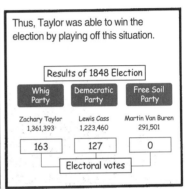

Results of 1848 Election		
Whig Party	Democratic Party	Free Soil Party
Zachary Taylor 1,361,393	Lewis Cass 1,223,460	Martin Van Buren 291,501
163	127	0
Electoral votes		

After Taylor entered the White House as President,

What should we do about the resisting Indians?

true to his military background, he aggressively tackled political issues.

Crush them!

Later on, Abraham Lincoln said of Taylor:

Taylor won wars based on his resolute judgement and conviction, rather than strategy.

However, before he could accomplish anything as President, on Independence Day in 1850,

Doctor, call a doctor!

Taylor collapsed after suffering from stomach cramps brought on by overeating in humid weather. He died five days later.

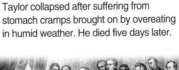

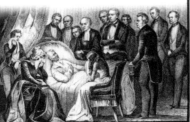

It had been only 16 months since his inauguration.

How could a general who beat all of his enemies

fail to overcome an illness?

ZACHARY TAYLOR 1784-1850

Zachary Taylor was born on November 24, 1784 in Orange County, Virginia.

Virginia again?

At that time, Virginia covered most of the southern United States.

He joined the army in 1808 and served as a career soldier for 40 years,

and then, from there, directly became President. He was the second President to die in office. Indeed, his career was a rare one.

Pretty unusual life, eh?

General | President

As a dutiful and courageous soldier, Taylor served with great distinction during the War of 1812 against Britain.

After the war, he focused on putting down Indians and won recognition for his merciless suppression of Indian uprisings.

To the Indians, he was a dreadful oppressor, the 'Grim Reaper.'

Curses fall on Taylor!

Taylor was known as 'Old Rough and Ready.'

It means that I was a 'rough, experienced and prepared officer.'

He earned this nickname through his rough and merciless destruction of opponents.

As an officer, he was always prepared to do just that to his opponents.

I'll smash to pieces anyone who wants a fight!

When war with Mexico became imminent over territorial issues,

Mexican border

a secret order from President Polk was delivered to Taylor.

Provoke Mexico to shoot first!

After receiving this order, Taylor immediately ordered his men to take action.

Cross the border and surround the Mexican village!

After illegally crossing the border, American soldiers naturally faced resistance from the Mexican Army.

After the gun fight began, Taylor reported the situation to the President.

I believe the enemy's animosity has reached such a level that we can now start the war.

The war will start soon. The first to strike will seize the advantage. We shall strike first!

The Americans started marching against the Mexicans without making a formal declaration of war.

What? The U.S. Army has attacked without declaring war?

Mexico was dealt a severe blow by this surprise attack.

In 1848, after the war, Taylor had become a hero.

Roar — Long live General Taylor! — Roar — Roar

Although the majority of the Whig Party members opposed the Mexican War that turned Taylor into a hero,

Hurray Taylor! Yeah — No war — THE WHIGS

the Whig Party nevertheles presented him as its 1848 presidential candidate.

We have to win the election anyway,

and there's no other candidate of Taylor's caliber who can defeat the Democratic candidate!

THE WHIGS

Taylor was the first President to have no experience as a legislator. He was totally inexperienced as a politician.

Z. Taylor		
Resume		X
State Representative		X
U.S. Representative		X
Senator		X
Governor		X

Although his wife prayed in earnest for her husband to lose the election,

Please have him remain here in his hometown...

high expectations were placed on Taylor to resolve the slavery issue with his soldier-like spirit and conviction.

Taylor will be able to resolve the slavery issue

that no one has been able to resolve yet.

South — North

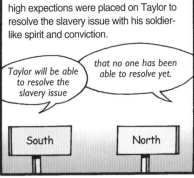

So he was elected as the twelfth U.S. President with balanced Northern and Southern support.

We support Taylor.

South — North

Although the Mexican War resulted in great territorial expansion for America,

it also brought along enormous problems, in particular a more serious showdown between the North and the South over slavery.

Honey, we have to register these children as ours.

The issue of whether or not states from the new territory would permit slavery

South   North

could shake the very delicate balance between the North and the South.

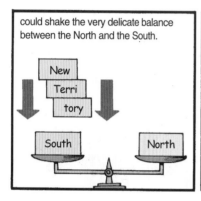

Taylor was from the South,

Slavery permitted South

Slaves needed for plantation work

Slavery outlawed North

Factory workers paid wages

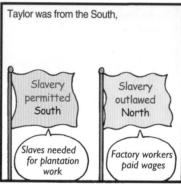

and he owned 80 slaves.

However, he viewed slavery from the perspective of the North,

I'm opposed to the expansion of slavery.

so it was made clear that new states joining the Union were to be free states.

Although territory where slavery already existed will be permitted to join the Union...

"States that haven't yet formally adopted slavery will not be permitted to join the Union as slave states!"

Petition for Entry into Union

Our state, which has become U.S. territory from Mexican territory, hereby submits this petition for entry into the Union as a slave state.

Rejected

Taylor's supporters in the South heavily resisted this policy.

This is clearly an open challenge to the South!

If the number of free states were to increase like this, that would break the balance between the North and the South, and such imbalance would disadvantage the South!

This is clearly an infringement of state rights, and we shall consider secession from the Union!

So, Mr. President, you want to play rough, huh?

To appease the South that was resisting and threatening secession from the Union,

Secession

Carrot!

Congress squabbled over whether to accept the Compromise of 1850, an argument that lasted until Taylor's death.

Compromise 1850

Yeah — YES! / Nay — NO!

In exchange for letting the people decide on whether to permit slavery, the slavery laws were to be strengthened to protect the interests of Southern slave owners.

1. The people shall determine whether to permit slavery in states newly joining the Union.

2. Strengthening of slavery laws / Restriction on aiding the escape of slaves / More stringent searches to be conducted for fugitive slaves

The Compromise of 1850 only temporarily stopped the inevitable great collision between the North and the South.

It only delayed the great collision by 10 years.

Whew~

In the afternoon of Independence Day in 1850, Taylor collapsed from stomach cramps brought on by overeating cherries and milk in the humid weather.

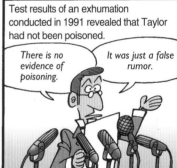

Oh!

My stomach hurts!

He died five days later on July 9. Based on the very poor hygiene conditions of Washington D.C. at that time, some say that he died of cholera,

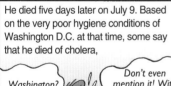

Washington?

Don't even mention it! With the mud and flies and mosquitos...

while, due to the sudden nature of his death, others continually speculated that he was poisoned.

It must have been poisoning...

by the group that opposed Taylor's policies.

Test results of an exhumation conducted in 1991 revealed that Taylor had not been poisoned.

There is no evidence of poisoning.

It was just a false rumor.

His sudden death must have comforted the pro-slavery faction within Congress

Whew~

Aw Shucks

South

North

because compared to Taylor, a Southerner strongly opposed to slavery,

Slavery must not be expanded!

his successor Millard Fillmore was pro-slavery despite being a Northerner.

The interests of Southern slave owners must be protected!

Millard Fillmore 1850~1853

From Tailor to the White House

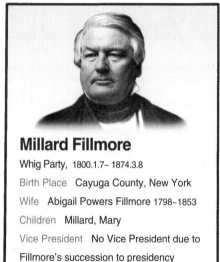

Millard Fillmore

Whig Party, 1800.1.7~ 1874.3.8

Birth Place   Cayuga County, New York

Wife   Abigail Powers Fillmore 1798~1853

Children   Millard, Mary

Vice President   No Vice President due to Fillmore's succession to presidency

---

Millard Fillmore was the second Vice President in U.S. history to succeed to the Office of President.

Compared to the deceased Taylor, he was viewed as more capable and receptive to compromise.

But the problem was that the nation was split over the issue of slavery,

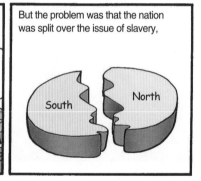

---

and there was no room for any leader to exercise his ability to reach compromise, regardless of his capability.

So although Lincoln's predecessors are politically viewed as incompetent leaders,

that may be an unfair assessment of those men given the circumstances they faced back then.

Unlike most other U.S. Presidents, Fillmore came from poor and humble origins.

He was born on January 7, 1800 in a log cabin in Cayuga County, New York.

Cayuga County

Due to his needy circumstances, he couldn't go to school and was apprenticed to a tailor.

With self-study, he subsequently became a lawyer in Buffalo.

Presidents who became lawyers through self-study

7th
Andrew Jackson

8th
Martin Van Buren

Like many young lawyers back then, Fillmore became attracted to politics.

Washington D.C.

Yes, I shall realize my dream in politics!

After a stint with the New York State Assembly, he served four terms as a U.S. Representative.

· 1883~1835
· 1837~1839
· 1839~1841
· 1841~1843

Whig Party

THE WHIGS

He lost the 1844 election for the governorship of New York,

Defeated!

but was nominated as the vice presidential candidate in the 1848 presidential election.

Candidate for President	Candidate for Vice President
Zachary Taylor	Millard Fillmore

It helped to have the ardent support of his New York electoral district.

Vice President from our state!

Go Fillmore!

Hurray Roar

New York State

It also helped that voters feared the radical nature of his competitors.

I'm sick and tired of this presidential candidate nonsense!

Those guys are too radical...

Let's flip society upside down!

Fillmore assumed the presidency within 16 months of becoming Vice President due to the death of Taylor,

ZACHARY TAYLOR

but there was almost nothing he could accomplish as an unelected President in the midst of the intense fighting between the North and the South over slavery.

What am I supposed to do?

South   North

Furthermore, at that time, Congress was dominated by the most prominent congressmen in U.S. history.

| Henry Clay | Steven Douglas | Jefferson Davis |

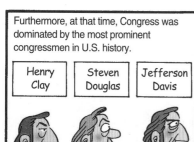

They overpowered the government and took the initiative in politics.

| John C. Calhoun | Daniel Webster |

Inevitably, after Fillmore became President, he had no choice but to acquiesce to the powerful Congress.

Congress

The presidency was weakened by Congress, which was divided along the lines of the North and the South. Congress incessantly fought over slavery. In such circumstances,

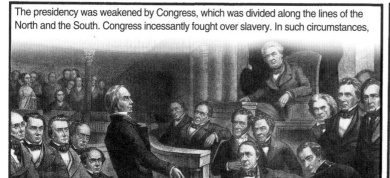

there was little that the President could do but watch the situation deteriorate.

NO!
ROAR
YES!
ROAR

However, when South Carolina started suggesting that it might secede from the Union,

We can no longer get along with the North!

Fillmore realized that he could no longer tolerate the situation and threatened to take strong military action.

If I face resistance that is too strong to overcome by law,

BANG

then it is my duty as President to use all means, including military force!

The secessionists calmed down for a while after seeing the resolute stand taken by the President.

!

That was pretty scary...

And the risk of division of the nation also eased a bit, for a while.

I guess he wasn't a pushover...

Whew...

Didn't know he had such a temper...

But that was just the beginning of more serious division and conflict.

Pretty impressive, eh?

War

As soon as he became President, Fillmore accepted the Compromise of 1850,

which made it very easy for Southerners to capture fugitive slaves.

Hey, this isn't even your state...

Southerners went so far as to capture and bring back thousands of slaves who had escaped to Canada.

Canada? I'll go as far as hell to get you back!

But Fillmore thought the Compromise of 1850 was the only way to resolve the confrontation between the North and the South,

Haven't you gone too far?

If you have a better way, let's hear about it.

and he attacked the many Northerners, who were opposed to this law, as too extreme.

Hey, slaves are personal property. Why is the North making such a big fuss over that?

I am the most American of all, so I am prepared to resist the extreme elements of the North!

Nevertheless, the Compromise of 1850 and the Fugitive Slave Act were seriously flawed because they did not allow a slave to even receive a trial,

I'm a freed slave but I was wrongfully kidnapped...

We have no jurisdiction to hear your case!

Court

nor did they provide for any mechanism that could protect even freed slaves in the North.

I told you I'm a freed slave!

You're mine now!

The law itself was incomplete and contradictory,

You think you can solve the problems by just siding with the South?

This is a completely unreasonable law that only benefits slave owners!

and insulting to the anti-slavery public opinion that strongly prevailed in the North.

We voted for him because he was a Northerner,

and now he's at the forefront of supporting slavery as President?

North

Roar
Roar

Fillmore, a passive abolitionist, eventually signed the Fugitive Slave Act into law.

This is the only way to preserve peace in America...

This angered the North and eventually destroyed Fillmore's chance of winning re-election.

Unfaithful traitor Fillmore!

Drive him out in the next election!

There was a small diplomatic victory that remains as an achievement of his administration. It was the opening of Japan.

With Britain's victory over the Qing Dynasty in the Opium War that lasted from 1840 to 1842,

European powers started their aggression against Asia and Africa.

The U.S. also sought to acquire colonies by joining the bandwagon,

but European nations such as Britain and France had already encroached upon China.

So there wasn't enough room for the U.S. to join the party.

The U.S. thus selected Japan, which was yet untouched by European powers,

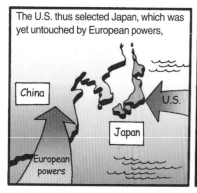

and, in 1853, sent Commodore Matthew C. Perry and four warships to Japan with demands that the country open up to trade.

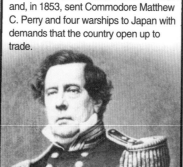

*Matthew Calbraith Perry (1794~1858)

In response, the next year, Japan concluded the U.S.-Japan Treaty of Amity and Commerce and ended its seclusion.

Perry was sent by Fillmore,

but the treaty was concluded during his successor Pierce's administration.

The opening of Japan led to the Meiji Restoration of 1868,

and served as a basis for Japan's emergence as a strong military power in East Asia.

But the U.S. was unable to further meddle with Japan because domestically it was heading toward the Civil War.

Fillmore left the White House in 1853 after failing to win the nomination as the Whig Party's presidential candidate.

If they won't give me the opportunity, then what can I do...

White House

The new President was elected from the Democratic Party, and, as such, Fillmore became the last Whig Party President.

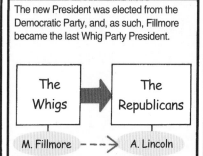

The Whigs	→	The Republicans
M. Fillmore	- - ->	A. Lincoln
Last President		First President

In 1856, he ran for President as a candidate for a small party, but suffered a crushing defeat with only eight electoral votes.

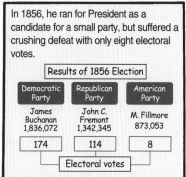

Results of 1856 Election		
Democratic Party	Republican Party	American Party
James Buchanan 1,836,072	John C. Fremont 1,342,345	M. Fillmore 873,053
174	114	8
	Electoral votes	

After his retirement, he returned to Buffalo, which was just like his second hometown, and dedicated himself to the local community.

How're you doing these days?

Not so bad...

He died there on March 8, 1874.

Lake Ontario

Lake Erie

Buffalo

New York State

New York City

Although he was an 'unsuccessful' President who failed to win recognition during his times, Fillmore was a capable and warm-hearted President.

Millard Fillmore

13th U.S. President

Failed to win nomination as candidate for re-election
Defeated in 1856 election
North-South problems worsened

After leaving the presidency, Fillmore visited the University of Oxford in Britain in 1855.

The University of Oxford offered him an honorary doctorate, but he modestly turned the offer down.

I lacked the benefit of a classical education.

No man should accept a degree he cannot read.

In contrast, when Andrew Jackson received an honorary doctorate from Harvard University,

Best day of my life!

No more regrets for not having gone to school...

Sniff

it is said that he shouted out the few Latin words he had memorized.

E pluribus Unum! Sine qua non

Don't ask me what it means!

It's like he's teaching fish how to swim...

Compared to Jackson, a man full of vanity and a sense of inferiority for his lack of schooling, Fillmore at least seems to have known his place.

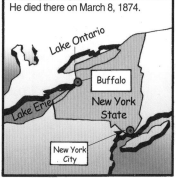

Franklin Pierce 1853~1857

Northern Traitor, Southern Sympathizer

Franklin Pierce

Democratic Party, 1804.11.23~1869.10.8

Birth Place   Hillsboro, New Hampshire

Wife   Jane Means Appleton Pierce 1806~1863

Children   Franklin Jr., Frank Robert, Benjamin

Vice President   W. R. King

As exemplified by his illustrious public career, Franklin Pierce led a remarkable life in public service.

Although Pierce was a kind and good person, and a skilled orator and pleasant drinking companion,

history records him as an incompetent President who was incapable of stopping the massive wave striking in the direction of the Civil War.

He is one of the several incompetent Presidents recorded in history, men whose efforts and will power were futile.

They lived in times during which no man could distinguish himself without resolving the North-South conflict,

which could be resolved only by an extreme measure like war.

Pierce was born as the governor's son in Hillsboro, New Hampshire.

He graduated from Bowdoin College and was admitted to the bar at the age of 23.

Helped by his family background, Pierce made his debut in Washington society and rapidly ascended the political ladder.

At a young age, he became a U.S. Representative as a Democrat, and, in his thirties, a U.S. Senator.

Wow, a rocket ride to success...

But his wife hated politics,

Franklin, I beg you to retire from politics.

The political world is too ugly and dirty.

So in 1842 (at the age of 38), he resigned from the Senate and left political life.

Stop grumbling and come with me!

Pierce fought in the Mexican War that broke out in the mid-1840s and rose through the ranks from private to brigadier general. However, there are no records that show he served with distinction.

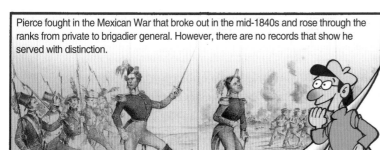

*Caricature depicting Pierce as a dull officer

After the war, despite his wife's opposition, Pierce returned to political life.

They say politics is addictive like drugs...

Once you get a taste of it, there's no way out!

In 1852, when her husband was nominated as the presidential candidate at the Democratic National Convention,

*Democratic National Convention back then

it is said that Mrs. Pierce fainted at the news. The shock was just too much for her.

Oh my~

If he serves as President during these chaotic times,

no matter how good a job he does, he'll just lose everything! Fool!

Why did the Democratic Party nominate Pierce as its presidential candidate?

The party highly regarded his undying loyalty to the party.

Loyalty, Sir!

Would he turn his back on us after he wins the presidency...?

Also, as a Southern sympathizer, Southern support was assured because he wasn't opposed to slavery.

SLAVERY YES

South

Since he was a Northerner, the Democratic Party also calculated that he would receive Northern support as well.

We shouldn't elect a Southerner as President, right?

I'm a Northerner

North

Pierce, who was adept at clique politics, took advantage of the 'machine' system.

whisper

whisper

So in the 1852 presidential election, Pierce defeated war hero Winfield Scott.

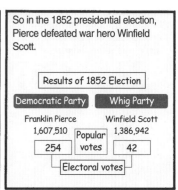

Results of 1852 Election	
Democratic Party	Whig Party
Franklin Pierce	Winfield Scott
1,607,510	1,386,942

Popular votes

254	42

Electoral votes

But immediately after his inauguration, ominous signs showed up.

RUMBLE

Emboldened by the inauguration of a pro-Southern President, the South became more vocal.

With the President under our control,

let's put pressure on the North and secure a clear advantage!

Northerners who voted for Pierce also started complaining and resisting.

Those Southerners have already started!

They must think they now dominate the world!

Pouring oil on fire, Harriet Beecher Stowe published a novel entitled 'Uncle Tom's Cabin,'

Uncle Tom's Cabin

H.B. Stowe

prompting even Northerners who had been apathetic to slavery to actively oppose it.

Didn't know that slaves lived such a miserable life.

Such an inhumane system should be abolished right away!

Lightning and thunder now accompanied the clouds of a civil war.

There's no place to hide from the storm now...

RUMBLE

In addition, Southerners filled most cabinet posts.

Cabinet of F. Pierce

Secretary of State	William L. Marsh	S
Secretary of Treasury	James Guthrie	S
Secretary of War	Jefferson Davis	S
Secretary of the Navy	James C. Dobbin	N
Attorney General	Caleb Cushing	S
Secretary of the Interior	R. McClelland	N

Jefferson Davis, then named as Secretary of War, later on became President of the Confederate States of America. So you can imagine

*Mr. and Mrs. Jefferson Davis

the level of Northern discontent and the magnitude of the North-South conflict, which had now reached uncontrollable proportions.

We voted for this guy from the North, and he's just siding with the South!

He's just concerned about the breakup of the Union without regard to the North...

As for the sensitive and unavoidable issue of slavery,

Pierce tried to avoid it as much as possible.

Let's not further provoke each other. Let's just maintain the status quo.

But the Kansas-Nebraska Act that was enacted in 1854

Kansas-Nebraska Act
(1854)

Settlers shall determine whether to allow slavery in this territory.

Kansas is located north of latitude 36° 30'.

nullified the Missouri Compromise itself that was concluded in 1820.

Missouri Compromise

Nullified!

Slavery shall be prohibited north of latitude 36° 30'.

This prompted a small-scale civil war known as 'Bloody Kansas' in the Kansas Territory.

Kill them Southerners!

Drive out those Northerners!

Kansas

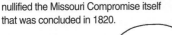

The pro-Southern Pierce's attitude eventually caused him to lose the support of the North and the nomination for re-election.

Screech

STOP

Like his predecessors, Pierce aggressively pursued diplomatic policies that expanded U.S. territory.

It is Manifest Destiny for the U.S. to expand its territory! We shall even resort to force to achieve expansion!

His biggest achievement was the Gadsden Purchase,

So you want to buy some land?

I'm President Pierce's special envoy J. Gadsden.

involving the purchase of 75,000km² of land in what is now southern New Mexico and southern Arizona from Mexico for $10 million.

California

Land purchased from Mexico

Gila River

Mexico

This purchase was greatly welcomed by the South

because it secured land for construction of a transcontinental railroad connecting the South and the Pacific Ocean,

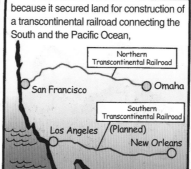

which could compete against the transcontinental railroad being constructed by the North.

But the Ostend Manifesto ended in failure while exposing America's belligerency.

In the 1850s, the slave uprising that occurred on the nearby Cuban island

instilled great fear in Southern slave owners.

Taking advice from his ministers to Spain, France and Britain,

Pierce announced the so-called Ostend Manifesto.

"If it is deemed that Spanish ownership of the Cuban island constitutes a threat to U.S. peace and independence, it shall be justifiable for the U.S. to take Cuba by force!"

As soon as the manifesto was announced, the North offered fierce resistance.

Thus, Pierce's plan to occupy Cuba eventually failed due to Northern opposition.

Pierce's pro-Southern disposition and policies designed to appease the South

turned out to be like pouring oil on fire.

At the 1856 Democratic convention, the Democratic Party nominated James Buchanan as its presidential candidate over Pierce.

The Bloody Kansas incident was the largest stain of his administration.

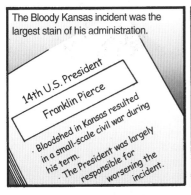

His submission to the powerful Southern faction in the party and his pro-Southern propensity

eventually drove the nation toward division and civil war.

After finishing his term, Pierce returned to his hometown in New Hampshire.

Even though he made an effort to not attract the attention of others,

he fiercely criticized Abraham Lincoln's policies.

Franklin Pierce was probably the best-looking President among all Presidents,

but he suffered from a respiratory illness throughout his life, and his sons all died before reaching adulthood.

Pierce himself wasn't mourned very much and was buried next to his wife who had thoroughly despised politics.

James Buchanan 1857~1861

Another Sacrificial Lamb of the North-South Conflict

James Buchanan

We can definitely solve the problem with this!

Love and side with the South

North-South Conflict

James Buchanan

Democratic Party, 1791.4.23~1868.6.1

Birth Place   Cove Gap, Pennsylvania
Wife   None (Buchanan was a lifelong bachelor)
Children   None
Vice President   C. Breckinridge

It's difficult to find another President who so thoroughly prepared himself in public office with such strong principles before entering the White House.

I'm a President prepared to resolve the North-South problems!

Even though Buchanan assured the nation that he would resolve the North-South problems,

I will devote all my efforts to the resolution of the issue of slavery

and mediate North-South conflicts and disputes.

---

the Civil War broke out only six weeks after his term ended.

BOOM

In fact, James Buchanan actually raised the likelihood of war.

War

His case exemplified the consequences of having an inappropriate person serve as President,

Shuffle~

---

regardless of his capability and experience.

I'm not up to the task!

Buchanan was born in 1791 in Cove Gap, Pennsylvania to a wealthy Scottish father and Irish mother.

At the age of 23 when he graduated from college, he was elected to the Pennsylvania House of Representatives,

Wow, at so young an age...

He's got a solid future in front of him.

and, before the age of 30, to the U.S. House of Representatives. He served five consecutive terms as a U.S. Representative before becoming elected as a U.S. Senator.

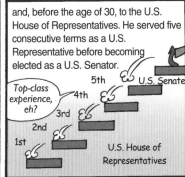

Top-class experience, eh?

5th — U.S. Senate
4th
3rd
2nd
1st
U.S. House of Representatives

Although Buchanan was the front runner for the presidential candidate nomination at the Democratic Convention in 1852,

Buchanan! Buchanan!

For presidential candidate!

he lost the nomination to the unknown Franklin Pierce, and finally garnered the nomination only in 1856.

By then, he had served in various major government posts, including ministers to Russia and Britain.

He played a role in the Ostend Manifesto...

as minister to Britain.

London

Like his predecessor Pierce, despite being a Northerner, Buchanan was pro-Southern in disposition.

North

South

Why did the Democratic Party nominate Buchanan—who resembled Pierce—as its presidential candidate when it had already failed with Pierce?

We chose a Northerner

and all he did was side with the South.

Buchanan will probably be different!

First, the Democratic Party needed Southern votes to win the election. There was no other Northerner who received as much support from the South as Buchanan.

Buchanan

Southern votes

Second, the party calculated that Buchanan's diverse international experience from his service as ministers to Russia and Britain would be helpful to American foreign policy.

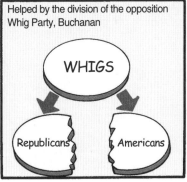

There ain't a politician who is as internationally experienced as Buchanan.

Helped by the division of the opposition Whig Party, Buchanan

WHIGS

Republicans   Americans

easily won the election and was inaugurated as President amid high hopes of the Democrats.

You didn't know standing divided only weakens you?

Dem

Rep.   Amer.

Panel 1: But contrary to the promises made to the Democratic Party,

I'll evenly appoint both Northerners and Southerners to my cabinet, taking into account party factions.

Panel 2: Buchanan appointed only his closest allies without taking into account the various factions that supported him.

This is a call for my buddies!

Pro-Buchanan faction gather here!

Those who think alike with me, come!

Panel 3: Thus, resistance arose in the Democratic Party,

So he's going to appoint only those persons who are aligned with him?

How dare he leave us out like this? We made him President!

Panel 4: not to mention fierce opposition in the North due to Buchanan's biased support of the Southern position.

Why this reverse discrimination of the North?

They cried out aloud, so I gave them another rice cake!

Panel 5:

Unless I pay closer attention to the South, they're going to talk of secession...

Do Americans eat rice cakes too?

Panel 6:

He said he'd 'mediate' Northern and Southern relations, but all he's doing is engaging in a sunshine policy in favor of the South only.

Out of fear of offending the South, he can't even say what's on his mind. He's just at his wit's end...

Panel 7: Out of his seven cabinet members, Buchanan chose four Southerner slave owners,

*Buchanan's cabinet

Panel 8: while two out of the other three were Northern supporters of the South.

Panel 9: No wonder the North was so critical of Buchanan.

Why don't you name your administration the 'Southern administration?'

Remember what Pierce got when he did what you did?

Panel 10:

Buchanan is a Southern sympathizer from the North! He's an anti-Northern, pro-Southern activist!

Buchanan shall fail as President! He will pay for his deeds!

Panel 11: His support of slavery was exemplified by his conduct in the Dred Scott* case.

*Dred Scott (1795~1858)

Panel 12: While the entire country focused on this case, which was fought out as a proxy war between the North and the South,

Slaves who have entered free states are no longer slaves! Regardless of

whether they have gone to free states, slaves are the property of their owners!

ROAR ROAR

Buchanan bribed the judge, among others, in his hometown Pennsylvania

We need to calm down the South to prevent the breakup of the Union.

to obtain a favorable judgment for the South.

South

North

This kind of one-sided pro-Southern disposition brought about fierce Northern resistance

Is the federal government the puppet of the South?

Isn't Buchanan a Northerner?

Buchanan has betrayed us!

and caused Buchanan to lose the presidential nomination for re-election.

No nomination for you!

In such circumstances, the Democrats would have had a hard time winning the election even if they had been united.

Democrats

Repub-licans

But Buchanan couldn't overcome his hatred of rival Steven Douglas,

Even if I have to split the party,

I won't support that guy for President!

and the Democratic Party eventually split up.

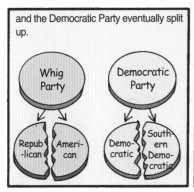

Whig Party

Democratic Party

Repub-lican

Ameri-can

Demo-cratic

South-ern Demo-cratic

In the 1860 presidential election, Buchanan's political foe Steven Douglas ran as the divided Democratic Party candidate,

I'm the legitimate presidential candidate of the Democratic Party!

DEMOCRATIC

while Breckinridge, Buchanan's Vice President, also ran.

A Southerner must become President...

Douglas must lose...

SOUTHERN DEMOCRATIC

Under these circumstances, the Republican Party's Abraham Lincoln managed to easily win the election.

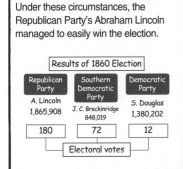

Results of 1860 Election		
Republican Party	Southern Democratic Party	Democratic Party
A. Lincoln 1,865,908	J. C. Breckinridge 848,019	S. Douglas 1,380,202
180	72	12
	Electoral votes	

The weak pro-Southern policies designed to appease the South and prevent secession could never be a solution,

South

so like Pierce, Buchanan only ended up raising the likelihood of war while failing in his bid for re-election.

Presidents who failed to become re-elected due to the North-South conflict
8th   Martin Van Buren
9th   W.H. Harris (died in office)
10th   J. Tyler
11th   J.K. Polk
12th   Z. Taylor (died in office)
13th   M. Fillmore
14th   F. Pierce
15th   J. Buchanan

With Lincoln's election, South Carolina seceded from the Union.

With a pro-Northern government in place, there's no reason to remain in the Union.

Although Buchanan emphasized the illegality of such action,

You... can't do... that... It's not... wrong... to say... that...

he didn't take any measure to stop South Carolina, thereby opening the possibility of further secession of Southern states.

Why are you letting them secede?

How could I stop them when they're walking out on us?

Instead, he blamed the North for the secession of the South.

I can well imagine why they're leaving the Union!

It's because of the excessive Northern interference in the issue of slavery in the South!

It's one thing for the North to not permit slavery. Why interfere in the affairs of other states whose freedom and rights are guaranteed?

Who cares if they permit slavery or have their women wear guns or pick their teeth with firewood? What does it matter to the North?!

Is that guy really a Northerner?

Watch your mouth Buchanan!

Whenever that guy opens his mouth he makes me nervous...

A President needs to spare his words!

Buchanan asked Lincoln on the way to the new President's inauguration ceremony.

I'm now leaving the presidency.

Are you happy that you've become President?

If I were leaving the presidency, I'd probably be happier.

The presidency is a really tough office.

If you are as happy in entering the White House as I shall feel on returning home, you are the happiest man in this country!

Having never married, Buchanan was the only bachelor President in U.S. history.

Bachelor President~

He was a prudent man but was also criticized as whimsical and opportunistic.

Need to maintain my approval rating...

Otherwise, I'll lose my votes...

At the same time, he was a very stubborn man who blindly pursued a path once his mind was made up.

Not that way, Sir!

Shut up! I'm gonna go my way!

He was not the type of impartial and neutral leader that America needed in the chaotic 1850s.

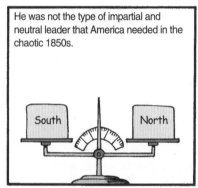

South

North

Buchanan refused to listen to Northern public opinion,

You're not hearing the North out...

Even if I were to take the time to drink tea and eat bread together with a Northerner, what would we talk about?

NO!

and only opened his ears to the South.

Let's move the administrative capital to the South!

We need to set Southern history straight!

Let's investigate and punish pro-Northern activities.

This only had the effect of fanning the bellicosity of the South.

He listens if we make demands!

He yields if we press him!

South

After leaving office, Buchanan devoted all his efforts to justifying himself,

I didn't do anything wrong, right?

Lincoln started the war!

I didn't start the war, right?

and continued to insist that the North was to blame for the Civil War.

It's a war that started after the South first attacked...

Didn't the North induce the South to attack?

U.S. history records him as a not-so intelligent person who made up for lack of ability by painful preparation.

Hard Work

In any event, he appears to have been a good man regardless of his support of slavery

Southern states are free to maintain slavery...

because he continued to acquire slaves from the South and free them in Pennsylvania, a free state.

but slavery is an inhumane institution!

Abraham Lincoln 1861~1865

Hero, Saint and Martyr: A Giant in U.S. History

Abraham Lincoln

Leader who won victory in war

Saint who declared the emancipation of slaves

Martyr who died at the bullet of an assassin

Established an undividable, unified nation

Emancipation Proclamation

Created a free nation for all!

Abraham Lincoln

Republican Party, 1809.2.12~1865.4.15

Birth Place   Hardin, Kentucky

Wife   Mary Todd Lincoln 1731~1802

Children   Robert Todd, Edward Baker, William Willis, Thomas

Vice Presidents   H. Hamlin 1861

Andrew Johnson 1865

In 1999, C-SPAN, a public service cable television station, conducted a poll on the popularity of U.S. presidents.

Which President do you respect the most?

At that time, there were a total of 41 Presidents to choose from (Bill Clinton, the 42nd President, was in office, and Cleveland had served as the 22nd and 24th Presidents).

Hmm, the President who I most respect is...

The ranking of the Presidents most respected by Americans was

No. 1	Abraham Lincoln	856
No. 2	George Washington	840
No. 3	Theodore Roosevelt	826
No. 4	Franklin D. Roosevelt	798
No. 5	Thomas Jefferson	793
No. 6	Ronald Reagan	771
⋮	⋮	⋮

The ranking of the Presidents least respected by Americans was···

No. 35	William Harrison	461
No. 36	Bill Clinton	455
No. 37	Millard Fillmore	437
No. 38	Andrew Johnson	428
No. 39	Franklin Pierce	410
No. 40	Warren Harding	385
No. 41	James Buchanan	366

Even in other polls, Lincoln is generally ranked as the most beloved and respected President by Americans.

What could be the reason for the polar difference between Lincoln's ranking and his predecessor James Buchanan's ranking···

Lincoln 16th

Ranked 1st

15th   Buchanan

Ranked last

Lincoln is a giant figure in U.S. history.

In fact, physically, he was the tallest of all U.S. Presidents

A. Lincoln	193cm
(Tallest)	

James Madison	162.5cm
(Smallest)	

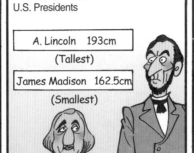

Regardless of nationality, the people wish to have a heroic leader capable of wisely leading the nation in times of crisis.

Dunno if you lead well because you're a hero,

or if you become a hero because you lead well...

It's no coincidence that these men are consistently ranked as Presidents most respected by Americans.

1. Lincoln

2. Washington

3. T. Roosevelt

4. F. Roosevelt

All of the so-called 'best Presidents' were in office at times when America faced crises and wars.

National Crisis

War

George Washington, the national father, gave birth to America by winning the Revolutionary War.

Revolutionary War

Theodore Roosevelt, a hero of troubled times, bravely fought at war and led America to wealth and power in the early 20th century.

Franklin D. Roosevelt saved a destitute America engulfed by depression,

Economy

and led his nation to victory in World War II, establishing the basis for America's emergence as a superpower.

Lincoln surpasses these three men in the rankings

LINCOLN

because he managed to preserve the Union that was on the brink of perpetual division—by waging a war that required enormous sacrifice.

Civil War

He played the greatest role in preserving America in its current form today.

Without Lincoln, America today

would just be 50 small and weak nations.

USA

U.S. History

Although Washington put together 13 states to found America as one nation,

The original American flag

what he created was a loose and imperfect Union that was at risk of breaking apart at any time.

From the very moment of its founding, America was plagued by endless conflict and enmity.

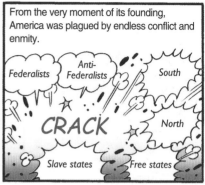

Federalists | Anti-Federalists | South

CRACK

North

Slave states | Free states

It was Lincoln who put an end to the incessant historical conflict and enmity by achieving victory at war.

Division
Confron-tation
Conflict
Enmity

What Washington left to the future generation was a nation that was at risk of becoming divided.

Barely put it together.

Freedom was a privilege for only a select few.

Caucasian

What Lincoln left to the future generation was an undividable, unified nation,

United States

and freedom for all, not just a select few.

Thus, Lincoln's greatest legacies are the preservation of the Union and the abolishment of slavery.

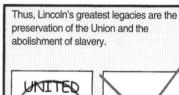

UNITED STATES OF AMERICA

SLAVERY

Lincoln was a hero who achieved victory at war, and a great leader who saved his country from a great crisis.

It's not necessarily viewed that way in the South...

Through the Emancipation Proclamation, he became revered as a virtuous saint.

Emancipation Proclamation

Because he was assassinated in office, Lincoln is also viewed as a martyr. He has become a legend in the hearts of the American people.

Lincoln perfectly matches the portrait of a leader wanted by the people,

Hero   Saint   Martyr

and he probably will be recorded forever in U.S. history as the most respected and beloved President.

Lincoln.

Abraham Lincoln was born on February 12, 1809 as the son of settlers in a log cabin in Hardin, Kentucky.

*The log cabin where Lincoln was born

His parents were illiterate,

and Lincoln himself received less than a year of formal school education.

It wasn't easy attending school in a frontier village.

A B C D E..

SCHOOL

However, he engrossed himself in self-study, prompted by his desire to escape from savagery on the frontier.

Without learning, I can't escape from this poverty and ignorance...

He even walked many kilometers to borrow books that were not readily available at that time.

Lincoln moved to Illinois, and at the age of 27 in 1836 became a trainee lawyer and entered politics.

Membership application

Whig Party

He married Mary Todd who possessed a much superior educational background.

*Portrait of Mary Todd in her youth

She had a complicated personality and wasn't very generous to her husband.

Abe!

Oh my!

Some say that Todd was a bad wife, but overall Lincoln is said to have led a happy marriage life.

*Photograph of Lincoln with his son

Anyway, what brought national attention to Lincoln were his debates with Steven Douglas, the powerful Democrat politician.

S. Douglas
vs.
A. Lincoln

105

Through the series of seven debates against Douglas, Lincoln immediately shot to prominence,

*Crowd gathered to listen to the debate

and garnered the nomination as the presidential candidate of the Republican Party and eventually became elected as the sixteenth President.

Hurray Hurray

Hurray

The debates helped out a lot!

Even though Lincoln was anti-slavery, he was prepared to yield as much as necessary to stop the division of the Union.

I'll do whatever it takes if I can stop the division of the Union!

In his inaugural speech, Lincoln emphasized that civil war was not in the hands of the President but in the hands of the dissatisfied South,

"In your hands, my dissatisfied fellow-countrymen, and not in mine, is the momentous issue of civil war!"

and made it clear that he had absolutely no intention to attack the South, nor to challenge the South over the issue of slavery.

I do not wish to go to war with the South!

Nor do I have any intention to provoke the South over slavery!

If the South were to remain in the Union and we can all join our hands together, the mystic chords of memory... will yet swell the chorus of the Union...!

However, the South responded by attacking Fort Sumter. The Civil War had started.

It became clear that the problems between the North and the South could not be resolved by dialogue and compromise. A battle using force was the only remaining option.

War wasn't what Lincoln wanted,

T H U M P!

but it was an inevitable step that helped solidify the Union. Eventually, the war turned out to be Lincoln's most significant achievement.

The festering wound finally burst open.

It wasn't Lincoln who burst open the wound.

Civil War

Although the likelihood of his re-election was almost non-existent, Lincoln won re-election in the 1864 presidential election, which was the first election in U.S. history to be held during a war.

Results of 1864 Election

Republican Party	Democratic Party
Abraham Lincoln Andrew Johnson	George B. McClellan George H. Pendleton
2,218,388	1,812,807

Popular votes

| 212 | 21 |

Electoral votes

The war circumstances helped the re-election of Lincoln, the nation's leader who was conducting the war effort.

You don't change your horse when crossing a river!

Meaning you don't replace a President during a war...

True to his countryside log cabin origin, Lincoln was very crude in appearance and manner.

The guy's just tall without any grace.

He's so boorish...

His voice was low and monotonous, while his hair was coarse as if he got a haircut with an ax.

Doesn't he even comb his hair?

Seems he doesn't care about his appearance.

After he became President, he started growing sideburns at the suggestion of a girl, but that didn't help much in improving his appearance.

That's a little better...

Still, his boorishness is helpless...

whisper   whisper

What most disconcerted the people around him was

You know what the log cabin people use to pick their teeth?

the outrageous jokes he would make that didn't suit the occasion and

With small logs!

HA HA HA HA HA

would embarrass those around him.

That's awkward~

He acted as if he were socializing with his Illinois country friends.

BURP~

His political foes criticized him as a 'real gorilla.'

GRUNT

Original gorilla!

Right after his second term started, on April 9, 1865, the Confederacy surrendered,

putting an end to the Civil War and, more importantly, the endless North-South conflict that plagued America since its founding.

Founding of America

North-South Conflict Period

The End

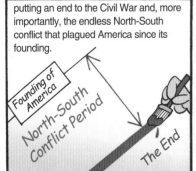

One week later, on April 15, Lincoln was assassinated by an ardent supporter of the Confederacy.

Bang

With his suffering and sacrifice, Lincoln protected the Union!

Andrew Johnson 1865~1869

First President to be Impeached by Congress

With you gone, I've gotten myself in quite a predicament!

Impeachment

Congress should take this opportunity to tame the President!

Why can't you do as Lincoln did?!

Andrew Johnson

Democratic Party, 1808.12.29~1875.7.31

Birth Place   Raleigh, North Carolina

Wife   Eliza McCardle Johnson 1810~1876

Children   Martha, Charles, Mary, Robert, Andrew Jr.

Vice President   No Vice President due to Johnson's succession to presidency

---

A strong light casts a dark shadow.

When Lincoln was assassinated right after he won the Civil War, he became revered as a hero, martyr and saint.

On the other hand, Andrew Johnson—who succeeded to the presidency—was left with an unbearably heavy burden to become a 'second Lincoln.'

Even though he was a Southerner from North Carolina, Andrew Johnson sided with the North,

I oppose secession!

Are you really a Southerner?

and although he was a slave owner in support of slavery, he also supported the preservation of the Union.

If you want to maintain slavery, then the Union must be preserved!

Yes to the Union

Yes to slavery

Evidently, he was a unique individual in many aspects.

Protect poor farmers!

Whites are superior to blacks!

Respect the Constitution!

Andrew Johnson, who as Vice President succeeded to the presidency, was born to a poor family in Raleigh, North Carolina.

Like Lincoln, he received almost no formal schooling,

and started his career as a tailor.

Johnson opened his eyes to the world after his wife Eliza tutored him to improve his literacy and imparted much knowledge to him.

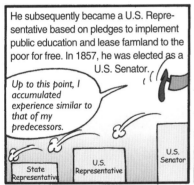

Johnson was a very skilled orator and politician.

After entering politics, in 1830 at the age of 22, Johnson was elected as mayor of Greeneville and soon thereafter a representative to the Tennessee House of Representatives.

He subsequently became a U.S. Representative based on pledges to implement public education and lease farmland to the poor for free. In 1857, he was elected as a U.S. Senator.

In 1861, after Lincoln was inaugurated, Southern states seceded one by one from the Union.

Among the senators from states that seceded from the Union, Andrew Johnson was the only senator to remain in the U.S. Senate.

The North applauded his courage,

and Lincoln named him military governor of Tennessee.

The Civil War period was his heyday.

In the 1864 presidential election, Johnson was selected as Lincoln's running mate and subsequently elected as Vice President.

Lincoln wins re-election!

Vice President is Johnson!

Johnson got off to the wrong start by entering his inaugural ceremony under the influence of alcohol and talking nonsense.

Lincoln came to Johnson's defense, claiming that Johnson wasn't a drunkard. Within one week, however, Lincoln was assassinated and Johnson inherited an unwanted presidency.

This is something that I really, really didn't want to happen...

The Johnson administration confronted very difficult problems, problems that really needed to be resolved.

Aftermath of Civil War

First, how would he reconstruct the ruined South?

Even though it had lost the war, there were still lingering discontent and hatred in the South. How would he appease the Southerners?

Second, how would he deal with the emancipated slaves?

You're free!

Even though the Southerners were shocked by their war loss and apprehensive of retribution by the Northerners over the assassination of Lincoln,

they were not prepared at all to treat blacks as 'human beings' based on the principle of equality.

A negro is still a negro!

Johnson himself was a white supremacist who did nothing to change the attitude of the Southerners.

A negro is no equal to the white man.

This emboldened the South, which started confronting the North again in Congress.

Johnson's the problem, that Johnson...

Don't tell the South what to do over blacks!

South

North

Meanwhile, racist organizations such as the Ku Klux Klan emerged and harassed blacks.

The Republican Party, which had argued for the repeal of slavery, attacked Johnson,

It's your fault! What's the use of the emancipation of slaves?

while the still defiant South also attacked Johnson who it didn't take seriously.

We'll never forget that you betrayed your brethren in the South!

More than any time in history, the presidency, under Johnson, came under challenge by Congress.

As time went by, not only Congress, but even his own cabinet started swaying Johnson and disobeying his orders.

The guy's powerless...

These circumstances culminated in the Stanton Affair that broke out in 1867.

Stanton Affair

Stanton, the Secretary of War, directly challenged the President by declaring that the allegiance of a military commander is owed to Congress, not the President.

I swear my allegiance!

Congress

How dare you declare that you owe your allegiance to Congress when the President is the commander-in-chief of the armed forces?

The Constitution provides that all powers are vested in Congress, so doesn't it follow that the military owes its allegiance to Congress that represents the people instead of the President?

This is an insult and challenge to the authority of the President. So you want to take this to extremes? You're fired as Secretary of War!

Dismissing Stanton, who declared his allegiance to Congress, is a challenge to Congress!

So these events came down to a direct showdown between the President and Congress,

So you want a fight, huh?!

resulting in the submission of a bill of impeachment against the President for the first time in U.S. history.

Impeachment

Let's drive him out of the presidency!

The House of Representatives voted in favor of the bill to impeach the President, and the Senate voted on whether to convict him.

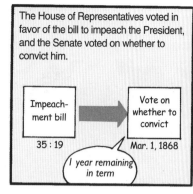

Impeach-ment bill	→	Vote on whether to convict
35 : 19		Mar. 1, 1868

I year remaining in term

A two-thirds vote of the senators present was required for conviction and removal of Johnson from office.

Out!

White House

Since the number of senators favoring conviction was much higher than two-thirds of all the senators in office,

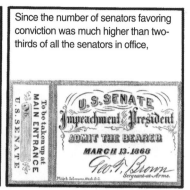

*Admission ticket to impeachment trial

it was taken for granted that Johnson would be kicked out of office.

Johnson's finally getting axed.

He wasn't suited to be President in the first place.

However, unexpectedly, Johnson was acquitted by one vote short of the two-thirds needed for removal of the President.

One vote short!

Acquittal!

This result was attributable to seven Republican Senators who voted against convicting Johnson.

No conviction!

NO NO NO NO NO NO NO

Weren't you in favor of his impeachment? Then why'd you vote against conviction?

Think about it.

We're all emotional right now and trying to kick Johnson out of office,

but if we were to leave this as a precedent, then Congress in the future would impeach the President at its whim. Wouldn't that make it difficult for the President to properly carry out his job?

Impeach-ment

I voted against Johnson's conviction to not leave a precedent that would chronically paralyze the powers of the President.

Since Johnson, there's been no other President who's been impeached in American politics (except Bill Clinton).

Nixon resigned before he was impeached...

Clinton narrowly escaped removal from office...

U.S. HISTORY

In any event, politically, Johnson sustained a severe blow for his impeachment.

For a guy who got impeached, he should know his place!

Why can't he learn? He's just being stubborn!

Even though he avoided conviction, Johnson not only suffered politically, but he also sustained a major blow to his reputation.

He's incompetent and arrogant!

He's the President who got impeached.

He finished his term in frustration and sorrow.

No one pays any attention to me...

The achievements of his term were

Andrew Johnson

Term: 1865~1869

Couldn't even dream of re-election...

the purchase of Alaska, which was twice the size of Texas, from Russia

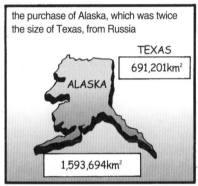

TEXAS
691,201km²

ALASKA

1,593,694km²

and the assistance he rendered in driving out the French army from Mexico—based on the Monroe Doctrine.

Didn't we tell you Europe is not welcome in the Americas?

Mexico

However, at that time, even the purchase of Alaska became the butt of jokes in Congress.

He's crazy. Why buy such a worthless piece of land?

Since Secretary Seward arranged the purchase, let's call it 'Seward's Icebox.'

Other than the political reasons behind the purchase,

We need to repel Russian power in North America

and restrain Canada (Britain) from making a major expansion to the Pacific...

Pacific Ocean

Canada

U.S.A.

not many people knew about the value of Alaska, which possessed unlimited natural resources.

I'll buy it back from you at 10 times what you paid.

I won't sell it to you even at 100 times!

Alaska

USSR

USA

Johnson, who possessed a booming voice and was rough spoken,

stubbornly stayed in politics to restore his reputation.

I can't fade away like this! Not even if I were to die!

After leaving the presidency, he was elected as a Tennessee State Senator right before his death.

The U.S. President as a state senator?

That's why they say you can't leave politics until the day you die.

On July 31, 1875, this man with many regrets passed away.

I alone suffered because Lincoln was so great...

A. Johnson
17th U.S. President

Ulysses S. Grant 1869~1877

Politically Inept War Hero

Sir, you need to get rid of your incompetent and corrupt associates!

My men aren't incompetent and corrupt!

Any criticism of them is a challenge to myself!

RACIAL CONFLICT

DISHONESTY CORRUPTION

Ulysses Simpson Grant

Republican Party, 1822.4.27~1885.7.23

Birth Place   Point Pleasant, Ohio

Wife   Julia Boggs Dent Grant 1826~1902

Children   Frederick, Ulysses, Ellen, Jessy

Vice Presidents   S. Colfax 1869

H. Wilson 1873

Ulysses Grant, who is recorded as one of the most brilliant generals in U.S. history, led the Union to victory in the Civil War.

With that background, he entered the White House with the most blessings.

I feel the heavy responsibility of the presidency,

but I accept it without any fear.

After leaving the army, however, Grant incompetently and ineptly led the nation. He barely finished his two terms that were plagued with scandal and disrepute.

Corruption   Scandals

Grant was born in Ohio as the son of a tanner.

He was baptized under the name Hiram Ulysses at a Baptist church.

You shall be named Hiram.

The young Grant didn't show any particular talent, so he decided to enter the U.S. Military Academy and become a soldier.

Hiram is a corny name.

At that time, he changed his name to 'Ulysses Simpson.'

Grant was a socially awkward loner at the military academy.

In 1843, he graduated from the military academy and was commissioned as an officer.

In 1846, when the U.S. went to war against Mexico to seize Mexican territory, the young officer Grant deplored the situation in tears,

The U.S. will turn into a graveyard for shamelessly starting this immoral war!

but he was a fine officer and showed he could expertly execute tactics and conduct bold operations.

:ROAR: ATTACK~!

After the war ended in 1848, Grant married Julia Dent.

* Grant's family

It is said that the Grants led a very happy marriage life.

He was so lonely *that he really loved his wife...*

But his happy marriage life had the effect of hurting Grant's military career

Honey!

Darling~

because Grant started drinking to overcome the loneliness of life in the barracks without his wife.

This led to heavy drinking and alcoholism, which caused him to become dishonorably discharged in 1854.

We don't need an officer like you!

Unemployed and broke, Grant lived a few years in Illinois to learn the leather trade of his father.

Once dreamed of becoming a general. Now I'm just a tanner...

But the Civil War that finally broke out was an opportunity from heaven that enabled Grant to splendidly revive his career.

BOOM

Unfortunately, he still drank heavily and couldn't overcome his alcoholism even after he was called back to service as an army commander.

Nevertheless, Grant was a tender and sensitive man who abhorred bloodshed.

Blood... Get rid of it!

He made his name as a fierce fighting general by capturing Fort Henry and Fort Donelson* and destroying the Confederate Army there.

He refused to negotiate with the enemy unless the enemy immediately and unconditionally surrendered.

Truce!

No truce. Your choice is to either surrender or fight!

* The Battle of Fort Donelson was one of Grant's greatest victories.

This earned Grant the nickname 'Unconditional Surrender' Grant.

General Grant

Unconditional Surrender!

After Fort Donelson fell, Grant also annihilated the Confederate Army at the Battle of Vicksburg*.

Due to these accomplishments, General Grant suddenly emerged as a great American hero, and Lincoln named him general-in-chief of all of the armies of the United States.

* Battle of Vicksburg (Mississippi): 1863.5.17~7.4

In 1865, as the victorious general, Grant accepted the surrender of General Robert E. Lee of the Confederate Army, thereby ending the Civil War. Andrew Johnson,

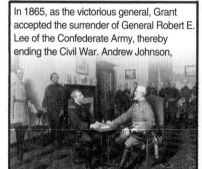

who had become President after Lincoln's assassination, was unable to garner his party's nomination as the presidential candidate for re-election due to his impeach-ment by Congress, among other things.

Impeach-ment

We can't work with Johnson!

The Republican Party naturally turned to the war hero Grant as its presidential candidate for the 1868 presidential election.

War hero Grant!

He can do it!

He's the general who made Lincoln a victorious President!

GR AN T

Grant easily defeated his opponent Horatio Seymore in a landslide,

Results of 1868 Election		
Republican Party		Democratic Party
U.S. Grant		Horatio Seymore
3,013,650	Popular votes	2,708,744
214		80
	Electoral votes	

and started his term in early 1869, an extremely chaotic time in America. His presidency during that period required enormous ability and courage.

USA

Racial issues concerning African-Americans (blacks) and Native-Americans (Indians), etc., created the most significant problems for the nation.

Lincoln's Emancipation Proclamation is just a piece of paper!

Nothing's been solved in the real world!

USA

Racial problems

In the South, blacks were blatantly stripped of their civil rights,

while groups such as the Ku Klux Klan surfaced to terrorize blacks.

In the West, armed Indian uprisings continued in response to the white man's persecution. To make matters worse,

the nation's rapid industrialization increasingly widened the gap between the rich and the poor and created social discord.

Once a resolute and courageous general on the battlefield, Grant deteriorated into an ineffective President in the White House.

In these difficult times, cabinet members placed all the responsibilities on the President for matters for which they may be held accountable. Their sole interest was to see which way the wind was blowing.

Grant wasn't respected much by his cabinet members

who were implicated in various unethical scandals.

The financial scandal that broke out during his term in 1872 dishonored the presidency and caused his approval rating to plummet.

In the election held that year, Grant barely managed to secure the nomination as the Republican Party's presidential candidate and win re-election.

His second term was marked by many scandals,

which left the nation in utter turmoil.

The President's private secretary was indicted for his involvement in a whiskey smuggling ring,

Hey, my share was really small...

and his Secretary of War was arrested for defrauding Indians and taking their land. Corruption was prevalent throughout the land.

What did I do wrong? Indian land is up for grabs...

However, Grant, a man of infinite integrity, wasn't very sophisticated in money matters. He continued to trust his corrupt associates to the end.

They're my colleagues.

They would never have done those things!

NO!

Whenever someone around him would become indicted, he would defend them even though doing so would hurt his reputation.

With such a naïve President governing America,

How could he be so ignorant?

It's impossible to teach him what to do!

blacks and Indians suffered at the hands of predators.

The wealthy, who accounted for only 1% of the total population, controlled one-seventh to one-eighth of the total national wealth.

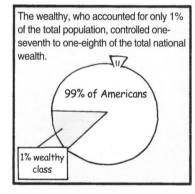

99% of Americans

1% wealthy class

The gap between the rich and the poor widened tremendously.

$

In particular, rampant dishonesty and corruption prevailed among public servants. This led the people to fiercely criticize the President.

ROAR   ROAR   ROAR

Corruption civil watch group

No to bribes

The Grant gov't is full of thieves

Still, the President couldn't grasp the situation.

What's all this fuss about? We're giving our best efforts and doing pretty well.

He refuted the allegations of corruption and treated attacks made on his subordinates as attacks on the government.

I won't tolerate any action to rock the President!

Claims of corruption by the press and the opposition are just political ploys!

His unyielding spirit blinded him to the corruption, while his hatred wrecked his ability to choose faithful subordinates, an ability that had made him a great man in the past.

You're either with me or against me!

Hmmp..

I need people who share my principles...

After Grant left the Presidency,

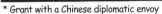
* Grant with a Chinese diplomatic envoy

he was swindled after lending his name to a brokerage company that was operated by a friend, and then subsequently went broke.

Bankruptcy

Some guys even swindle the President...

After declaring bankruptcy in 1884, Grant started writing his memoir to economically aid his family.

* Grant during his last years

He finished the manuscript a few days before he died of throat cancer on July 23, 1885.

cough

This book will pay off all the debts...

cough

Grant's memoir is considered as one of the finest memoirs in U.S. military history.

Personal Memoir of U. S. Grant

Ulysses Simpson Grant

He's known to have earned over $500,000 in royalties, adjusted for inflation.

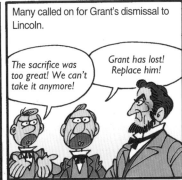

How do U.S. Presidents earn a living after leaving office?

They write memoirs and earn hundreds of thousands of dollars.

U.S.   Presidents

Even for the legendary great general Ulysses Grant, there were bad memories from the battlefield.

In June 1864, when the Civil War was drawing to an end, 45,000 out of 118,000 men were killed in battle during a one-month period at the Battle of Petersburg.

Petersburg

Many called on for Grant's dismissal to Lincoln.

The sacrifice was too great! We can't take it anymore!

Grant has lost! Replace him!

However, Lincoln firmly turned them down.

I can't spare this man!

He fights!

A great leader recognizes a great military commander.

But from Grant, we know that it's difficult for a lion on the battlefield to transform himself into a wise man of politics.

It's much more difficult being a good president

than a good general.

Ulysses S. Grant

Rutherford B. Hayes 1877~1881

Morality Politician Out of Touch with Reality

Rutherford B. Hayes

Republican Party, 1822.10.4~1893.1.17

Birth Place   Delaware, Ohio

Wife   Lucy Ware Webb Hayes 1831~1889

Children   Birchard, Rutherford Jr., Joseph,
George, Fanny, Scott, Manning

Vice President   W. A. Wheeler

Compared to other Presidents, Rutherford Birchard Hayes was unique in two ways.

First, he was a staunch humanitarian and moralist.

He was good-hearted and honest to a fault.

In particular, he gave warm consideration to the Indians and other minorities.

Many Indians are suffering due to

broken promises made by the white man and unjust laws!

Second, he was elected as President in the most ridiculous election in U.S. history.

The presidency was stolen!

How in the world could a sham like this happen?

Specifically, although he lost the popular vote by a large margin to the Democratic candidate,

Results of 1876 Election

Republican Party	Democratic Party
Rutherford B. Hayes	Samuel J. Tilden
4,034,311	4,288,546

Popular votes

185	184

Electoral votes

---

he strangely won the election by a razor-thin margin of one electoral vote.

This is ridiculous! To have won by one electoral vote!

Ever since Western expansion started, Indians were endlessly persecuted and driven from their hometowns.

Eventually, the situation blew up in an armed uprising by the Indians. An Indian coalition and the U.S. Army led by Colonel George A. Custer

It's time for a fight~!

fought for over a year at the Little Bighorn River.

bang
Bang *bang* *bang*
bang

Little Bighorn River

After becoming President, Hayes changed the policy of unilateral persecution of the Indians to a policy of persuasion and engagement.

Persuasion · Engagement

Sunshine Policy

Young Indians were offered educational and job opportunities,

Let's live side-by-side!

Educational opportunities | Job counseling

and, instead of driving them out to Indian reservations, the government made offers to allocate land and grant citizenship to them.

Allocation of land | Granting of citizenship

However, like other pledges made during Hayes's term, none of these pledges were actually implemented.

It was a lie!

I knew it was going to be like this...

Although Hayes talked of humanitarian, exemplary and Christianity-based goals,

Humanity,
Love thy neighbor

the results were always non-humanitarian and un-Christianlike due to the powerful Congress, an institution that ironically represented Christians...

Interest of the white man!

NO!

Congress

Rutherford Hayes was born in Delaware, Ohio and raised by a mother with strong morals.

Morality, ethics, way of the man, love, action.

He graduated from Kenyon College in Ohio at the top of his class, and then graduated from Harvard Law School three years later.

After he started a law practice, he became interested in political reform, social justice and life as a humanitarian.

Political reform!

Social justice!

Humanitarianism!

* Hayes around 1845

Hayes, who stood at the forefront of the anti-slavery movement, married Lucy Webb, a modern woman and one of the first women to receive a college education.

She also was very active in the prohibition and anti-slavery movements.

Alcohol NO   Slavery NO

After she became First Lady, she categorically banned alcohol in the White House and served only lemonade, for which she earned the nickname 'Lady Lemonade.'

"Lady Lemonade"

Hayes became increasingly politically ambitious,

As a man, to realize my dreams...

Washington D.C.

but due to the outbreak of the Civil War, instead of pursuing his dreams in politics, he volunteered for service in the army and became a major _____ in an artillery unit.

During his four-year service with the army, he was wounded five times. In the year he was honorably discharged as a brigadier general, he was elected as a U.S. Representative.

In 1867, Hayes was elected as Governor of Ohio. He was re-elected twice to the governorship, and then selected as the Republican Party's presidential candidate.

Republican candidate R. B. Hayes

Democratic candidate S. J. Tilden

The Republican Party faced a difficult situation due to the rampant dishonesty and corruption of Grant's presidency.

ROAR

Let's get rid of and replace the incompetent and corrupt gov't!

It needed a 'clean and moral' candidate who could stand against the fierce attacks of the Democratic Party.

Meritorious war service, reformist governor image, importance of Ohio in the election!

Rutherford Hayes

However, the public was disgusted with the corruption of the Grant adminis- tration, and voters had abandoned the Republican Party.

Republican Party   NO!

It appeared that the Democratic Party would regain power for the first time in 16 years since 1856.

Democratic Party

16th Lincoln
17th Johnson
18th Grant
Monopolization
of power
by the Republicans
This was bad!

In fact, the Democratic candidate Tilden won more popular votes than Hayes.

Hurray

The Democrats have won in a landslide!

Moreover, the Democratic Party had secured 184 electoral votes, 18 more votes than the 166 electoral votes secured by the Republican Party.

The Democrats will now win no matter what!

Demo-crats	Republi-cans
184	166

However, it was yet undecided which party had won the 19 electoral votes allocated to three states that were controlled by the Republicans.

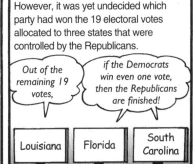

Out of the remaining 19 votes,

if the Democrats win even one vote, then the Republicans are finished!

Louisiana | Florida | South Carolina

The entire nation focused on the ballot counting.

These 19 votes will decide the next President!

A special electoral commission consisting of a total of 15 members from the House, the Senate and the Supreme Court engaged in tiresome debates and arguments,

We can't possibly decide because the difference in the number of votes is so small!

We made scores of counts but the results are different each time...

It's been several months, but we haven't been able to announce the winner...

Mumble   Washington D.C.   Grumble

and reached a strange conclusion two days before the inauguration.

It's difficult to decide because the vote count is so close,

So let's decide based on the ratio by which each party is represented in the House.

and the new President needs to be inaugurated the day after tomorrow.

Since the ratio of seats held by the Republican Party and the Democratic Party is 8:7, with the Republican Party holding more seats,

Republican seats	:	Democratic seats
8		7

---

based on the unit rule system under which the party with at least one more vote wins all of the electoral votes, we hereby recognize that the undecided 19 votes have been won by the Republican Party!

Boy, even I can tell this is unreasonable...

Thus, the Democrats have won 184 electoral votes, and the Republicans 166 + 19 = 185 electoral votes. So it is hereby declared that Hayes is the President!

Bang bang bang

Naturally, this decision turned the entire nation upside down.

That's ridiculous...!

So a round off was made just like that?

They've stolen the presidency!

There even appeared signs that an uprising may occur in the South.

We can't tolerate these Northern Republicans!

Let's recover the stolen presidency!

Hayes was barely able to take office by making assurances to the Southerners.

I'll end military rule in the South,

and rebuild the economic infrastructure of the South.

Also, I promise to select many, many Democrats in my cabinet!

Rrrrr

Hmmp

In 1877, the inaugural year of Hayes, America was undergoing a severe depression.

* Inauguration of Hayes

When the four major railroad companies significantly increased fares while reducing wages by a whopping 10% to make up for losses,

workers stirred up great riots in July of that year.

Increase wages!

ROAR
ROAR

Here and there, striking workers and federal troops collided as if they were fighting a civil war.

Bang bang bang bang

In some places, federal troops joined the striking workers to fight against fellow federal troops. The nation was in utter chaos.

Boom

Kaboom

Hayes resolutely sent in federal troops to put down the strikes and uprisings.

Actions that destroy safety and order will not be tolerated!

Hayes became the second President after Andrew Jackson to send in federal troops to handle labor problems.

Federal army: Regular army used in wars against other nations

Federal reserve: Reserve force used to maintain public security in the states

There was also a lot of friction between Hayes and Congress.

Who do you think the President is, anyway?!

An idiot!

Grrrrrr

Hayes vetoed bills sent to him by Congress as many as seven times. He had an extremely antagonistic relationship with Congress.

NO NO NO NO NO NO NO

This guy really wants to fight to the extremes...

Congress

Meanwhile, his humanitarian side was displayed regarding the Chinese.

As the number of Chinese workers greatly increased due to the construction of railroads and development of gold mines, anti-Chinese sentiments surged.

There're too many Chinese! We should stop an additional influx of Chinese!

Although Congress enacted a law restricting Chinese immigration, Hayes firmly refused to sign it into law.

It was only yesterday when we were bringing them over in truckloads!

NO!

What Hayes inherited from Grant was a very weakened presidency,

extreme partisan confrontation and antagonism

and totally rotten and stinking bureaucrats.

Hayes tried to free himself from all those things with his high moral principles, but eventually gave up on running for re-election and left the White House after serving only one term.

After leaving the presidency, he worked for a philanthropic organization dedicated to the improvement of education of blacks and whites,

and also served as a trustee of Ohio State University

and worked for human rights of prisoners as the chairman of the National Penitentiary Commission.

Although Hayes' friends also considered him as a failed President who didn't possess the ability or talent required of a President,

the writer Mark Twain, a man of his times, judged him differently.

"As each day went by, he became a more outstanding and greater man!"

Hayes is famous for having kept a diary every day during his lifetime.

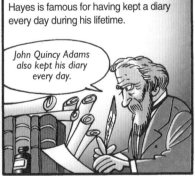

Hayes's diary remains to this day, including the diary entries he kept when he was almost fatally wounded at the Battle of South Mountain in 1862.

James A. Garfield 1881

Corrupt Politician Assassinated while Fighting Corruption

James Abram Garfield

Republican Party, 1831.11.19~1881.9.19

Birth Place   Orange, Ohio

Wife   Lucretia Rudolph Garfield 1832~1918

Children   Eliza, Harry, James, Mary, Irving, Abram Jr., Edward

Vice President   Chester A. Arthur

President Rutherford Hayes judged James Garfield as follows:

In all of U.S. history, there was no man like Garfield

who started from such humble origins and achieved so much as he did,

U.S. HISTORY

"even when compared to Abraham Lincoln and Benjamin Franklin!"

As Hayes said, Garfield overcame poverty on his own,

poverty

---

and led a career as a scholar, general, clergyman, etc.

James A. Garfield
Resume

-Dean of Williams College
-Preacher, evangelist
-General
-U.S. Representative
-Politician
-Etc., etc.

His career was most diverse and illustrious compared to other U.S. Presidents,

WOW~!

Garfield

---

but he became the second President to be assassinated in office, less than four months from the date of his inauguration.

Bang

James Garfield was born in 1831 as the son of poor farmers in a log cabin in Orange Township near Cleveland, Ohio.

His father died two years after his birth, so his mother had to work hard as a laborer in the fields and as a cleaner.

A 'lazy' boy, Garfield spent his time reading novels, neglecting the poverty surrounding him and wandering in a fantasy world.

Boy... I envy those rich kids...

Garfield tried to overcome poverty by leaving home at the age of 16 and working as a crew on a small boat that sailed up and down a canal, a job he held for six weeks.

He fell into the water no less than 14 times, as a result of which he suffered a severe bout of fever and cold.

While nursing for Garfield, his mother convinced him that he needed an education.

James, the only way to overcome poverty is to learn.

Here's $17 that I saved. I want you to go to school and use this as your tuition.

Convinced by his mother, for the first time in his life, Garfield opened his eyes to learning and studied very hard.

When he ran out of the $17 his mother gave him, Garfield continued his studies by working as a carpenter and tutoring students.

Mr. Garfield, you must be really tired.

While continuing his studies, he also taught at his school,

U.S. history is totally different from the history of other nations...

and became a disciple and preacher of the 'Disciple of Christ' church with the goal of becoming a clergyman at the wish of his deeply religious mother.

Let us pray!

Disciple of Christ

In 1856, Garfield graduated from Williams College, after which he went on the fast track working as a professor and dean, among other things.

Williams College President

During that process, Garfield became aware of the immorality of slavery.

Slavery

Despite his mother's opposition, Garfield entered politics and, in 1859, was elected as an Ohio State Senator.

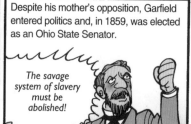

The savage system of slavery must be abolished!

OHIO

In 1862, he was elected as the youngest U.S. Representative and continued as a congressman in the House of Representatives for 17 years.

17 years

I was a 9-term congressman since a U.S. Representative serves a 2-year term!

During the Civil War, he also accumulated military experience by volunteering for service in the army. Eventually, he was promoted to the rank of major.

Charge!

He was immensely popular due to his diverse experience, intellectual character and convincing oratorical power.

James~

We love you~

Hey, I must be really popular...

GARFIELD

He had no enemies since he professed a centrist policy line. He emerged as a key figure in the political world of Washington D.C.

Centrist · Moderate Conservative

I'm neither radical

nor ultra-conservative!

Garfield became a bigshot within the incumbent Republican Party and was eventually seduced by bribes from the corrupt politicians of the Grant administration.

You know what's in this box, right?

APPLE

With seven children, he was a powerful politician who lacked the financial means.

Only idiots turn these down. Well, I'm counting on you.

APPLE

Such reality made Garfield compromise with the times.

I know it was inappropriate,

but I was so pressed for money, I couldn't resist the temptation.

For example, he would receive a dividend from a company in which he hadn't even invested a penny,

This is $329, your dividend.

This is a bribe! I never made an investment...

and take a $5,000 honorarium from a company that had received favors from him. Even though these kinds of bribery scandals surfaced,

Please! Keep them coming...

they were not so severe to prevent his candidacy and election as President.

To build a war chest,

it's just inevitable. Even if its illicit money...

The 1880 presidential election was the most closely contested race up to that time.

The situation was so tense that New York became the deciding factor in the election.

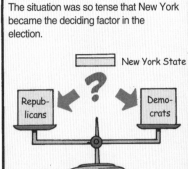

New York State

New York was controlled by spoils system office hunters and brokers. Garfield ended up compromising with these persons.

Let's do a deal.

The powerful New York Senator Conklin!

In exchange for making promises to hand out government jobs, Garfield was able to win the election.

You're going to give us the vice presidency and a few other cabinet posts. You better keep your promise!

OK!

The guy's selling gov't jobs.

In this extremely close election, the popular vote was won by only 1,898 votes.

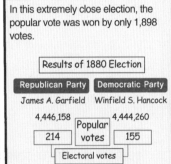

Results of 1880 Election	
Republican Party	Democratic Party
James A. Garfield	Winfield S. Hancock
4,446,158	4,444,260
214	155

Popular votes

Electoral votes

Although Garfield won the election, he was haunted by the deal he made to hand out government jobs.

Where's my job!

The obligations he owed limited his presidential powers.

As Secretary of Defense, I'm going to appoint...

No way, that post belongs to us!

Eventually, Garfield made up his mind that it was necessary to break the deal he'd made before the election.

If I hand out government jobs like I promised during the election,

I won't be able to accomplish anything. I'll be a puppet in their hands!

Naturally, this decision greatly angered Garfield's supporters to whom he promised government jobs.

He's not keeping his promise!

He's breaking the deal he made!

On July 2, 1881, less than four months from his inauguration, Garfield was assassinated by Charles J. Guiteau, one of his disgruntled supporters.

BANG

Garfield put up an excruciatingly painful fight for 11 weeks, but the doctors failed to find the bullet lodged in his body.

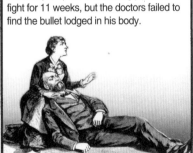

On September 19, at last, he died from his gun-shot wound that was complicated by blood poisoning.

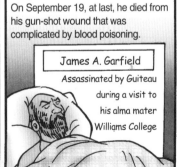

James A. Garfield

Assassinated by Guiteau during a visit to his alma mater Williams College

It isn't easy to judge Garfield, who was a complex and contradictory man.

* Portrait of Garfield with his family

At first, although he was a strict moralist who rejected the unbridled materialism that prevailed during the period of dishonesty, corruption and money politics,

Morality politics

Absolutely no bribes accepted

he subsequently compromised with such dishonesty and corruption and turned into a realist.

Behind his back...

$

One side of him was a reformist while yet another side of him was a grafter.

REFORM

MONEY... OK!

While Garfield earned a reputation as a corrupt politician,

Dishonesty Corruption

he is also seen as a martyr assassinated for his fight against dishonesty.

Garfield, elected 20 years after Lincoln's 1860 election, was assassinated while in office.

16th Lincoln   19th Garfield

Assassinated

William McKinley, elected 20 years later in 1900, was also assassinated while in office.

25th McKinley   Elected in 1900

Assassinated

To this day, these assassinations remind the Washington political world of the curse of 'Tecumseh.'

Presidents have experienced misfortune every 20 years.

Hasn't the curse of Tecumseh been broken?

Tecumseh was the chief of the Indian Shawnee Tribe,

who was killed in battle by William Harrison (9th President), the general who made his name in campaigns against the Indians.

Old Tippecanoe* (nickname)

W. Harrison

It is said that he left a curse, which mysteriously came true.

Every 20 years, the American President elected in a year ending with '0'

will be cursed and die while he's in office!

* This nickname originated from the Battle of Tippecanoe against the Indians (see chapter on President Harrison).

The first person to exerience Tecumseh's 'zero (0) year curse' was William Harrison who was elected in '1840' and died in office due to an illness.

Elected in 1840

W. Harrison

Died of illness

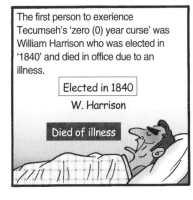

Abraham Lincoln, elected in '1860,' was assassinated in 1865 during his term.

Elected in 1860

A. Lincoln

Assassinated

Bang

James Garfield, elected in '1880,' was also assassinated.

Elected in 1880

J. Garfield

Assassinated

William McKinley, elected in '1900,' was assassinated too.

Elected in 1900

W. McKinley

Assassinated

Bang

And Warren Harding, elected in '1920,' died in office due to an illness.

Elected in 1920

W. Harding

Died of illness

Likewise, Franklin Roosevelt, elected in '1940,' died in office due to an illness,

Elected in 1940   F.D. Roosevelt

Died of illness

while John F. Kennedy, elected in '1960,' was assassinated.

Elected in 1960

J.F. Kennedy

Assassinated

We then go on to Ronald Reagan, elected in '1980,' who survived an assassination attempt.

Elected in 1980

R. Reagan

Assassination attempted

Having barely survived the assassination, he became the first President elected in a year ending with '0' to finish his term.

Thought I'd never make it...

Whew~

And now we come to George W. Bush, the 43rd President elected in '2000.'

Elected in 2000

G. W. Bush

?

Perhaps he will not experience Tecumseh's curse,

The President's bodyguards must be really concerned!

I don't think such a superstitution would apply in the 21st century...

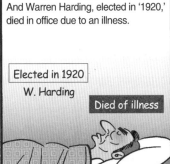

but would you call the misfortunes experienced by the Presidents elected every 20 years just a coincidence?

1840
1860
1880
1900
1920
1940
1960
1980

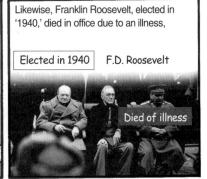

Chester A. Arthur 1881~1885

Defender of Presidential Dignity

Chester Alan Arthur

Republican Party, 1829.10.5~1886.11.18
Birth Place North Fairfield, Vermont
Wife Ellen Lewis Herndon Arthur 1837~1880
Children William Lewis, Chester Alan,
Ellen Herndon
Vice President No Vice President due to
Arthur's succession to presidency

Chester Alan Arthur was the fourth person to succeed to the presidency due to the death of the President.

13. Fillmore

10. Tyler

17. Johnson   21. Arthur

Although the Vice President is next in line to the presidency in case the President cannot carry out his duties,

Vice President

President

---

fundamentally, the vice presidency is an unessential office.

Vice President

President

In the past, the vice presidency was usually the consolation prize awarded to the faction that lost the fight for supremacy in the party.

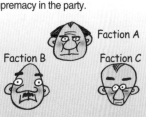

Faction A

Faction B   Faction C

A person from the winning faction would run for the presidency, while a person from the faction that failed to place first would get to run for the vice presidency.

Faction A   Faction C

Candidate for President   Candidate for Vice President

Thus, it was an office that went to the second most powerful faction in the party.

1   2

So once a Vice President ascended to the presidency, he would fiercely fight for his faction against the faction that had produced the former President.

Our faction is now in control!

No way! Our faction made the President!

Tyler and Fillmore fought hard against other factions in their parties,

Even though the President died, our faction must stay in control!

The new President's faction should rule!

SMACK CRACK

while Johnson too exerted tremendous effort in the fight against party factions and Congress.

Impeachment

Garfield, who died six months after his inauguration, was nominated as his party's presidential candidate through a compromise with the corrupt Senator Conklin.

In exchange, my faction will take the vice presidency.

In exchange, Conklin chose Chester Arthur from his faction as the vice presidential candidate.

Candidate for President
J. Garfield

Candidate for Vice President
C. A. Arthur

So you can see that Arthur was made Vice President as a result of the political compromise between Garfield and Conklin, the party's strongman.

Arthur

Conklin faction

Vice President

Garfield's death rocked the American political establishment.

What? Arthur from the Conklin faction is now President?

The powerful Conklin is behind President Arthur! His faction will now prevail!

Contrary to these concerns, however, Arthur cut all ties with his benefactor Conklin,

I'm done with corrupt politicians.

and didn't appoint members of his faction to important government posts.

No cronyism!

The Arthur Faction
We ♥ Arthur

This decision stirred up great anger and resentment among his many supporters,

TRAITOR!

but Arthur faithfully continued the policy line of his predecessor,

Follow me!

Garfield Policy Line

There will be no change of course!

and got rid of cronyism in personnel matters. By doing so, he became highly regarded for empowering the presidency.

Connections

Solicitation of gov't jobs

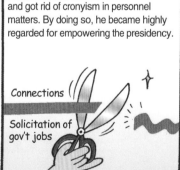

Moreover, in 1833, he signed into law the Pendleton Civil Service Act, which prohibited the exchange of government jobs based on factions, personal connections, negotiations and deals.

Pendleton Civil Service Act

Spoils system outlawed.
Government jobs to be filled based on merit

G. H. Pendleton
Chairman of Senate Civil Service Reform Committee

By doing so, Arthur brought an end to the spoils system.

Spoils system=handing out jobs as rewards to supporters

Gov't job

He is praised for establishing a modern administration system based on competition and merit.

The Pendleton Act was designed to create a clean government run by civil servants

with integrity. It's commonly referred to as the Magna Carta of the U.S. civil service system.

Pendleton Act

However, Arthur himself was a product of his times. While he appeared to be 'suitably' cleanhanded, he was also a 'suitably' corrupt bureaucrat who accepted whatever came his way.

President Hayes once dismissed Arthur from his job as Chief of the New York City Custom House on suspicion of corruption.

Corrupt civil servants out!

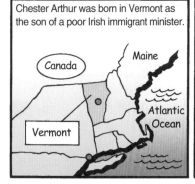

As a career politician, he believed he deserved such side money.

Hey, am I the only one who makes money on the side?

Come on, it wasn't that much...

Chester Arthur was born in Vermont as the son of a poor Irish immigrant minister.

Canada

Maine

Vermont

Atlantic Ocean

At the age of 25, he became a lawyer and joined the Republican Party for which he worked very hard.

※ Arthur in 1859

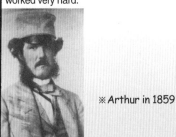

His career took off as a bureaucrat when people recognized his hard work ethic and good judgement.

With the backing of the influential Rosco Conklin, Arthur became the candidate for Vice President, and, after Garfield's death, the President.

President

Historians judge Arthur as a man of responsibility and a President who ousted corrupt bureaucrats and greatly expanded U.S. foreign trade,

Corrupt bureaucrats

---

and also as a more capable and successful President than his predecessor Garfield, the one actually elected to the presidency. However, Arthur is not so well remembered by the American people.

Popularity of Presidents

28th James Garfield

34th Chester A. Arthur

Arthur is also viewed favorably for restoring the 'dignity of the presidency.'

The President's lack of power was shown in the impreachment of Johnson by Congress.

Arthur, however, was successful in restoring the dignity of the presidency that had fallen to its nadir during the Grant administration,

in part due to his stately and presidential aura.

He was a tall man with an imposing physique weighing 112kgs,

and always perfectly and splendidly dressed.

He was known by the nickname 'gentlemanly boss.'

Boss!

Arthur also enjoyed good food and wine,

This wine is excellent!

and was famous for never working more than six hours a day.

The President is entitled to some free time!

Any time before 10 am. and after 4 p.m. is for my personal enjoyment!

CLOSED

Being overweight, Arthur suffered from a number of diet-related diseases. He passed away from such a disease within two years of leaving office.

Diabetes, obesity, arteriosclerosis, liver disease...

Arthur lived as a widower in the White House because his wife passed away before he became Vice President.

Widower President

Besides that, memories of his presidency gradually faded away, and he is remembered only as a mediocre President in domestic politics.

Chester Arthur...

Uh, I think there was such a President.

Meanwhile, Arthur exercised his veto power numerous times against Congress to preserve the dignity of the presidency.

I'll make sure Congress doesn't take the President for granted!

For example, he vetoed the law that restricted Chinese immigration for 20 years,

Let's stop Chinese immigration for 20 years.

No way!

Chinese Exclusion Act 20 years

so the exclusion period was reduced to 10 years.

Then how about 10 years...

Well, I'll accept that so Congress can save face.

Compromise 10 years

Chester Arthur is also known to have had a pretty bad relationship with the press.

Everything's the fault of the press!

I'm doing very well but they're just trying to find fault with me...

Because Arthur feared and despised the press,

What is this? The press is making distorted reports! It's evil!

he avoided all press conferences and interviews.

I wish I could reform the press

and get rid of all the newspapers.

Interview

It was no surprise that the press didn't like him either.

He's always blaming the press!

He just sides with papers published by cronies!

He's always cooking up ideas to persecute the press!

Arthur was always negatively portrayed as an incompetent President.

The President hardly works and just plays.

The President just blames the press all the time.

However, according to biographer Thomas Reeves, despite his large frame, Arthur had a soft side.

Hey there~

According to Reeves, Arthur was sentimental and romantic and prone to tears.

I feel so sorry for the hero of the story.

His delicate side surfaced here and there,

This portrait doesn't belong here.

and, as a refined and elegant man, he showed deep interest in the interior design of the White House.

When Arthur first entered the White House after Garfield's death, he was astonished by its very poor maintenance.

I can't live in a house like this. Repair the White House right now! It's not befitting of a presidential residence!

During the three-month repair period, he lived outside of the White House.

That's why they take the President for granted!

White House

Vacant room available

He also commissioned the best designer of the times to design the main entrance of the White House.

That top designer was Louis C. Tiffany, the master of the then most popular Art Nouveau style.

Tiffany Co. Jewels

Tiffany remains to this day as one of the most highly regarded design houses...

Furthermore, he commissioned Tiffany to design the chinaware used in the White House.

※White House dish designed by Tiffany

Arthur's expensive tastes had the effect of boosting the dignity and class of the President and the White House.

According to Historian William Seale, "history remembers only a few things about Arthur."

21st President Arthur... Signed the Pendleton Act into law...

C. Arthur

"That includes his expensives tastes!"

Yeah, this was a President with very expensive tastes.

He was also stylish, and loved good food...

Snap

After the assassination of Lincoln, mourning the loss of a great leader, American society

Oh, Lincoln, Lincoln ♥

Is there another Lincoln?

didn't give his successors the opportunity to shine.

Whoever runs for President would be no match for Lincoln...

Lincoln,

Lincoln,

It was Chester Alan Arthur who greatly contributed to the restoration of the fallen dignity and majesty of the presidency.

I'm a President too!

Grover Cleveland 1885~1889, 1893~1897

Foe of Organized Labor

ROAR
ROAR

ROAR
WAGE INCREASES

ROAR

* Caricature of the rise of the labor union (1886)

Grover Cleveland

Democratic Party, 1837.3.18~1908.6.24

Birth Place   Caldwell, New Jersey

Wife   Frances Folsom Cleveland 1864~1947

Children   Ruth, Esther, Marion, Richard, Francis

Vice Presidents   T. A. Hendricks 1885

A. E. Stevenson 1893

Grover Cleveland is the only U.S. President who served two non-consecutive terms.

1885	1889	1893	1897

22nd	Lost election	24th

23rd
Benjamin Harrison

Between Presidents Lincoln and Theodore Roosevelt, American historians consider Grover Cleveland

16. ● A. Lincoln— 1861
17. ◆ A. Johnson
18. ◆ U. Grant
19. ◆ R. Hayes
20. ◆ J. Garfield
21. ◆ C. Arthur
22. ● G. Cleveland
23. ◆ B. Harrison
24. ◆ G. Cleveland
25. ◆ W. McKinley
26. ● T. Roosevelt— 1901

---

as the most capable and important President during the period of disorder that followed the Civil War.

After Lincoln and until Theodore Roosevelt,

Ulysses Grant is the only President who won re-election.

However, Cleveland was a conservative politician.

Cleveland implement-ed justice from his conservative and old-fashioned perspective.
-Dean Atchison

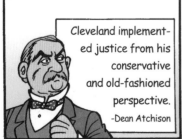

It was his firm belief that the President owed a duty to prevent misfortunes from occurring to the nation

Preparation
Prevention

---

rather than to promote good for the nation.

Crisis

Many politicians are unable to say no to what is wrong,

but Cleveland had the conviction to say no without hesitation.

He is remembered as a courageous, upright and responsible President.

At 125kgs, Cleveland was the second heaviest among all U.S. Presidents after twenty-seventh President Taft.

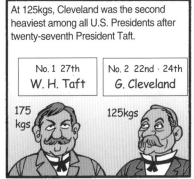

No. 1 27th	No. 2 22nd · 24th
W. H. Taft	G. Cleveland

175 kgs

125kgs

Having fallen in love with a young woman 27 years his junior,

Is that his... daughter?

he's also the first President to wed in the White House.

Special report!
News flash!

21-year old First Lady!

Grover Cleveland was the fifth of nine children born to a Presbyterian minister in Caldwell, New Jersey.

Whew, another one...

Let's give our... thanks in prayer.

WAH~

At the age of 16, he left school and went to work when his father died.

Papa, you left me nothing...

Sorry son...

Even though he didn't go to college, he studied law on his own and passed the bar in Buffalo.

So... even without a college degree,

self-study → lawyer → President is the way to go!

U.S. Presidents

After entering politics, he joined the Democratic Party.

Common people constituents

Upper class, wealthy constituents

Democratic Party

Republican Party

People highly regarded his honesty and conviction.

No way! You can't do that!

That stubbornness!

He was seen as a politician neutral from the 'machine' factions. This helped him win the Buffalo mayorship and New York governorship (1882).

Man with a conviction!

Impartial from machine politics!

Cleveland was successful as New York Governor, and his reputation and popularity led to his nomination as the Democratic presidential candidate.

By a slim margin, he beat James Blaine, the candidate from the corrupted Republican Party, in the 1884 presidential election.

Results of 1884 Election		
Democratic Party		Republican Party
G. Cleveland		James G. Blaine
4,874,621	Popular votes	4,848,936
219		182
	Electoral votes	

Cleveland's election ended the Republican Party's 24-year monopolization of the White House, which had continued since Lincoln's 1860 election.

Democratic Administration

In this election, the biggest campaign issue was each candidate's record of military service in the Civil War.

Veteran
=
Patriot

At that time, whether or not it was on his own volition, a politician must have served in the war to be considered as a 'patriotic' politician.

Draft evader!

You're no patriot! You're just selfish!

However, Cleveland was unable to serve due to family circumstances. His political adversaries attacked him for this.

How could a draft evader like yourself run for President!

I told you it wasn't on purpose!

Two of his brothers served in the army, so he had to take care of his two sisters and mother at home.

If all the men went off to war, who would've fed the family?!

Thus, Cleveland obtained an exemption by paying $150 and sending off a Polish immigrant in his place pursuant to the Conscription Act then in effect.

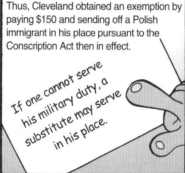

If one cannot serve his military duty, a substitute may serve in his place.

Even though he didn't violate the law, it was a serious moral flaw for a presidential candidate to have evaded the draft.

DRAFT SCANDAL

Nevertheless, Cleveland's opponent Blaine, the Republican candidate, also had sent off a substitute to the war,

Hey! This guy didn't serve too!

so the so-called 'draft scandal' didn't have a big impact on Cleveland.

Who is he to criticize me for not serving?

So, in the end, the Democratic Party took power after defeating the Republican Party that had seemed invincible for years.

Boy, that was close...

He would never have become President if he ran for President in Korea.

WHEW~

Cleveland ran for re-election in the 1888 presidential election. Although he won the popular vote against the Republican Party candidate,

Results of 1888 Election	
Democratic Party	Republican Party
G. Cleveland	Benjamin Harrison
5,534,488	5,443,892
Popular votes	
168	233
Electoral votes	

he failed in his re-election bid because he lost the electoral vote. Refusing to give up, Cleveland persisted, however,

Wait and see

I will win back the White House!

and got even with his nemesis Benjamin Harrison in the 1892 presidential election by defeating him and winning the presidency again.

During the period encompassing his two-term presidency, public servants including the President suffered from a severe loss of prestige in America, while Congress held political power.

The times were difficult as the nation was unable to overcome an acute economic depression.

H·E· *L·P·...*

Depresssion

* Cleveland on the way to his inauguration (person waving his hat on the coach, on the right-hand side)

Unprecedented extreme labor unrest continued throughout his term, and

Increase wages!

Help the jobless!

Improve labor conditions!

ROAR ROAR ROAR

in 1886, the American Federation of Labor, a federation of labor unions, was established. Labor movements had increased in size and become more systematic.

AFL
American Federation of Labor

Confrontation between capitalists and workers increasingly worsened, and, in some cases, resulted in violence such as in the case of the Haymarket Affair.*

* Haymarket Affair: Labor-management dispute that occurred in Chicago in 1886

Cleveland's most noteworthy policy was his strong non-interventionist economic policy.

Freedom of the Markets
No intervention by the government!

He also firmly rejected the assertion that the state must come to the aid of the poor.

Why should the state help the poor?

It's the people who should help the state! It shouldn't be the other way around!

Cleveland's views were reflected in the inaugural speech given by future Democratic President John F. Kennedy.

Ask not what your country can do for you.

Ask what you can do for your country.

It was no wonder that the workers fiercely opposed Cleveland's policies.

Cleveland pays no attention to the hardships of the poor and only sides with the industrialists!

Is Cleveland the President of the wealthy only?!

During his term, America experienced the most serious labor struggles in its history.

ROAR
ROAR
ROAR

Cleveland's second term was dominated by an economic depression.

* Caricature of Congress dominated by robber barons

As his term got off to a start, 600 banks failed and were closed down, triggering a severe recession.

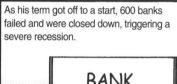

BANK

Bankruptcy

In 1895, the government almost went bankrupt when its reserve fell to a mere $413 million.

Treasury

Cleveland had no alternative but to borrow money from bankers like J.P. Morgan.

Mr. Morgan, lend the nation some money...

He managed to urgently borrow $62 million and take other such measures,

Boy, this is demeaning.

which severely tarnished his upright image. He was viewed as having sold out to the banks.

Just look at how his attitude has changed!

He's now a puppet of the banks.

Where's all that pomp of his?

From its founding to the Civil War, U.S. history was dominated by the North-South conflict over slavery,

Founding   North-South conflict   Civil War

but thereafter the focus shifted to the gap between rich and poor caused by abrupt industrialization

World Wars

Conflict between rich and poor   Racial conflict

and the unbridled capitalism and resulting economic depressions. These issues brought on great challenges for the Presidents.

Economic depression

Nevertheless, the presidency's dignity, which was considerably restored after Chester A. Arthur's presidency,

was further strengthened by Cleveland.

He freely used his veto powers and vetoed no less than 414 bills passed by Congress during his term.

Later on, Woodrow Wilson, the future Democratic presidential candidate and President, spoke highly of Cleveland.

Woodrow Wilson

28th President

"Johnson, Grant, Hayes, Garfield and Arthur were all tied down by Congress and unable to do the work they were supposed to do."

"Cleveland singularly played a decisive role among all the Presidents from 1865 (the year of Lincoln's death) to 1894. He was the only President to act as a true leader during that period."

It is said that Cleveland first met his wife Francis Folsom in 1864, immediately after her birth.

After his partner and Francis's father Oscar Folsom died in 1875,

Cleveland served as the executor of his estate and took care of his family. It is not clear, however, when Cleveland and Francis Folsom became lovers.

In August 1885, the 48-year old President Cleveland proposed to the 21-year old Francis.

She willingly accepted his proposal, and the first ever wedding in the White House took place.

Benjamin Harrison 1889~1893

Gifted Public Speaker, Not So Gifted President

Benjamin Harrison

Republican Party, 1833.8.20~1901.3.13

Birth Place **North Bend, Ohio**

Wives **1. Caroline L. Scott Harrison 1832~1892**

2. Mary S. L. Dimmick Harrison 1858~1948

Children **Russell, Mary, Elizabeth**

Vice President **L. P. Morton**

Benjamin Harison was a grandson of ninth President William Harrison.

Benjamin.

Grandpa!

His father was John Scott Harrison, a U.S. Senator.

That's a helluva family...

To trace his ancestry even further, one of his great grandfathers was a signatory of the Declaration of Independence.

Virginia
Carter Braxton
Thomas Jefferson
Benjamin Harrison (1726~1791)
Francis Lighthood Lee
Richard Henry Lee
Thomas Nelson
George Wythe

Harrison was born into such a traditional and distinguished political family.

What's your family business?

Politics!

Even though he possessed a keen intellect and remarkable oratorical skills, which charmed the public,

Even though TV makes the modern-day President,

in the old days, a booming voice and skilled oratory made a politician.

---

curiously, he didn't possess the skills required of a great President.

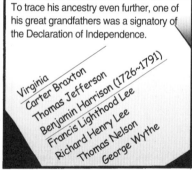

* Caricature of Harrison wearing his grandfather's hat that is too big for him

He was seven when his grandfather William Harrison was inaugurated as President (1841).

ROAR

Grandpa's now President~!

Raised in a family of career politicians, Harrison spent his entire life in politics.

POLITICS

The only time he ventured out of politics was for military service during the Civil War

If I were to avoid military service♪

I would be questioned about it throughout my political life!

Volunteer Station

---

alongside General Sherman.

Promoted to Colonel within three weeks of my commission as a second lieutenant!

What kind of background does that guy have...?

After his discharge from the army, even though he twice ran for Governor of Indiana and failed on both tries,

Governor

he managed to get elected as a U.S. Senator in 1881 due to his 'family background.'

U.S. Senate

Harrison Family

However, he lost even that office after his defeat in the 1887 election.

Another loss!

The Republican Party still nominated Harrison as its presidential candidate at the Republican National Convention the next year.

They've nominated Harrison, the perennial loser?

Republicans nominate Harrison

It was a really big upset for him to defeat the popular incumbent President Cleveland and take the White House.

Cleveland

Other than his superb oratorical skills, he didn't possess any special ability,

Oratory is the only thing he's good at...

but he was backed by the resources of the Republican Party and financial support of industrialists.

$$$$$$$

Republicans Industry

He was also helped by the state of the world economy that was moving towards protectionism.

Cleveland

Harrison

Free trade

Protectionism Custom barriers

Benjamin Harrison was born as one of the 13 children of John Scott Harrison in Ohio.

Although he spent his childhood at the 24,000km² farm 'Point' bequeathed to him by his President grandfather,

due to the deterioration in his family's financial condition, he was unable to attend a well-known college on the East Coast and completed his college studies in Ohio.

It's expensive to study on the East Coast, so I have no other choice...

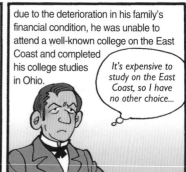

During college, Harrison distinguished himself in debate clubs due to his prominent oratorical skills.

He was nicknamed 'glacier' for his cold personality,

He's so cold...

but his public speaking charmed audiences, and he was able to win many verdicts as a lawyer.

Ladies and gentlemen, please return a not-guilty verdict for the defendant.

It was no surprise that the Republican Party recruited him into the political world.

Let's recruit that Harrison.

After losing a number of elections, he ended up promising his wife that he would end his career in politics.

Honey, I'm finished with politics...

So he focused on lawyering and continued to win big cases.

The Republican Party, which highly regarded his popularity, recruited him back to politics.

At that time, the Republicans were looking for a candidate to oppose the reform-minded Democratic President Cleveland.

Democratic Party
Cleveland

Reform

They badly needed a candidate with a reputation for integrity who could help the Republicans discard their image as a corrupt party.

Republican Party
Harrison

Integ-rity

Unlike the majority of Republicans who were smudged with bribes and dishonesty and corruption,

Harrison stood out in the Senate as a man of integrity.

No way, I have my grandpa's honor to keep!

Eventually, the Republican Party nominated Harrison as its candidate in the presidential election of 1888,

presidential candidate
Benjamin Harrison

vice presidential candidate
Levi P. Morton

Republican Party

and commenced an intense election campaign to regain the presidency from the Democratic Party.

* Harrison giving an election speech

The Republicans resorted to slandering and faultfinding and all other kinds of false propaganda to bring Cleveland down.

He evaded the draft...

Faultfinding

Slander

False rumors

Republican Party

As their nastiest and darkest means of false propaganda, the Republicans attempted to alienate English-American and Irish-American voters from each other.

Those English are the enemy!

Those Irish are savage...

When a Republican strategist sought advice on the election from the British Ambassador,

From the perspective of Britain, which candidate is the preferred candidate?

British Embassy in U.S.

the British Ambassador replied that Britain prefers Cleveland who supported free trade.

Well, if you ask, we're in favor of Cleveland...

The Republicans extensively publicized this reply in its election campaign.

Cleveland is pro-British!

Britain supports Cleveland!

This caused the anti-Britain Irish-American voters in the populous New York State to turn their backs on Cleveland.

WHAT?!

Although Cleveland—who was ahead in the polls—also won the actual popular vote,

Cleveland won 90,596 more votes!

he lost the electoral vote and the White House to Harrison. This phenomenon reoccurred in the year 2000.

Victory

Harrison's inauguration was held in pouring rain just like the inauguration of his grandfather.

Oh, Almighty God, give me the wisdom, strength and faith...

It is said he delivered an unimpressive inaugural speech.

Give the people equality and justice, peace and love...

Why can't he just shut up in this pouring rain. It's all just mumbo jumbo...

After his inauguration, instead of developing into a great President, he was constantly dominated by the people who had made him President.

Remember who made you President?

Of... course.

Harrison signed into law the McKinley Tarriff Act of 1890 that raised protectionist trade barriers.

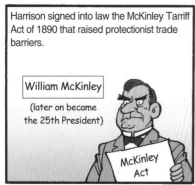

William McKinley

(later on became the 25th President)

McKinley Act

This statute greatly raised tariffs on imported goods and, in turn, their prices.

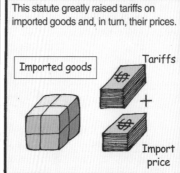

Imported goods

Tariffs

+

Import price

The goal was to make U.S. products more price competitive.

Price

Imported goods

U.S. goods

But as the prices of imported goods skyrocketed, so did the prices of other goods.

Price of imported goods

Price levels

The U.S. economy fell into a severe depression,

Prices

Jobless

as a result of which Harrison suffered a crushing defeat to Cleveland in the 1892 presidential election.

It's the economy, stupid!

Rep

Dem

To prevent large enterprises from monopolizing the markets by recklessly increasing their size,

Large enterprises

Small-and-medium enterprises

Harrison signed into law the Sherman Antitrust Act.

This became the weapon of choice of Theodore Roosevelt 10 years later.

Sherman Antitrust Act 1890

Nevertheless, his effort had no dampening effect on secret and illegal mergers and collusions.

Let's pretend we're doing... and do...

The government's too incompetent to find out about it.

Harrison returned to Indianapolis after failing in his re-election bid.

Results of 1892 Election	
Democratic Party	**Republican Party**
G. Cleveland	B. Harrison
5,551,883	Popular votes	5,179,244
277	Electoral votes	182

During his presidency, Harrison lost his first wife.

Sorry to hear that the First Lady passed away...

Funeral

White House

Despite the opposition of his children, he remarried Mary Dimmick who was 25 years his junior.

What's the big deal...

Cleveland married a young woman 27 years his junior...

He was 63 when Mary gave birth to another daughter for him in 1897.

How cute~

Is she his daughter or granddaughter...?

The old man's still virile...

Due to his easygoing personality, Harrison disliked embarking on new projects.

Is that really necessary?

As an orator, even though he was at ease in front of a crowd,

With patriotism and justice in the hearts of all the people...

he wasn't at ease in dealing with people on a personal level.

Hmm...

This is pretty awkward...

People who knew him well have said "Harrison had a sense of humor, but didn't know how to use it.

Ha ha ha ha

He could charm thousands of people with his oratory,

WOW~

but he turns anyone into an enemy the very moment he meets that person."

What a turnoff...

There are four families that have produced two Presidents.

2nd	John Adams (father)
6th	John Quincy Adams (son)
9th	William Harrison (grandfather)
23rd	Benjamin Harrison (grandson)
26th	Theodore Roosevelt (uncle)
32nd	Franklin D. Roosevelt (nephew)
41st	George Bush (father)
43rd	George W. Bush (son)

The Adams family is more highly regarded than the Harrison family in history.

Adams family

Harrison family

Bush family

Where would this family fit in?

William McKinley 1897~1901

Architect of American Imperialism

William McKinley

Republican Party, 1843.1.29~1901.9.14

Birth Place   Niles, Ohio

Wife   Ida Saxton McKinley 1847~1907

Children   Katherine, Ida

Vice Presidents   G.A. Hobart 1897

Theodore Roosevelt 1901

William McKinley served as President toward the end of the 19th century as imperialistic world powers were redrawing the world map.

He was the first President to win re-election after the 20-year period that followed Grant's presidency. No President had won re-election during that period.

19th Hayes	(one term)	1877~1881
20th Garfield	(assassinated)	1881
21st Arthur	(one term)	1881~1885
22nd Cleveland	(one term)	1885~1889
23rd Harrison	(one term)	1889~1893
24th Cleveland	(one term)	1893~1897

He is recorded in history as the architect of the 'American Empire.'

His words and thinking didn't leave a lasting legacy,

*McKinley giving a speech

but it's significant that McKinley led the U.S. during an important transitional period leading into the 20th century.

The U.S., which is the world's only superpower in the 21st century, started to rapidly develop into a world power during McKinley's presidency.

McKinley's home state Ohio produced six out of the seven Presidents* elected from 1868 to 1920.

18th Grant
19th Hayes
20th Garfield
23rd Harrison
25th McKinley
27th Taft

*Only those elected to the presidency in an election

Many electoral votes are allocated to Ohio, which joins together the Eastern, Southern and Midwestern states.

Ohio possesses evenly and well developed agricultural, mining, manufacturing, retail and other industries. In 2004, Ohio also decided Bush's re-election.

McKinley started out as frontrunner U.S. Representative from Ohio. He then won the governorship of this important state, which is capable of deciding presidential elections.

Of course, it also helped that he served with great distinction in the Civil War. Military service was a prerequisite to success in politics during his times.

In June 1861, he enlisted in the army as a private at the young age of 18.

He was promoted to second lieutenant for his exploits at the Battle of Antietam.

He also served as the adjutant of Colonel Rutherford B. Hayes (19th President) of the Union Army, and was promoted to major in 1865 at the age of 22.

McKinley, a gentleman, was a devout Christian.

He took meticulous care of his epileptic wife throughout her life, a trait that also helped his political career.

His political philosophy was driven by his efforts to overcome economic crises.

High tariffs will help workers live comfortably, provide farmers with stable markets and give the people a high standard of living!

However, the McKinley Tariff Act of 1890 worsened the economic crisis,

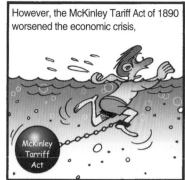

and was blamed for the 1893 depression and the economic recession that followed.

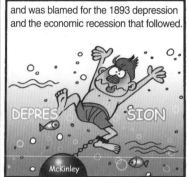

After Harrison's failure to win re-election due to the McKinley Act, and following the end of Cleveland's second term that was marked by extreme labor movements,

the Republicans and the Democrats battled each other in the 1896 presidential election.

On the economic policy front, the two parties clashed over protectionism and the gold standard.

We must return to protectionism and adopt the gold standard system.

Gold Standard System

Monetary system that pegs or fixes the value of a nation's currency unit to a fixed amount of gold bullion.

Under a gold standard system, the value of a currency unit always remains constant.

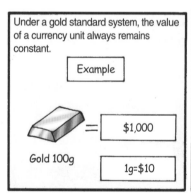

In a difficult economy, if the value of money appreciates, that appreciation would, in turn, reduce wages and prices. This is unfavorable to the workers.

On the other hand, since the gold standard system always preserves the value of money, it's favorable to the wealthy elite and industrialists.

In contrast, the Democrats argued for the adoption of a free silver system by which the government could print as much money as was needed.

A free silver system would increase the money supply and result in inflation, but also reduce the value of the debt of farmers and workers.

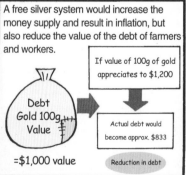

Thus, the free silver system was favorable to the workers and unfavorable to the wealthy elite and industrialists.

At the 1896 Democratic National Convention, presidential candidate William Jennings Bryan made one of the best speeches ever given at a national convention.

"You shall not press down upon the brow of labor this crown of thorns, you shall not crucify mankind upon a cross of gold."

However, in fear of a Democratic government, American industrialists supported McKinley in droves.

If Bryan becomes President, he's going to crack down on industry.

He'll make life miserable for us through anti-market policies!

During the 1896 presidential election campaign, McKinley spent the most money ever spent in a campaign up to that time,

Democratic candidate Bryan's war chest	Republican candidate McKinley's war chest
	$3.5 million~$16 million (estimated)
$500,000	

and won the election by the largest margin since Grant's election in 1872.

Results of 1896 Election

Republican Party	Democratic Party+ Populist Party
William McKinley	William. J. Bryan
7,108,480	6,511,495
271	149+27

Popular votes

Electoral votes

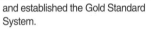

The 1896 election was the first modern election in terms of its budget and size, among other things.

My investment in the Gold Standard System paid off...

I spent more money than I could ever dream of...

After his inauguration, McKinley started implementing new protective tariffs

Climb
this wall
if you can~~

Tariff Barrier

USA

and established the Gold Standard System.

GOLD STANDARD SYSTEM

Meanwhile, he faced great difficulties in the foreign policy arena.

BOOM

USA

Cuba

As Cuban revolutionaries fought against Spain to free Cuba from colonial rule,

ROAR

Independence

Drive out the oppressors!

neighboring America was eventually called on to intervene in the Cuban problem.

Are you just going to wait and see?

There're significant American assets in Cuba...

McKinley, however, turned down the demands for intervention.

I've fought in wars and seen heaps of corpses.

I don't wish to see any more victims of war.

NO!

In February 1898, a U.S. warship docked at Havana Harbor exploded. Angry Americans blamed the Spanish military, heating up public opinion and resulting in demands for war.

Pressured by public opinion, the U.S. declared war on Spain even though Spain had agreed to most of the U.S. demands.

It's war!

Cuba

*An investigation later on revealed that the accident stemmed from an explosion in the engine room.

McKinley, a devout Christian, defined this war as a righteous crusade on behalf of the American people and God.

In the name of God

and the American people, we will punish evil.

As a realist in economic affairs, he also viewed the war as an opportunity for economic development.

When the war ends,

we will have to defend what we desire!

Profits

Spoils of war

The war ended with a U.S. victory in just five months.

*The U.S. Marine Corps in battle

Through this war, the U.S. gained control over Puerto Rico, Guam and the Philippines,

Philippines

1898 Ceded to U.S.
1902 U.S. rule begins
1941 Occupied by Japan
1945 Recaptured by U.S.
1946 Achieves independence

and joined the club of imperialist nations that controlled overseas colonies.

*The U.S. Army marching in Beijing in 1900

The Spanish-American War greatly improved the status of the presidency.

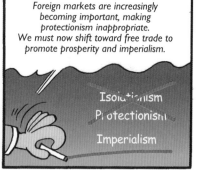

White House staff increased from 6 to 80.

Spokesperson of the President appointed.

The White House became a fundamental source of all news.

According to the White House, the Iraqi War...

TV

McKinley's policies greatly changed as well.

It's no longer possible to maintain isolationism, nor is it desirable!

Isolationism
Protectionism

Foreign markets are increasingly becoming important, making protectionism inappropriate. We must now shift toward free trade to promote prosperity and imperialism.

Isolationism
Protectionism
Imperialism

With prosperity and imperialism as his campaign slogans, McKinley proved to be extremely popular in the 1900 presidential election.

He defeated the Democratic candidate Bryan and easily won re-election.

Results of 1900 Election	
Republican Party	Democratic Party
William McKinley	W. J. Bryan
7,218,039	6,358,345	Popular votes
292	155	Electoral votes

In September 1901, on his way back home after a visit to the West in celebration of his re-election,

McKinley attended the Pan-American Exposition in Buffalo,

where he was assassinated by anarchist Leon Czolgosz. He became the third President to die by an assassin's bullet.

Czolgosz was aware that McKinley was famous for profusely shaking the hands of the people.

Czolgosz hid himself in the exposition crowd and shot McKinley twice as the president approached him.

I support anarchism because it pursues true freedom of mankind!

Imperialism and hegemonism persecute the freedom of mankind!

Bang   Bang

McKinley led America during the transitional period from the late 19th century to the early 20th century.

*The McKinleys

He was the first President to declare America's imperialism.

IMPERIALISM

Half a century later, America won the two world wars

and emerged as the world's only super power, and a great economic and military power.

It was McKinley who raised the flagpole that would fly the flag of this world empire.

The flag of the greatest nation will fly on this flagpole.

Theodore Roosevelt 1901~1909

The Trustbuster

Regulation
Collusion
Large enterprises
Trusts
Monopoly
M&A
Small-and-medium enterprises

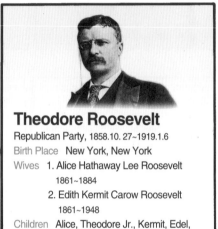

Theodore Roosevelt

Republican Party, 1858.10. 27~1919.1.6

Birth Place   New York, New York

Wives   1. Alice Hathaway Lee Roosevelt
           1861~1884
        2. Edith Kermit Carow Roosevelt
           1861~1948

Children   Alice, Theodore Jr., Kermit, Edel, Archie, Quentin

Vice President   C. W. Fairbanks

Surveys of the most popular U.S. Presidents always return the same results.

No. 1   Abraham Lincoln

No. 2   George Washington

No. 3   Theodore Roosevelt

It's fair to characterize Lincoln and Washington as 'respected' Presidents rather than 'popular' Presidents,

Washington = National Father

Lincoln = Preserver of Union

---

whereas Theodore Roosevelt was indeed the most popular President. He was indeed a character.

Teddy!

YAY!   Teddy!

YEAH!

President Roosevelt was also known by his initials TR and, occasionally, Teddy, a nickname he hated.

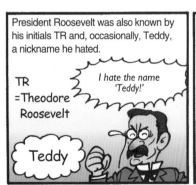

TR = Theodore Roosevelt

I hate the name 'Teddy!'

Teddy

This multi-faceted man who possessed a fiery temper and defiant spirit

ARRRRRGH...

---

is forever imprinted as a legendary hero in the minds of Americans.

He was a remarkable man...

Who's to stop Teddy!

Born into a patrician and wealthy family, TR was raised in an affluent environment.

*Teddy as a New York State Assemblyman in 1882

When he was a child, he suffered from a host of health problems such as nearsightedness and asthma,

so he came to enjoy sports, nature and history to overcome his ailments.

I can't lose this battle with myself!

By the time he graduated *magna cum laude* from Harvard University at the age of 22, TR had already written a history book.

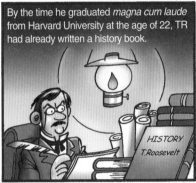

HISTORY
T.Roosevelt

After a stint in law school, TR joined the Republican Party and started his political career as a New York State Assemblyman in 1882 at the age of 24.

Republican

POLITICS

When he was 37, in 1895, President McKinley appointed him as Commissioner of the New York City Police, which helped him build a national reputation.

Loyalty, Sir!

When the Spanish-American War broke out in 1898 over the Cuban problem,

Cuba

TR personally organized and led a volunteer cavalry known as the Rough Riders.

He led the Rough Riders to victory at the Battle of Kettle Hill and returned to America as a war hero.

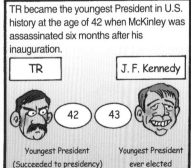

*Teddy as a cavalry leader

Helped by his national reputation, he was immediately elected New York Governor after his return,

Teddy! Yeah!
Teddy! Roar
N.Y. STATE

and then nominated and elected as Vice President in the 1900 presidential election.

President
William McKinley

Vice President
Theodore Roosevelt

TR became the youngest President in U.S. history at the age of 42 when McKinley was assassinated six months after his inauguration.

TR		J. F. Kennedy
42	43	
Youngest President (Succeeded to presidency)		Youngest President ever elected

The young TR had built up a brilliant resume before ascending to the presidency. He was a scholar, naturalist, farm owner and

public servant, army colonel and war hero, not to mention Governor of New York.

THEODORE ROOSEVELT
T R

As President, he confronted major corporations that had grown like dinosaurs. Their heavy-handed business practices had become a major problem.

Large Enterprises

Major corporations built monopolies by acquiring weaker corporations through collusive backroom deals.

Small corporations

Large corporations

By monopolizing markets and fixing prices, they caused great harm to the markets.

Monopoly

I'm going to wipe out all of my competitors!

Market

The government, however, had made only empty threats against the monopolistic enterprises that were like a horse on the loose.

Antitrust!

I can't just go on bluffing forever...

Having veered out of control, the corporations became increasingly arrogant as they wantonly usurped the national wealth.

BURP

This phenomenon accelerated the polarization between the rich and the poor,

Poor man

Rich man

and stirred up anger and hatred against large corporations in American society.

It was TR who took action to rein in the laissez faire economy.

Regulation

With the Sherman Antitrust Act, he attacked Morgan, Rockefeller and other large corporations,

TRUST

and effectively checked the expansion of Standard Oil, American Tobacco and Dupont, among others.

*J. P. Morgan, Rockefeller, Carnegie and TR (in the boat on the left)

Naturally, TR's popularity skyrocketed. The sky was the limit.

He won re-election in the 1904 presidential election by defeating the Democratic candidate in a landslide.

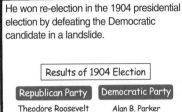

Results of 1904 Election		
Republican Party		Democratic Party
Theodore Roosevelt		Alan B. Parker
7,626,593	Popular votes	5,082,898
336		140
	Electoral votes	

The voters had supported his position that advocated for government regulation and supervision over industry in a rapidly industrializing society.

However, just because he imposed sanctions on capitalism, that doesn't mean TR was an anti-capitalist.

ME?

I'm an absolute protector of the market!

Even though he himself was a capitalist born and raised in a capitalist family,

Bourgeois Family

he believed that if capitalism went to extremes and lost the ability to restrain abusive business practices of large enterprises,

Mer Large enterprises ger

socialism, which was then sweeping throughout the world, would take root in America.

Workers of the world, unite!

In order to prevent the entrenchment of socialism in America, we must monitor and supervise capitalism so that it can function properly!

Internally, TR worked hard to prevent illegal corporate mergers and, externally, made strong efforts to promote U.S. leadership abroad.

He restarted construction of the infamous and greatly delayed Panama Canal,

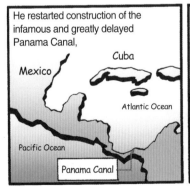

Cuba

Mexico

Atlantic Ocean

Pacific Ocean

Panama Canal

and mediated the Treaty of Portsmouth that formally ended the Russo-Japanese War in 1905,

Hey, let's resolve this conflict through dialogue.

for which he won the Nobel Peace Price.

But he ordered his special envoy Taft to conclude a secret pact with Japan's Katsura

and tacitly consented to Japan's annexation of Korea!

Roosevelt

TR's tragedy started when he selected his friend and former aide Howard Taft as his successor.

He's a pretty docile guy...

H. Taft

Taft was easily elected President with the help of the popular TR.

Results of 1908 Election

Republican Party		Democratic Party
William H. Taft		William J. Bryan
7,676,258	Popular votes	6,406,801
321	Electoral votes	162

Contrary to TR's expectations, Taft proved to be feeble and, in TR's view, went the wrong direction.

Overcome by disappointment, TR eventually became exasperated.

What is this? Everything's been ruined!

I can't leave Howard alone. I need to become President again and rectify these wrongs!

So TR ran for president again in the 1912 presidential election. Doing so created a rift within the Republican Party,

CRACK

Republican Party
W.H. Taft

Progressive Party
T. Roosevelt

and Woodrow Wilson was able to play off one side against the other to win the presidency.

President

TR was always the man in the news. Stories about TR and his family always attracted the interests of Americans.

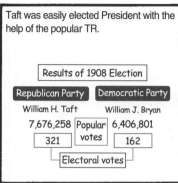

*TR with his family around 1903

In 1917, during World War I, Roosevelt made a request to President Wilson.

I'll lead a volunteer cavalry division

and fight in the European front.

Of course, Wilson refused his request.

Old man, think about your age.

The guy's senseless...

More than anyone else, TR worked hard to preserve the natural environment.

He prohibited forestry development in more than 200 million acres (eight times the size of the Korean peninsula) and created many national parks.

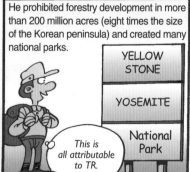

YELLOW STONE

YOSEMITE

National Park

This is all attributable to TR.

In 1902, when TR went bear hunting in Mississippi, he found a baby bear but refused to shoot it.

I don't have the heart to shoot a baby bear...

A reporter named Clifford Berrymen reported the incident with a cartoon,

Washington Post

Teddy and the Baby Bear
The President draws the line

and Morris Mitchtom, a Brooklyn, New York toy store owner, named the doll on display in his store as 'Teddy,' TR's nickname.

TEDDY BEAR

This is how the ever-popular 'Teddy Bear' was born.

Among the three Presidents who assumed the presidency due to the assassination of their predecessors, TR is considered as the most capable and vigorous President, and also the one with the broadest outlook.

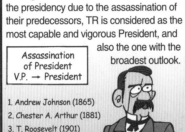

Assassination of President
V.P. → President

1. Andrew Johnson (1865)
2. Chester A. Arthur (1881)
3. T. Roosevelt (1901)

A big fan of sports, he would box with John Sullivan in the White House,

and run obstacle races with high-ranking politicians.

Gasping for their breath, overweight congressmen and ambassadors always trailed behind TR.

Mr. President, can we slow down a bit?

gasp gasp gasp

TR tested the power and limits of America.

USA

Full with passion, he expanded the power and limits of his nation.

USA

A relative who knew him well once said of him,

He would want to be the groom at a wedding,

"and the dead man at a funeral!"

HI !

TR always wanted to be the life of the party!

William Howard Taft 1909~1913

Overweight President Overshadowed by His Predecessor

Hey, you're going the wrong way!

Get out of the way! You're no longer President! I am!

William Howard Taft

Republican Party, 1857. 9.15~1930.3.8

Birth Place   Cincinnati, Ohio

Wife   Helen Herron Taft 1861~1943

Children   Robert, Helen, Charles

Vice President   J. S. Sherman

History remembers William Howard Taft as the most overweight President.

160~175kgs

He was a good and jovial man, but lacked the smarts.

Ho ho ho ho

CHILL

Why's he laughing?

Contrary to his own assessment, Taft wasn't very successful.

I'm a successful President!

Really?

Although Taft intensely disliked politics, he was a career politician.

I hate politics!

But this is the only job I can hold...

He wasn't a very ambitious man, but still built an impressive resume.

· Federal judge
· 1st U.S. Governor-General of the Philippines
· Cabinet member
· Chief Justice of United States

The only elected office that he ever held was the U.S. presidency.

Wow, the man ran for only one elected office

and that was the presidency!

Time and again, his weight has become the topic of quiz shows and the butt of jokes,

What was Taft's weight when he was at his heaviest?

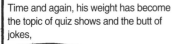

ABC Quiz
① 140kgs
② 160kgs
③ 175kgs

and a favorite subject of history professors to attract the attention of students.

Did you know that one day Taft...

Blink

When Taft made his first inspection of the Philippines, America's newest colony, he sent a telegram to Secretary of War Elihu Root,

I had to walk all day but fortunately I was able to ride a horse for 40kms.

to which Root sent the following reply:

How's the horse?

Boy, to ride a horse with that heavy body...

Taft was born in 1857 in Cincinnati, Ohio. He graduated second in his class from Yale University.

Michigan

Cleveland
Columbus
Indiana
Cincinnati
Kentucky

Pennsyl-vania

West Virginia

Ohio

Even before his graduation from Cincinatti Law School*, he was admitted to the Ohio bar.

License

He must've studied hard.

*School for training legal professionals

Taft entered Ohio politics, and also became a federal judge.

My lifelong wish is to become the Chief Justice of the United States!

U.S. Supreme Court

In 1900, Taft went to the Philippines, the colony acquired from Spain, to serve as its administrator and oversee the establishment of a civilian government.

I was also called the governor-general.

*Taft in the Philippines

In the Philippines, Taft spent four years and gained a reputation as a fair and able administrator.

PHILIPPINES
U.S.A.

He greatly contributed to establishment of the Philippines as a new territory of the U.S. without shedding blood.

We're a friend of the Philippines!

In 1904, President Roosevelt appointed Taft as Secretary of War.

I need you as a cabinet member!

And in 1905, as the President's special envoy, he played a role in concluding a secret agreement with Japan.

Katsura-Taft Agreement

Katsura—W. H. Taft

After its war victory against Russia, Japan suddenly emerged as an East Asian power.

In order to achieve its ultimate goal of expanding into China proper, Japan sought to annex the Korean peninsula as an advance base for China.

The U.S., which gained the Philippines through its war victory over Spain, wished to avoid conflict with Japan.

So the Japanese Prime Minister Katsura and Roosevelt's special envoy Taft concluded a secret agreement to recognize each other's colony.

In exchange for the U.S. tacitly consenting to Japan's occupation of Korea,

we will recognize the U.S. occupation of the Philippines.

As a result, the U.S. controlled the Philippines, which was an important strategic outpost in Asia,

while Japan proceeded to annex the Korean peninsula without hindrance.

Taft was a true follower of Roosevelt, who he deeply respected.

He did his best to serve TR as TR's right-hand man.

That way!

Yes, Sir!

It was natural that TR made Taft his successor and supported his candidacy for the presidency.

It's now your turn to run for President!

Helped by the popular TR, Taft easily defeated the Democratic candidate to win election as the twenty-seventh U.S. President.

Results of 1908 Election		
Republican Party		Democratic Party
William H. Taft		William J. Bryan
7,676,258	Popular votes	6,406,801
321		162
	Electoral votes	

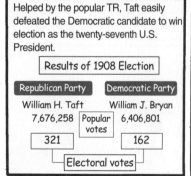

Before his election to the presidency, Taft showed absolute obedience to TR. But things changed after the election.

Howard, what's wrong with you?

Taft, now President, was no longer a member of TR's cabinet but the most powerful man in America.

Well, I'm now President!

Taft's inaugural speech is known to have been most lethargic and tiring.

My fellow – Citizens...
Anyone who has taken
the oath I have just taken
must feel a heavy weight...

TR hoped that Taft would become an ambitious and resolute President,

BOOM

This is what I pictured...

but he ended up becoming dominated by a few powerful Senators

who influenced his political decisions.

...Tell them to do this...

...I was told to do this... so do it!

The disappointed TR raged against Taft over the issue of replacing a Taft <u>cabinet</u> member.

...How could he appoint an idiot like that to his cabinet? Taft made him a cabinet member

just because he went to his alma mater!

Through a close associate, TR requested that Taft replace a corrupt cabinet member.

TR said to replace him...

Taft instead fired TR's associate, and by doing so greatly provoked TR.

I'm now the President!

So you're fired!

I'm not upset at Taft because he now occupies the White House! I'm upset because he's not governing well!

It's not that I'm upset that he's President. I just can't stand the fact that he's not doing his job as President well!

After returning from a lengthy trip to Africa, TR prepared to run in the 1912 presidential election.

An old friend has returned as an enemy...

Teddy's back!

TR for President Again!

Having severed his relationship with Taft, TR fiercely attacked Taft,

We can no longer entrust this country to Taft, who is an idiot and fool!

and this led to the breakup of the Republican Party.

TR

Repub   lican

Facing TR's continuing attacks, Taft fought back.

Well, yes, I might be a fool and a puppet,

but even a mouse will bite a cat when it's cornered. I won't decline the presidential candidacy anymore just because of TR's attacks!

When Taft received the nomination over TR at the Republican National Convention,

Taft receives nomination

YEAH   YAY

TAFT

TR organized a new party consisting of Taft's Republican opponents and ran for President.

Did you think I'd just fade away?

You've lost your sense of morality!

Pro-gressive Party*

Repub-lican Party

*Also known as the Bull Moose Party

The fractured Republican Party was defeated by a wide margin by the Democratic Party's Woodrow Wilson, who was a virtual newcomer to politics.

Results of 1912 Election		
Democratic Party	Progressive Party	Democratic Party
W.H. Taft	T. Roosevelt	W. Wilson
3,486,333	4,119,207	6,293,152
8	88	435
Electoral votes		

In early 1913, Taft left the terribly stressful White House and returned home.

It was a miserable time in my life...

WHITE HOUSE

After leaving the presidency, Taft lectured at his alma mater Yale University,

and in 1921 was appointed as the Chief Justice of the United States, a position he had coveted all his life.*

You really wanted this, didn't you?

YES, SIR!

*Appointed by 29th President Harding

History views him much more favorably as Chief Justice than President.

He was more suited to serve as Chief Justice than President.

Bang
bang bang

Many amusing anecdotes are told of Taft's heavy body frame.

He once got stuck in the White House bath tub,

HELP!

so a special tub (210cms x 120cms) had to be ordered for him at the White House. It was large enough to fit three male adults.

During his term, the only consolation to the unhappy Taft was food.

Despite his wife's pleas for him to go on a diet, such pleas did nothing to quell his voracious appetite.

You're going to kill yourself eating like that!

If you take this away, I'll mobilize federal troops!

He would hide his food or sneak out of the White House for snacks.

I can tolerate Teddy, but I can't stand hunger...

White House

Whenever he was on the road, he would request that a sumptuous feast be served on his table.

A special menu unknown to the First Lady... OK?

Of course, Mr. President!

During his term, Taft's weight ballooned by a whopping 50kgs over two years.

The needle on the scale won't move any more...

While he was campaigning in the 1912 election, he set a record by reaching 355 pounds (175kgs).

Huff

puff

Whew... Is politics worth all this trouble...?

Huff puff

The extreme election battle of 1912 between Taft and his former boss and leader TR yields diametrically opposing historical views of the two men.

1912

TR Taft

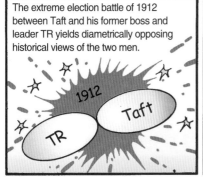

Compared to the active and progressive Roosevelt,

T. Roosevelt (Teddy)

Forceful · Adventurous
Active · Progressive
Hero of troubled times

history views Taft as a passive and needlessly conservative President.

W.H. Taft

Easygoing ·
Incompetent
Passive · Old fashioned
Helplessly
conservative

The stronger the light is shone against Teddy Roosevelt, a 'pop star' forever enshrined in the hearts of Americans,

Teddy! ROAR

TR

ROAR

the darker the shadow is cast against Taft, a man with an obscure, negative and conservative image.

TR

Despite all of this, the decisions that Taft made as Chief Justice of the United States show that in some respects he was much more progressive than Roosevelt.

Woodrow Wilson 1913~1921

Messenger of World Peace, the American Way

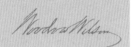

Woodrow Wilson

Democratic Party, 1856. 12. 28~1924. 2. 3

Birth Place   Staunton, Virginia

Wives   1. Ellen Louise Axson Wilson

1860~1914

2. Edith Bolling Galt Wilson

1872~1961

Children   Margaret, Jessy, Eleanor

Vice President   T. R. Marshall

Woodrow Wilson was originally known as Thomas Woodrow Wilson after his grandfather.

He changed his name to Woodrow Wilson by discarding the name 'Thomas' after graduating from Princeton University.

Having witnesses the atrocities of the Civil War from a very young age,

Wilson despised war and upheld preservation of peace as his primary goal. It was a crusade-like mission to him.

Thus, Wilson made every effort to stay out of World War I that broke out during his term.

He worked hard to achieve world peace after the end of the war that America had inevitably entered.

A Southerner born in Staunton Virginia, Wilson was primarily raised in the Carolinas.

His father was a Presbyterian minister with considerable oratorical skills.

Father, I believe!

Naturally, Wilson received a thorough training in oratory from his father.

Father, I believe!

What he practiced was not the content of his oratory but the style of its delivery, *i.e.*, oratory that could touch the hearts of people.

To make a speech that touches the hearts of people,

technique is more important than content! Do you get that?

In 1879, he graduated from Princeton University and started studying law, after which he pursued an academic career.

There ain't anything else to do...

As a college professor, he taught politics and law.

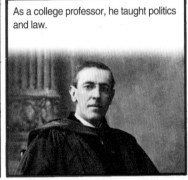

*Wilson during his days as a Princeton Univ. professor

Wilson's health was frail, as he suffered from nervous breakdown, indigestion and headaches, among other illnesses.

Oh, my stomach...

Oh, what a headache...

Later on when he became President, he experienced great difficulties due to his health problems.

How could a President be so sickly?

With his brilliant oratory, Wilson stood out in politics and took center stage with his election as Governor of New Jersey in 1910.

Ladies and Gentlemen! Do you believe in my words?

His star suddenly rose with his nomination as the Democratic presidential candidate in 1912.

VOTE WILSON FOR PRESIDENT

WOODROW ILSON

DEMOCRATS

Due to the discord and conflict between Taft and Teddy that fractured the Republican Party,

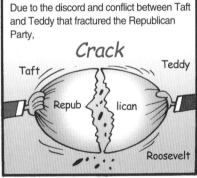

Crack

Taft

Teddy

Repub lican

Roosevelt

Wilson, almost a newcomer to politics, easily won election to the presidency.

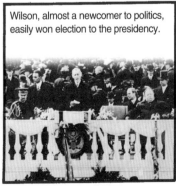

*Wilson's inauguration in 1913

During his first term, World War I broke out in Europe. It was the then-largest calamity that ever occurred to humankind.

Wilson, however, declared America's neutrality and made every effort to stay out of the war.

In 1915, when a German submarine torpedoed and sank the Lusitania, a British ship,

*Newspaper reporting on the sinking of the Lusitania.

more than 100 Americans on board were killed. American public opinion increasingly cried out for war,

but Wilson just issued a stern warning to Germany without entering the war.

Wilson's 1916 election campaign slogan was that 'he kept American out of war.'

*Election campaign (1916)

With this campaign slogan, Wilson won re-election,

Results of 1916 Election	
Democratic Party	Republican Party
Woodrow Wilson	Charles Evans Hughes
9,126,300	8,546,789

Popular votes

277	254

Electoral votes

but he was inevitably pushed into the war due to the Zimmerman incident.

Zimmerman Incident*

*Germany's attempt to enlist Mexico as an ally against the U.S. in WWI

Wilson asked Congress to declare war on Germany, citing protection of democracy in the world as the reason.

Toward the end of the war, on January 8, 1918, Wilson announced the Fourteen Points, his plan for the post-war world order.

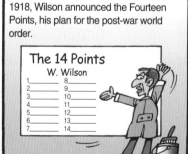

The 14 Points
W. Wilson

At its core was the establishment of a multilateral association of nations.

Major Points of the 14 Points
· Abolishment of secret treaties
· Principle of self-determination of peoples
· Establishment of League of Nations

After World War I ended in November 1918 with the surrender of Germany,

Wilson arrived in Paris early the following year. Praised as the savior of Europe, he played a key role in the conclusion of the Treaty of Versailles.

*Wilson at the Versailles

Under Wilson's initiative and American leadership, the League of Nations was created,

but Congress opposed America's entry into the League of Nations.

It's questionable whether the Treaty of Versailles will actually work,

and the principle of self-determination will sanctify all national borders.

NO!

This means that America will have to give up its overseas territories. It fundamentally blocks America from expanding overseas.

Congress

White House

So President Wilson should yield and reconsider U.S. entry into the League of Nations.

No way!

If Congress fails to recognize my will to preserve peace, I will directly appeal to the American people!

Wilson then went on a public speaking tour to win the support of the American people. He traveled 16,000kms throughout the nation.

*Wilson giving a speech on his public speaking tour.

On September 26, 1919, he collapsed and was incapacitated in Pueblo City, Colorado.

I worked too hard with my frail body...

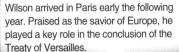

Wilson refused to resign even though he became confined to his bed.

I won't resign even if I die!

It's so hard to give up power, isn't it...?

Until he regained some mobility, the First Lady, Edith Wilson, served as his steward.

*Edith assisting Wilson in his work

In 1920, Wilson was awarded the Nobel Peace Prize. He was more favorably viewed internationally than domestically.

See, the world recognizes my contributions...

Wilson cried out for peace and declared an anti-imperialist stance,

and America declared that it would not expand its territory by even one inch with military force.

Despite all such rhetoric, America frequently invaded other countries in South America to uphold its interests.

More than any other President in U.S. history, Wilson frequently utilized military force to intervene in the affairs of other countries.

He is also seen as having utilized military force most opportunely.

Thus, peace (and democracy) that he so vigorously asserted to the world

was not peace between equals,

but peace the American Way.

For this reason, America was unable to join the League of Nations, the very organization that was created by its initiative.

Not a very social person and with almost no friends, Wilson greatly relied on his first wife Ellen Axson.

But Ellen was more interested in gardening than serving or socializing with people as First Lady.

She died of nephritis in the White House in August 1914.

On the train ride back to his hometown, Wilson all along sat next to his wife's coffin.

Honey, what will I do now...

clunk

clunk

Seven months later, Wilson proposed to Edith Bolling Galt, a widow, in Washington D.C. They were married two months later.

Will you become my First Lady?

He became another President to marry in the White House.

Wow, he's marrying less than a year from the death of his first wife!

The loneliness must've been hard on him!

2nd First Lady

After Wilson's incapacitation, his second wife Edith served as his steward for the next six months.

Handle that matter this way.

Yes, Mr. President... no Madame!

His views on freedom and world affairs as seen the 'American way' also surfaced in his views on African-Americans.

Descendants of slaves...

Wilson was a white supremacist.

How can blacks be equal to whites? The white man is racially superior to the black man!

It is said that he even praised a movie that favorably depicted the Ku Klux Klan.

Wow

That was great~!

Even though he didn't persecute African-Americans to promote white supremacy,

What do you want me to do?

Do as you see fit.

---

he ignored the inhumane persecution of African-Americans in the South.

Things happen in life...

If Wilson had seen the world from a more flexible perspective and compromised with Congress and joined the League of Nations,

Let's compromise!

Congress will agree to U.S. entry into the League of Nations!

World War II may have been avoided,

With the U.S. in the League of Nations,

it wouldn't have been easy to start the war...

---

and humankind may have shed less blood.

League of Nations less the U.S.
= no substance
= little more than a name
= war!

Warren G. Harding 1921~1923

Ordinary Leader during Ordinary Times

Warren Gamaliel Harding

Republican Party, 1865.11.2~1923.8.2

Birth Place Corsica, Ohio

Wife Florence King Harding 1860~1924

Children None

Vice President Calvin Coolidge

In surveys of popular U.S. Presidents, Warren Gamaliel Harding's place is always at the bottom.

He wasn't very smart, didn't stand out very much and even lacked leadership skills.

On top of that, he suddenly died in office without leaving any lasting legacy.

Historians question how such a person could have ascended to the presidency.

His case shows that it isn't always the best person that rises to the highest office in the land.

In fact, he was neither motivated nor qualified to become President.

Harding was born in Corsica, Ohio on November 2, 1865.

He studied law and, when that didn't work out, dabbled in various jobs but was unsuccessful.

Eventually, he became a journalist by serving as the editor of a small town newspaper in 1884.

In 1891 at the age of 26, Harding married the daughter of a prominent local banker.

His wife Florence King was a divorcee with two children.

She was a strong and politically ambitious woman who played a key role in Harding's entry into politics.

After entering politics, with the backing of Harry M. Daugherty, the powerful Ohio Republican,

he was elected Governor of Ohio and, subsequently, U.S. Senator.

During his six-year term as a U.S. Senator, Harding was a second-rate legislator who didn't accomplish much.

When he was a senator, he approached Theodore Roosevelt who had left the Republican Party and was seeking to run for President again.

TR promised the vice-presidency to the obedient and submissive Harding,

but Harding's dream for the vice-presidency was dashed due to TR's death prior to the 1920 presidential election.

The 1920s was probably the most corrupt period in U.S. history.

Reform!

Reform!

Reform!

Wilson

$

Because the bed-ridden Wilson refused to resign, the economy was in bad shape and the approval rating of the President at rock bottom.

I won't resign even if I die!

Tell them the economy will be OK as long as I'm around!

It was almost certain that the presidency would shift back to the Republicans for the first time in eight years.

Power

Democrats

Republicans

Naturally, prominent Republicans sought to secure the Republican presidential candidate nomination for the 1920 election. No one was prepared to make any concession.

I'm Leonard Wood, the legitimate heir of TR!

I'm Frank Rhoden, the Illinois Governor!

I'm Hiram Johnson, the U.S. Senator from California!

Wood   Rhoden   Johnson

Despite undergoing a turbid nomination process, it was completely unpredictable who would become the Republican candidate.

I'm never going to concede the candidacy!

The party leadership then agreed that the party would vote to select the candidate.

Since no one's going to concede,

let's see who's the strongest

by putting this to a vote among party representatives!

But when the vote failed to produce a candidate after as many as nine voting rounds,

7th round
X

8th round
X

9th round
X

the exhausted faction leaders reached a compromise.

I'm too tired I can't take this anymore.

This is gonna kill us! I wanna go home!

We weren't able to produce a candidate after nine rounds, so a candidate backed by any one faction won't be nominated anyway! Let's just select a third person who we can all agree on!

Wouldn't Warren Harding be the most acceptable candidate?

That mediocre senator? The wishy-washy guy?

Well, wouldn't he at least do as we say when he becomes President?

OK! Then let's decide quickly and go home!

Strangely, this is how Harding became the Republican presidential candidate in 1920.

What? I've been nominated as the presidential candidate?

Yeah! They decided on you in a smoke-filled room!

Harding wasn't smart, but at least he knew his limitations.

I know I'm not a great man!

My biggest worry now is what to do if I become elected President!

Although he was pushed into the candidacy, he waged a fierce campaign.

Ladies and Gentlemen!

What America needs is not a hero but a healer of the scars of the war!

And surprisingly, he won in a landslide.

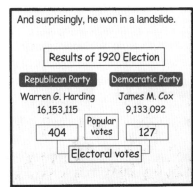

Results of 1920 Election

Republican Party	Democratic Party
Warren G. Harding	James M. Cox
16,153,115	9,133,092

404	Popular votes	127

Electoral votes

The reason for his victory? At that time, America lacked real leadership after Wilson's incapacitation.

The nearly crippled Wilson is refusing to resign,

and the First Lady is acting in his place! That ain't right!

Due to the aftereffects of the war, the unemployment rate and prices soared. America was in need of a new leader.

Prices

Unemploy-ment

Compared to the big-shot Republicans with corrupt images, the unknown Harding probably made a fresher impression.

Who's that man Harding?

Since he's unknown to us, he's probably not another corrupt Republican.

After his election, it is said that Harding wasn't happy at all that he had moved into the White House.

I'm not cut out for this job...

This isn't my place...!

White House

But at least he delivered an impressive inauguration address.

My Countrymen,

Ask not what your country can do for you. Ask what you can do for your country.

Hey, John F. Kennedy, the thirty-fifth President, said that...

Kennedy's only four years old (born 1917)!

Then that means Kennedy plagiarized Harding's speech...

Harding himself wasn't original. He plagiarized Cleveland's* speech!

It's the people who should help the state! It shouldn't be the other way around!

*Grover Cleveland (22nd · 24th President)

From the very start, the Harding administration encountered difficulties over personnel problems.

This won't move us forward!

Personnel affairs

Harding named his poker friend Albert B. Fall as a cabinet member,

He won that office in a poker game!

Secretary

This is favoritism!

and appointed Harry M. Daugherty, a supporter and wheeler and dealer, as his spokesperson.

YES!

The personnel selection from his cronies is worrisome...

Such partial and unreasonable personnel selections stirred up negative public opinion in America.

Are gov't jobs spoils of war?

They're all 'parachute appointments'!

ROAR   ROAR

USA

Fortunately, nothing much happened domestically or internationally during his term.

Z Z Z

As an uncharacteristic President, Harding was lucky to have served as the nation's leader during an uncharacteristic period.

*Harding (front row middle) and Thomas Edison (second from left)

When his health significantly deteriorated in the spring of 1923, his doctors recommended that he take some time off.

Spend a few months in Alaska.

But with the 1924 presidential election looming, the Republican Party wouldn't let him get some rest.

What rest?

The people hated Wilson because he was weak. You need to show that you're strong!

Pushed on a national speaking tour, he collapsed in a train from Seattle that was headed toward San Francisco.

Mr. President!

Mr. President!

He died in a San Francisco hotel on August 2, 1923.

6th President to die in office

During his presidency, American society was in disorder, with the Prohibition Act in place and all sorts of crime plaguing the nation.

Prohibition Act*

(1919~1933)

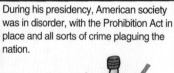

The executive branch was so rotten that Harding came to be infamously known as the 'head of the most corrupted executive branch.'

*Prohibited manufacture, sale and transportation of intoxicating liquors

But the really serious things started to surface after his death.

Scandals

It became known that his private life wasn't befitting of a President.

...So he was ...to a woman known as...?

They say he had a sleazy private life.

Aside from the scandals with several women, in 1927, a woman claiming to be Harding's daughter shook the U.S. by publishing her story.

The President's Daughter

Nan Britton 1927

Also, in 1930, rumors spread that Harding was poisoned to death by his wife and doctor.

Did you hear that rumor?

It was strange that he died so easily.

whisper   whisper

They turned out to be false rumors, but the rumors still perpetuated a negative image of Harding.

The book turned out to be untrue!

The Strange Death of President Harding

Also, the gloomy days of the Harding era

Bang bang bang

Bang bang bang

have been made into various novels and movies, among other things,

Only Yesterday F.L. Allen

Incredible Era S.H. Adams

Masks in a Pageant W.A. White

which have deeply imprinted the Harding era as an era of corruption, dishonesty and disorder in the minds of Americans.

Prohibition Act   Bank Robbers   Al Capone   Mafia

Harding

From as late as the 1960s, Historians started viewing Harding in a different light, but that didn't completely change his image.

Harding

Alice Roosevelt Longworth (TR's daughter), known for her stinging tongue, once said of Harding:

He wasn't a bad man.

He was just an idiot.

He was an ordinary man who achieved only ordinary things.

You're lucky I didn't take advantage of the presidency!

The fact that U.S. history records him as the 'most ordinary President' is probably the 'trait' that distinguishes him from other Presidents.

Hey, did I say I wanted to be President...?

Warren Gamaliel Harding

Calvin Coolidge 1923~1929

Laissez-fairist who Narrowly Escaped the Great Depression

Whew... I finished my job safe and sound...

PRESIDENT

Calvin Coolidge

Republican Party, 1872.7.4~1933.1.5

Birth Place   Plymouth, Vermont

Wife   Grace Anna Goodhue Coolidge
1879~1957

Children   John, Calvin Jr.

Vice President   C.G. Dawes

Three Presidents died on the American Independence Day (July 4),

2nd	John Adams	†
3rd	Thomas Jefferson	†
5th	James Monroe	†

---

but Calvin Coolidge was the first U.S. President who was born on that day.

July 4, 1872

Independence Day

The first and only one.

His opponents sarcastically referred to him as the 'President who slept throughout his five-year term.'

Sleeping again during a meeting...

Zzzzz

Calvin Coolidge was born as the son of a grocer.

Coolidge SHOP

After graduating from Amherst College, he joined the Republican Party.

Amherst College

Republican Party

He then walked a path similar to those walked by his predecessors.

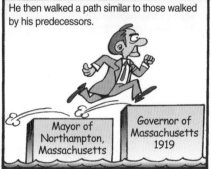

Mayor of Northampton, Massachusetts

Governor of Massachusetts 1919

In the early 1920s when he served as Governor, America was dominated by violent labor movements with strikes occurring incessantly.

There was serious confrontation between capitalists and workers, not to mention the government and labor unions.

Protect the interests of workers!

Illegal strikes and demonstrations will not be tolerated!

When the American Federation of Labor (AFL) went on strike in Massachusetts,

ROAR UNITE! ROAR

WE STRIKE

AFL

AFL AFL

Governor Coolidge immediately sent in the National Guard to forcefully break up the striking workers.

He solemnly declared to the AFL leader Samuel Gompers:

There is no right to strike against the public safety by anybody, anywhere, anytime!

There is no right to strike against the public safety by anybody, anywhere, anytime!

With these words, Coolidge became the newest national hero overnight!

Hey~ I liked that!

I feel so relieved that he said that!

Citizens tired of the continuing demonstrations and strikes applauded his resolute stance.

Coolidge~ Cool

Naturally, this overnight sensation became a star among the Republicans.

Coolidge's doing very well!

Let's keep our eyes on him. He's presidential material!

All of a sudden, Coolidge was nominated as the vice-presidential candidate and won the 1920 presidential election as Warren G. Harding's running mate.

Harding Coolidge

When Harding suddenly died after 900 days in office, Coolidge was staying at his father's house in his hometown,

Where's the Vice President?

Go look for him! NOW!

where he was woken from his sleep to receive the news that he had become President. After all, he was the 'President who slept through his five-year term.'

Sir! Mr. President! Sir~

Bang bang

Coolidge's father woke his son up to inform him that he had become President.

Son, you're now the President.

His father made him take the inaugural oath under a kerosene lamp in front of the grocery store's cashier register.

Put your hand on the Bible and take the oath.

I will abide by the Constitution...

Wonder if there will be another one who takes the oath in front of a grocery store cashier register?

As soon as he returned as President to Washington D.C., Coolidge started campaigning for the 1924 presidential election

Now that I've become President, I'm going to do it right!

The next election is only about 400 days away...

and solving the problems left by his predecessor President Harding.

America's biggest problem is

business itself, whether large or small...

America was dominated by corrupt public servants and a dog-eat-dog business environment marked with large mergers and market monopolization.

The first action he took was to oust corrupt public servants.

Need to get rid of corruption first...

His first target was Harry M. Daugherty, who as a Harding supporter and wheeler and dealer rose to be Attorney General,

and Albert B. Fall, who as Harding's poker friend rose to be Secretary of the Interior.

Secretary of the Interior

Although Daugherty was just fired, Fall was prosecuted for accepting bribes from oil executives.

You illegally took money from oil companies

Uh... you're not going to...

Fall became the first incumbent cabinet officer to become arrested for abuse of authority.

Incumbent cabinet officer arrested!

The restoration of the people's trust in public office is considered as Calvin Coolidge's greatest achievement.

Calvin~ You're so charming!

Good job~!

Held in such high regard by the people, Coolidge was easily elected for a second term in 1924.

Results of 1924 Election	
Republican Party	Democratic Party
Calvin Coolidge	John W. Davis
15,719,921	8,386,704

Popular votes

| 382 | 136 |

Electoral votes

But as President, Coolidge's big weakness was his ignorance about the economy.

*President Coolidge and Secretary Hoover

All he knew about the economy was 'saving.'

We need to be frugal and reduce consumption.

The only road to becoming a rich man is to faithfully save money!

Saving

Whenever he opens his mouth, all he talks about is saving...

Hey! Did Carnegie and Rockefeller become tycoons through saving!

As a layman when it came to the economy, Coolidge entrusted all economic affairs into the hands of Treasury Secretary Andrew Mellon.

Please take care of the economy.

YES, SIR!

True to his background as a former industrialist and business tycoon, Andrew Mellon implemented pro-business economic policies.

So the government took a laissez-faire economic policy approach to help businesses operate freely.

Because everthing's determined by the market.

Future President Ronald Reagan hung a portrait of Calvin Coolidge in the White House. This portrait was very special to Reagan

because he respected the Coolidge administration's laissez-faire policies.

Laissez-faire Free markets

Yet, such laissez-faire economic policies failed to stem a speculative boom in the stock market.

Stock prices

It's a buy! Buy!

Stock Market

The stock market suddenly crashed in October 1929, after a serious bubble burst following an unprecedented boom in stock investments.

Stock Market

bubble

bubble

Coolidge can hardly escape criticism that he contributed to the unprecedented and devastating Great Depression that followed.

GREAT DEPRESSION

Meanwhile, Coolidge made efforts to preserve world peace and, in particular, worked hard to improve relations with Germany.

If we keep rebuking Germany, it'll start another war.

The Germans were on the verge of suffocating from excessive reparation payment obligations resulting from its defeat in World War I.

Coolidge's policy was to give some breathing room to Germany. If Germany were to be left in such a state, it would claim again that there was no alternative but war.

This is the only way out!

So in 1924, based on a proposal made by Charles G. Dawes, Germany's reparation payments were greatly reduced.

Mr. President, this is the best solution!

This measure helped stabilize Germany's economy and appeared to have the effect of reducing the likelihood of another international crisis.

No double-dealing, OK?

Whew~

For such contribution, Dawes won the Nobel Peace Prize.

1925
Nobel Peace Prize

Charles G. Dawes
+
Sir Austen Chamberlain
(British Prime Minister)

Another achievement of the Coolidge era was the enactment of a law that prohibited the use of war as a national policy tool.

Policy

War

America's gesture for peace toward the world was also awarded the Nobel Peace Prize.

We won't use war as a means

for U.S. policy!

PEACE

But this law became obsolete.

Panama invasion

Cuban invasion

Vietnam War

PEACE

PEACE

Afghanistan invasion

Iraq War

Coolidge was famous for his terseness in speech and writing.

Honey, what does that moon bring to your mind?

Sleepiness.

On average, Washington used 51.4 words in a sentence while Lincoln used 26.6 words.

The Union must be preserved under any circumstance blah blah...

Under any circumstance, the Union blah blah, that's it!

In comparison, Coolidge is known to have only used 18 words.

Can you speak with so little words?

Yes!

Toward the end of his term, probably sensing his plummeting approval rating, Coolidge suddenly announced his decision not to run again for re-election.

I won't run for President in the next election.

This decision threw the Republican Party into a panic because the party hadn't sought out another candidate.

What're we supposed to do...?

Throughout his life, Calvin Coolidge was a pretty lucky man.

He lost only one election among the 20 elections he ran for during his life.

'Defeat in election' doesn't appear in my dictionary...

That loss came from an insignificant election for a trustee position for a school steering committee.

Well, it doesn't feel good, but it's not an important position...

With such luck, it appears that he considerably enjoyed life in government.

Mr. Coolidge, what is your hobby?

My work as a public official!

But he was most lucky that he left the presidency at the most opportune moment.

Less then a year after he left office, the Great Depression engulfed the nation. For the moment, he was able to avoid responsibility.

After leaving the White House, Coolidge completed his 247-page memoir.

While the Great Depression that followed his departure continued to ravage America, he died at the age of 60 on January 5, 1933.

Mrs. Coolidge, returning from the grocery store, found him dead on the floor from a heart attack.

Calvin!

Many Americans were saddened by his death, but he wasn't missed by them.

Bong bong

Herbert C. Hoover 1929~1933

Competent Leader Swamped by the Great Depression

Herbert Clark Hoover

Republican Party, 1874.8.10~1964.10.20

Birth Place   West Branch, Iowa

Wife   Lou Henry Hoover 1875~1944

Children   Herbert Jr., Allen

Vice President   C. Curtis

There rarely was a President entering the White House who was so talented and faced such high expectations of the people as Herbert Hoover.

But Hoover showed that remarkable ability could mean nothing if a leader blossomed in the wrong times.

The fundamental reason of failure of a capable President isn't attributable to the times

It's because the weather changed!

No way...

---

but the refusal to accept reality as it is. He left a message to the future generation

There's a concern that the economy might deteriorate and result in a depression.

What're you talking about? As long as I'm here, don't worry about the economy!

on what are the consequences of taking pains to distort reality and failing to accurately assess the situation.

Our economy is fundamentally strong!

The media is just needlessly creating unrest!

Hoover showed through his failure that to be effective, a leader must honestly acknowledge what has to be acknowledged and request the help of the people.

Nothing to worry about!

Don't trust you!

Hoover was a capable mining engineer,

and a great administrator and organizer. So great that he was called the 'Great Engineer.'

Hoover, "The Great Engineer"

Contrary to the people's expectations and his ambition that he would become a 'great President,' Hoover became another tragic victim of the Great Depression.

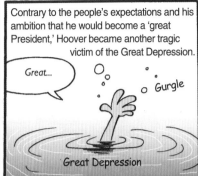

Great...

Gurgle

Great Depression

Born in West Branch, Iowa on August 10, 1874, Hoover was orphaned when he was nine years old. After years of self-study,

First President to be born west of the Mississippi River!

Minnesota

Iowa

Mississippi River

Kansas

Missouri

he majored in mining engineering at Stanford University, and built a remarkable career as a mining engineer and international businessman.

Burma Mines Ltd.

Australia Zinc Corporation

Russia Mines Copper, zinc, silver, lead

He was a true global trotter, with his work taking him to all corners of the world, including China, Africa and Australia.

5 trips around the world!

He even proposed to his wife by telegram from Australia.

I want you to bear my child!

Wow, to propose by telegram from such a faraway country...

He was also fluent in Chinese so that he spoke in Mandarin* with his wife to prevent eavesdroppers from listening into their discussions on sensitive matters.

不辣的西餐法國料理?

好!

*The standard Chinese dialect

By his thirties, Hoover was already a millionaire with his own company.

$ $

It's no wonder the U.S. government selected such a capable man with national fame.

For your country...

During the Wilson administration, Hoover displayed his talent handling food rationing during World War I. Even after control of

He was called 'Uncle Hoover.'

Uncle Hoover doesn't like leftover food.

the government shifted to the Republican Party from Wilson's Democratic Party, President Harding named him Secretary of Commerce.*

Party affiliation doesn't matter!

*1921

187

Secretary Hoover successfully undertook relief efforts to aid Belgian refugees after World War I

Hoover's a humanitarian.

Refugee
Relief
USA
Belgium

and cleared the way for the Saint Lawrence Seaway.

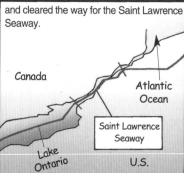

Canada
Atlantic Ocean
Lake Ontario
Saint Lawrence Seaway
U.S.

He also built the Boulder Dam in the then-largest dam construction works. This dam was renamed 'Hoover Dam' in 1947.

He was acknowledged as a forceful secretary who formulated and implemented decisive and broad policies.

Vroom Vroom

Policies

He continued to serve as a cabinet member in the Coolidge administration that succeeded the Harding administration,

Wilson   Harding   Coolidge

and in 1928 naturally emerged as the established presidential candidate of the Republican Party.

Hoover!   Hoover!   Hoover!

Republicans

Americans had high expectations for Hoover because they had suffered from the severe recession and economic stagnancy of the Coolidge era.

During this bad economy,

Hoover'll do something.

Of course, it's Hoover!

Hoover promised to fulfill their expectations with 'affluence.'

A Chicken in every pot,

a car in every garage!

As expected, Hoover was elected without any difficulty.

Results of 1928 Election	
Republican Party	Democratic Party
Herbert C. Hoover	Alfred E. Smith
21,437,277	15,007,698
444	87

Popular votes

Electoral votes

At least in March 1929 when he was inaugurated, the New York Times praised the new President.

He's a trustworthy leader of versatile talents!

However, the rough waves of the Great Depression that started with the collapse of the stock market on October 24 that year

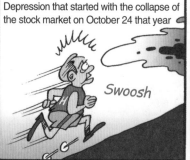

Swoosh

caused Hoover to precipitously fall in standing from a competent President with high expectations of the people to the least successful President.

HOOVER

Great Depression

To be fair, the Great Depression that started in 1929 wasn't Hoover's fault at all.

Market monopolization by large corporations, repeated mergers prompted by endless greed and corrupt public servants...

Bubble

Bubble

monopoly

merger

corruption

degradation

These various factors, which had accumulated over several decades, simultaneously exploded in the form of 'market failure.'

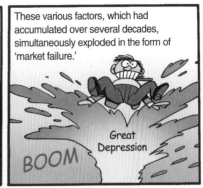

Great Depression

BOOM

Hoover, showing only confidence, played down the seriousness of the Great Depression.

Well, it's going to be bad for a while, but we'll recover.

It's no big deal, so don't make such a big fuss!

The fundamentals of the American economy are very strong, so it's clear the economy will soon recover!

The economy will recover on its own, so the press shouldn't be too critical!

Either he doesn't sense the crisis or he's trying hard to ignore it...

Contrary to Hoover's guarantee, however, the economy collapsed at a frightening speed day by day.

Economy

It's getting better... bet... b...

The number of the jobless increased to 1 million in December 1929, the year the Great Depression started.

*People standing in line to receive food aid

Within three years of his term, that number increased to 13 million. In other words, one out of four Americans in the labor force was jobless and without food.

Increase in jobless

1 million

13 million

The situation worsened to such an extent that hungry workers in rags filled the streets, and shantytowns built by people evicted from their homes spread across the city. The people—calling these shantytowns 'Hoovervilles'—criticized Hoover's policies.

Hooverville.

*A slum in New York City

The public blamed Hoover, who had entered office with the highest expectations of the people. Suddenly, he was now perceived as the main cause for bankrupting the nation's economy.

Hoover!

Hoover ruined it all!

During his term, the nation's economy was almost bankrupted.

We've fallen from the wealthiest nation in the world to a beggar nation...

HELP!

Toward the end of his term in late 1932, the steel industry, which was America's largest industry, recorded a productivity rate of only 13%.

100%

13%

Hoover became the butt of jokes as his approval rating plummeted to rock bottom.

The depression is over?

Does that mean Hoover's finally dead?

He became the target of even stronger criticism for using force to disband veterans who were demonstrating in Washington D.C. in 1932.

Old soldiers? They must be hopelessly conservative, right?

Sir, they're World War I veterans.

The World War I veterans, whose livelihoods became harder due to the depression, requested that the government pay them their promised bonuses,

We're at risk of starving to death!

Let us buy food with the promised bonus!

ROAR   ROAR

and camped out and demonstrated in front of the Capitol in Washington D.C.

When Hoover sent in U.S. Army forces led by Douglas MacArthur to forcefully dispel the demonstrators,

the little remaining public sympathy and support for him completely disappeared.

How could he club the veterans?

So he wants to go to extremes?

Although Herbert Hoover was a competent man, he ended up as an ill-fated President abandoned by the American people.

NO MORE HOOVER!

We hate Hoover!

Belatedly realizing the gravity of the situation, Hoover spent all his energy on quickly 'reviving the economy.'

Whoo

Whoo

Economy

He devised economic reform plans and tried to revive ailing corporations by lending them enormous amounts of money.

Corpora-tions

$

His government also pumped vast amounts of money into the market in strenuous efforts to revive the collapsed economy.

*Caricature of the failed policies to revive the economy

Although these policy measures were not as strong as the measures of his successor Roosevelt,

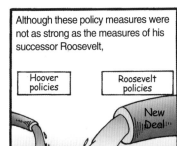

| Hoover policies | Roosevelt policies |

New Deal

back then, they were bold measures comparable to the New Deal policies.

U.S. Economy

However, Hoover's efforts failed as the economy didn't recover.

Whew... I should've paid attention to the economy and public welfare before it became too late...

It's so hard to revive the economy once it has collapsed!

He tried hard to bail out only corporations, while looking away from the travails of individual Americans.

Relief must be provided to the people.

We must help them overcome their debt and joblessness.

That we can't do! It goes against the American spirit to pioneer every aspect of one's own life!

If the state assists the individual citizen, that would cloud the strong American individualism, making the state and the individual citizen weak spiritually and morally!

He's talking all this nonsense!

People are dying right now, but he's just speaking of these lofty ideals!

Instead of bread, we must give hope to the people. Hope is the only way to overcome these difficult times! It's the only assistance we can provide!

Have you seen a dying person revive himself with hope alone?

It's like he's saying if there's no bread, the people should eat cake!

Uh   Uh

In the end, Hoover suffered a crushing defeat to the Democratic Party's Franklin D. Roosevelt in the 1932 presidential election.

Results of 1932 Election	
Democratic Party	Republican Party
Franklin D. Roosevelt	Herbert C. Hoover
22,829,501	15,760,684

Popular votes

| 472 | 59 |

Electoral votes

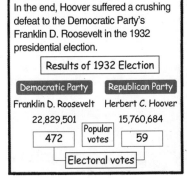

After leaving office, he continued to deny his blunders. Instead, he sought to justify himself by criticizing Roosevelt's policies.

Roosevelt's policies will fail!

I was right!

Hoover was a President cut out for ordinary times. Ultimately, he's seen as a leader who was competent but not appropriate for times of crisis.

You can't slice an apple with a long sword...

Franklin Delano Roosevelt 1933~1945

Creator of the New Deal

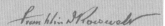

Our tax money!

New Deal

The needy, support the Democrats!

3rd term, 4th term, rule for life...

The wealthy, shut up!

Franklin Delano Roosevelt

Democratic Party, 1882.1.30~1945.4.12

Birth Place Hyde Park, New York

Wife Anna Eleanor Roosevelt 1884~1962

Children Anna, James, Franklin, Eliot,
Franklin Delano Jr., John

Vice Presidents J. N. Garner 1933
H.A. Wallace 1941
Harrry S. Truman 1945

Franklin Delano Roosevelt (FDR) is the most controversial President among all U.S. Presidents.

FDR was a great President!

No! He was just a lucky man of ambition!

He was the first and last President in U.S. history to win election four times; he occupied the White House for 12 years.

1st	1933~1937
2nd	1937~1941
3rd	1941~1945
4th	1945~Death

As a result of his prolonged one-man rule, Congress passed the Twenty-second Amendment to the U.S. Constitution that sets a two-term limit for the President.

22nd Amendment to the U.S. Constitution (1951. 2. 26)
No person shall be elected to the office of the President more than twice... (Under this law, no person may serve as President in excess of eight years.)

In any event, FDR pulled the nation out of two of the worst national crises in its history,

Economic Crisis

World War II

---

and firmly elevated the U.S. into the strongest power in the world. For these achievements, he is seen as one of the greatest Presidents.

USA No. 1

It can't be denied that FDR and his family were loved by the American public back then as true friends of the people.

ROAR **FDR!**
ROAR
FDR!

FDR was born as the only son of parents devoted to his education in Hyde Park, right in the middle of New York City.

*The house where FDR was born

His father James, a wealthy railroad businessman, was a descendant of a Dutch immigrant who had emigrated to New Amsterdam (what is now New York City) in the 1640s.

Dutch name

Roose velt
Roose (Rose)   velt (felt)

Anglicized name **Rose + field**
(Field of roses)

His mother was from the wealthy and distinguished Delano family of New York.

That's why I'm known as Franklin Delano Roosevelt.

*FDR (age 12) with his mother Sara

Befitting his status as the only son born into a patrician and wealthy family, during his childhood, FDR received his education from private tutors without going to school.

Young master, it's time for your mathematic lessons.

Receiving a privileged education, he was raised as a young noble.

Almost every year, he traveled with his family to Europe and broadened his knowledge of the world.

It's as if he was a little 'prince!'

In any case, you've got to be born to good parents...

His placid and flexible father always emphasized to FDR the importance of having a sense of responsibility.

You need to be a man who knows how to take responsibility for his actions...

His strict mother was a significant influence on him throughout his life.

MAMA!

Yes, my son!

At the age of 14, FDR entered Gorton School, a well-known private school. After graduating from Gorton,

Gorton Boarding School

FDR entered Harvard University. Due to his shy and unsocial personality, it's said that he didn't have many friends.

Instead, he played sports and worked for the school newspaper and engaged in other extracurricular activities to overcome his loneliness.

Swoosh

FDR made it clear that he wasn't the scholarly type.

I enjoy wandering around here and there,

but don't like studying in isolation.

After graduating from Harvard, he entered Columbia Law School with no intention of receiving a degree.

What's the use of a master's or doctoral degree? I'm not going to be a professor anyway...

Road to scholarship

Instead, FDR obtained a license to practice law and started working for a New York law firm.

New York Law firm

At this time, the young FDR met and married Eleanor Roosevelt, the niece of the then-incumbent President* and a distant cousin.

*Theodore Roosevelt (TR: Teddy)

Eleanor is remembered for her work on the women's movement for which she is most respected by Americans.

*Mrs. Roosevelt at the UN Commission on Human Rights in 1947

But when she discovered that her former secretary Lucy Mercer and FDR were having an 'inappropriate' relationship,

How could you...!

she and her husband ended up living separate lives.

If you weren't President, I would've divorced you immediately!

White House

FDR, bored by the monotonous life as a lawyer, entered politics.

Yawn~

I'm irritated and bored by doing the same things every day!

In 1910, he started out his political career with his election to the New York Senate.

N.Y. SENATOR

Thereafter, his political career blossomed. In the 1912 presidential election, he supported Wilson against his relative TR. After Wilson's election, Wilson named FDR Assistant Secretary for the Navy.

Wilson! Wilson!

Hey nephew! How could you go against another Roosevelt?

In the 1920 presidential election, he was nominated as the candidate for Vice President,

1920 Presidential Election

	Harding	Coolidge
Republicans		
Elected		
	Cox	FDR (age 38)
Democrats		
Defeated		

but his party was defeated by Harding and Coolidge of the Republican Party.

Thud

Defeat...

However, there was a more serious misfortune than the election defeat awaiting FDR.

NO

While vacationing at his summer vacation house in Campobello in 1921, FDR fell into cold water

and suffered permanent paralysis from the waist down.

What? I can't walk on my two feet again? No!

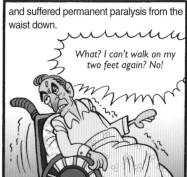

But he didn't despair and instead underwent strenuous therapy.

I won't give in to my destiny.

After he recovered sufficiently enough to move around, albeit with some help,

he returned to the political world to the great surprise of the people.

FDR
CAME BACK!
He's back...

In 1928, as the economy continued to deteriorate, FDR was elected as Governor of New York.

During his two terms, FDR was praised as the 'best governor,' as he proved his remarkable ability.

Franklin
Delano
Roosevelt

When he was finally nominated as the Democratic presidential candidate in 1932, he pledged his 'New Deal' policies.

New Deal

FDR defeated the extremely unpopular Hoover and was elected as the thirty-second President. He easily won re-election four years later.

Results of 1936 Election	
Democratic Party	Republican Party
FDR	Alfred M. Landon
27,757,333 Popular votes 16,684,231	
523	8
Electoral votes	

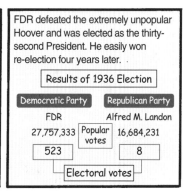

Even though the New Deal policies have been criticized for inducing socialism and communism in America, such policies

Planned economy
Gov't intervention
Priority in distribution

Socialist-style planned economy

Adoption of communism!

New Deal Policies

are viewed as ultimately having preserved capitalism, since America was protected without undergoing anything extreme like Nazi Germany's totalitarianism or Russia's communist revolution.

Totalitarianism	Militarism	Communism

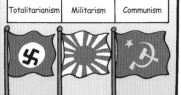

The general consensus, however, is that the U.S. economy recovered due to wartime demands brought on by World War II rather than New Deal policies.

Capitalism

New Deal Policies

When World War II broke out in 1939, FDR declared America's neutrality.

Neutrality

We won't interfere in a European war!

Nevertheless, although the majority of Americans fiercely opposed U.S. participation in the war,

We wasted our national resources by entering the previous war* for nothing!

We should never again interfere in another outside war!

ROAR   ROAR

*World War I

FDR openly provided war supplies and made low-interest loans to Britain. By doing so, he had already stepped into the war.

Results of 1940 Election	
Democratic Party	Republican Party
FDR (3rd term)	Wendel L. Willkie
27,313,041	22,348,480
Popular votes	
449	82
Electoral votes	

After the U.S. entered World War II in December 1941 with Japan's attack of Pearl Harbor,

FDR commanded the war during the last 52 months of his life until his death.

General Eisenhower to London,

and General MacArthur...

He was the supreme strategist, tactician and commander.

*With Stalin and Churchill in 1945

Even though FDR was successful in winning re-election to a fourth term in 1944, setting the record as the longest-serving President,

A general doesn't change his horse during a war!

Will we turn America into a monarchy by allowing perpetual rule by one man?!

he died of cerebral hemorrhage within one month of his inauguration on April 12, 1945, just before the surrender of Germany.

Results of 1944 Election	
Democratic Party	Republican Party
FDR (4th term)	Thomas E. Dewey
25,612,610	22,017,617
Popular votes	
432	99
Electoral votes	

Under his command, World War II ended in victory for the U.S. and the Allies, but there's a lot of criticism for his conduct before and after the war.

Foremost, despite the ruthless killing of the 6 million Jews in Europe,

HELP :

FDR ignored their plight and didn't take any action. Also, while he

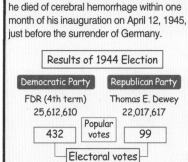

We're neutral.

The Jewish problem is something we can't interfere in.

There's no benefit in provoking the Nazis.

left alone German- and Italian-Americans, FDR implemented a policy of racial discrimination by ordering the harsh internment of Japanese-Americans.

We're American citizens too...

Japanese Internment Camp

He also played down the ambitions of the Soviet Union,

as a result of which Soviet influence greatly increased. This contributed to the development of the Cold War between the East and the West.

Nevertheless, the FDR era is recorded as the most successful era in U.S. history.

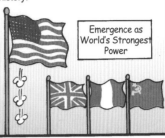

There were a number of women in FDR's life who greatly influenced him.

First, his wife Eleanor played a decisive role in FDR earning the people's respect. She was like a mother of the state.

*Roosevelt's family

Even after FDR's death, she greatly influenced America with her various social activities.

*With JFK in 1962

FDR's mother Sara lived nearby her son and was an influence on him until her death in 1941.

Eleanor's secretary Lucy Mercer was the very person who practically ended FDR's marriage life,

but she was FDR's lifelong companion who stayed by his side even when he died.

FDR's secretary Missy LeHand worked for FDR all her life. She died while still in his employ in 1941.

In the absence of the First Lady in the White House, FDR and Eleanor's daughter Anna

played that role in place of her mother.

*FDR's pet dog Fala

Harry S. Truman 1945~1953

Little Big Man who Took America to Center Stage

Anti-communism

NATO

USA & WESTERN EUROPE

KOREA

Harry S. Truman

Democratic Party, 1884.5.8~1972.12.26

Birth Place Lamar, Missouri

Wife Elizabeth Virginia Wallace Truman
1885~1982

Children Margaret

Vice President A.W. Barkley

In 1944 when Harry Truman was elected as Vice President, no one even imagined that he would become President.

I thought Roosevelt would serve for at least 20 years...

Roosevelt dies

Truman succeeds to presidency

Nevertheless, he became President 83 days after he was inaugurated as Vice President.

I shall abide by the Constitution...

Breaking expectations that he would be overshadowed by his luminous predecessor,

Lincoln

Johnson

Truman is recorded in history as a great President who opened a new era for America.

World

Compared to the America that FDR left with him,

FDR

Truman built a safer, more stable and more prosperous America.

Truman was born in 1884 in a small village named Lamar in Missouri.

His middle initial 'S' isn't really an initial but just the alphabet 'S.'

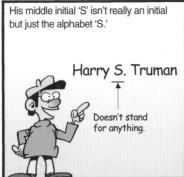

Harry S. Truman

Doesn't stand for anything.

It's said that his father just inserted an 'S' because his paternal and maternal grandfathers' names started with 'S.'

Samuel
Simon
Steve

Having read too many books from a young age, Truman's eyesight significantly deteriorated.

He couldn't pursue his dream of entering the U.S. Military Academy due to severe nearsightedness.

NO!

West Point

After graduating from high school, he didn't go to college and worked various odd jobs.

Can't find a suitable job...

He then enlisted in the Missouri Army National Guard as a second lieutenant, after passing an eye exam by memorizing the eye chart.

A C D
B F G
... ...
... ...
... ...

B, F, G, T, O, K, U...

You've got great eyesight!

Truman fought in World War I as an artillery officer in France and was discharged as a captain.

In 1919, he married Bess Wallace*, his high school sweetheart, and opened a haberdashery.

*Elizabeth V. Wallace

His marriage life was happy, but his business went under in less than three years.

Perhaps I'm not cut out to be a businessman...

Out of Business

Afterwards, he entered politics and worked as a district court judge (1922~1934).

Bang

His honest and diligent personality and thorough sense of responsibility eventually paved the way for his election as a U.S. Senator in 1934.

U.S. Senator

Truman served as a U.S. Senator for 10 years until 1944 when he became Vice President. While a Senator, he served as Chairman of the U.S. Senate

Is that something like the Chairman of National Defense Commission in North Korea?

That's totally different in nature.

Special Committee to Investigate the National Defense Program. He wasn't a very prominent or active Senator, but just a fairly good one.

That's the very reason why I was nominated for Vice President, a man who has to be on standby all the time.

Enormously difficult choices that could decide the fate of humankind were awaiting Truman when he suddenly became President after FDR's death near the end of the war.

CHOICE

The atomic bomb had been under development under the code name 'Little Boy' from the times of FDR.

Little Boy

Nuclear Bomb

Truman had to decide whether or not to drop the atomic bomb on Japan.

1. Nuclear — Loss of hundreds of thousands of lives

2. Continuation of war, Advance of Soviet military — Non-nuclear

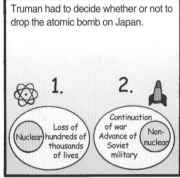

On this occasion, Truman made a quick decision.

Drop the atomic bomb on Japan!

That's the only way to quickly end the war.

So in August 1945, the atomic bomb was dropped on Hiroshima and Nagasaki in Japan.

*The B-29 bomber Bocks Car that dropped the atomic bomb on Nagasaki

On August 15, Japan unconditionally surrendered. The surrender completely ended the prolonged World War II.

However, Truman was criticized over and over by historians for using the atomic bomb.

He committed an atrocious act that was a crime against humanity!

Atomic bomb victims are suffering day by day!

*Hiroshima bombsite

Domestically, Truman implemented policies known as the Fair Deal policies.

FAIR DEAL

Equitable distribution

These policies were extensions of FDR's New Deal policies,

New Deal

Tax money

Relief

Welfare

$

and played a significant role in stabilizing the U.S. economy after World War II.

Re-education and job placement, etc., for veterans

US Economy

$ Taxes

After World War II, the world entered an era of ideological contest between the free world and the communist camp.

Due to Stalin's expansionism, the red wave of communism spread throughout the world.

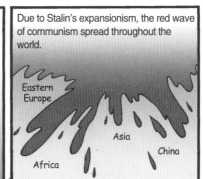

Eastern Europe

Asia

China

Africa

Truman, who was thoroughly anti-communist, took resolute action.

The communization of the world is absolutely unacceptable!

He proclaimed the 'Truman Doctrine,' which started the Cold War between the United States and the Soviet Union.

Truman Doctrine

Anti-communism

"The United States will provide assistance to whichever nation fighting against communism."

-Harry S. Truman

Meanwhile, he implemented the 'Marshall Plan' in the war-ravaged Europe

Marshall Plan

· Poverty is the shortcut to communization.
· Post-war Western Europe suffers from poverty.
· Western Europe is to be revived with U.S. assistance to prevent communization and secure markets for U.S. goods.

by providing massive aid, which played a decisive role in reviving the economies of the European nations in the free world.

Thank you!

Marshall Plan

$

Western European economies

But due to concerns that another war might break out as a result of the intensifying U.S.-Soviet conflict,

Wouldn't this lead to World War III?

We never know when a war might break out between the U.S. and the Soviet Union...

and that enormous aid funds were being provided to foreign countries, the number of dissatisfied voters increased to such an extent that

What's so special about Europe...

Truman's expenditures have no end in sight!

ROAR

ROAR

USA

there weren't many people predicting Truman's victory in the 1948 presidential election.

Truman's never going to be re-elected.

We shouldn't vote for Truman who's bankrupting the U.S. economy!

On election day, the Trumans went to bed early, thinking that the election was lost.

Harry, you're going to bed already? Aren't you going to check the counting of the votes?

It's a foregone conclusion. Let's just forget about it and get some sleep.

The next day morning, Truman was woken by the news that he had won.

Sir, Sir! You've won!

That day, a Chicago newspaper made history by famously misreporting 'Republican candidate Dewey defeats Truman.'

DEWEY DEFEATS TRUMAN

*Truman in smiles holding the *Chicago Tribune* with the incorrect reporting

During his second term, Truman spent almost all of his time wrestling with the Korean War.

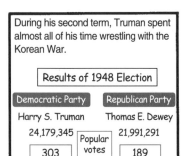

Results of 1948 Election	
Democratic Party	Republican Party
Harry S. Truman	Thomas E. Dewey
24,179,345	21,991,291

Popular votes

303	189

Electoral votes

On June 25, 1950, the North Korean army crossed the thirty-eighth parallel and launched a major attack on South Korea.

Truman quickly sent U.S. troops to prevent South Korea from falling to the communist troops.

Dispatch of U.S. Troops

Utilizing the United Nations, Truman brought in other countries and turned the Korean War into a U.N. war from what had virtually become an American war.

American soldier!

No, I'm a U.N. soldier!

UN

Until FDR, America only reluctantly got involved in global wars,

Help me!

but on the occasion of the Korean War, America transformed itself into a nation that took the initiative and control over global wars.

USA

As the Korean War dragged on for nearly three years, the public cried out for a quick end to the war.

This'll turn into a World War III!

End it quickly!

How long will this endless war of attrition last?!

General MacArthur, commander of UN forces, pushed for an attack of Manchuria and the use of the atomic bomb. When MacArthur openly challenged the hesitant Truman,

*Truman meeting with MacArthur

Truman, fearing the breakout of World War III, summarily fired the general.

Old soldiers never die. They just fade away...

In preparation of communist aggression,

Anti-communism

Truman set up the North Atlantic Treaty Organization in 1949,

NATO

North Atlantic Treaty Organization

while in response the Soviet Union and other Eastern European communist countries established the Warsaw Treaty Organization, intensifying the Cold War between the two sides.

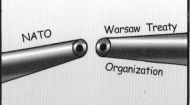

NATO

Warsaw Treaty Organization

After his term ended, the Truman leaving the White House in 1953 was no longer a 'Little Man.'

I was nicknamed 'Little Man' due to my small height.

WHITE HOUSE

*168cms/75kgs

He was a giant who had saved the Western world from communism!

Little big man!

After retiring from politics, he turned to writing, which occupied much of his time until he died in Independence in 1972.

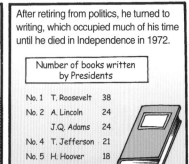

Number of books written by Presidents		
No. 1	T. Roosevelt	38
No. 2	A. Lincoln	24
	J.Q. Adams	24
No. 4	T. Jefferson	21
No. 5	H. Hoover	18

During his term, however, there were many important events that he was unable to stop from occurring.

Out of fear that a collision with the Soviet Union might start World War III,

So you want to go at it, huh?

he helplessly stood by and watched the Soviet Union communize Eastern European countries one by one.

Poland

Rumania

Czechoslovakia

Bulgaria

Hungary

Albany

Yugoslavia

After a long civil war, in 1949, the Chinese Communist Party drove the Nationalists to Taiwan

Taiwan

and communized China. Truman was unable to take any measure to stop that.

Establishment of People's Republic of China 1949

So conservative Republicans fiercely criticized him for such failures.

Truman's weakness resulted in the hand over of

Eastern Europe and China to the communists!

Still, Truman was an anti-communist who stopped the communization of the Republic of Korea.

NO!

Unification by communization with force

USA

Later on, Winston Churchill is said to have confessed to Truman:

To tell you the truth, I underestimated you,

and I didn't like the fact that you had become President in place of FDR.

But you have defended Western civilization better than anyone else!

Dwight D. Eisenhower 1953~1961

Preserver of World Peace amid the Intensifying Cold War

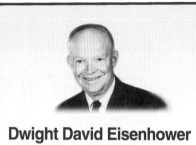

Dwight David Eisenhower

Republican Party, 1890.10.14~1969.3.28

Birth Place **Denison, Texas**

Wife **Mary 'Mamie' Geneva Doud Eisenhower 1896~1979**

Children **Doud, John**

Vice President **Richard M. Nixon**

A Gallup Poll has showed that 'preservation of peace' was the most significant achievement of Eisenhower, otherwise known by his nickname 'Ike.'

He ended Truman's Korean War, albeit in the form of an armistice,

Cease-fire line

---

and restrained an arms buildup. These measures had the effect of promoting peace.

Allocate budget money to us so we can build weapons.

No, if weapons increase, so will wars.

As a hero who led his nation to victory in World War II and a career soldier who spent his entire career in the military, Eisenhower knew the ins and outs of the military establishment very well.

You think you know the military better than I do?

Thus, since he had great insight into how the Defense Department maneuvered to win allocations of defense spending,

So what tricks do you plan to use this time to win the defense budget?

---

he was able to block such maneuvers and stop an arms buildup during the Cold War, and preserve world peace.

The President's sitting on top of our heads...

Ever since the founding of the United States, there were five war hero generals who became President after the respective wars they fought in.

1 Wash-ington	9 Har-rison	12 Taylor	18 Grant	34 Ike

Among these five, only two—Washington and Eisenhower—became successful Presidents who satisfied societal demands in the post-war eras.

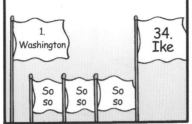

Eisenhower was a far cry from the image of a fierce, battle-hardened general.

Instead, with his magnanimous, easygoing and warm smile, he had the appearance of a kind next door neighbor.

I LIKE* IKE

*Election campaign slogan

Nevertheless, with his fundamentally strong leadership skills, he was a leader who got things done once he got started.

Eisenhower was one of the seven sons of a German-Swiss protestant family that emigrated to America in escape from warring Europe.

Both his parents were working class citizens who didn't receive a regular education. His father worked as a technician in a cream factory.

His parents, who wished for Ike's success, didn't object to Ike entering the military academy even though doing so contradicted with their religion.

Perhaps this is the will of God...

Ike played football at West Point* and in 1915 graduated 61st out of 164 cadets.

*U.S. Military Academy

He married Mamie while he was stationed at Fort Sam Houston in Texas.

*Mamie and Ike

During World War I, he didn't fight overseas and was assigned to an armored unit.

*Captain Eisenhower during World War I

He then graduated first out of a class of 275 at the Command and General Staff College in Kansas, which was an essential grooming ground for future generals.

Dwight D. Eisenhower 1st in class!

Eisenhower's next assignment was to accompany General MacArthur to the Philippines as his chief military aide in 1935.

Eisenhower!

Yes, Sir!

Philippines

When America entered World War II, he was assigned to the General Staff in Washington,

and in June 1942, he became Supreme Commander of U.S. Forces and from London commanded operations to occupy North Africa, Sicily and Italy.

*Ike with General Patton

British Prime Minister Churchill and FDR named Ike as the Supreme Allied Commander of Allied Forces after deciding to carry out a landing operation in Normandy.

Ike successfully pulled off the operation in Normandy, the largest ever military operation in history,

which was the decisive moment of the war that eventually led to the German surrender on May 7, 1945.

Eisenhower returned as a hero who led his nation to victory in World War II. He was more highly praised than even Washington himself.

ROAR IKE ROAR IKE

However, just like Washington, Ike also sought out retirement.

Now that the war is over, my job is over too.

I will now live my life as an ordinary man, not as a general.

In 1948, out of uniform, Eisenhower became president of Columbia University, but two years later became the Supreme Commander of the North Atlantic Treaty Organization.

University President

NATO Supreme Commander

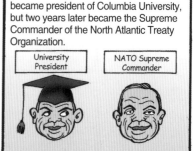

It was no surprise that the Republican Party tried to recruit this great war hero as its presidential candidate.

We need to end the 20-year rule of the Democratic Party!

Only Eisenhower can do that!

The Republicans were finally able to convince Ike who had repeatedly turned them down. Ike retired from the army in June 1952

I'm not interested in politics.

This is important to save democracy. We need to stop the prolonged one-party rule.

and was nominated as presidential candidate in July, after which, 'of course,' he was elected as the thirty-fourth President of the United States.

Results of 1952 Election

Democratic Party		Republican Party
Adlai E. Stevenson		Dwight D. Eisenhower
27,314,992	Popular votes	33,936,234
89		442
	Electoral votes	

His first task was to end the Korean War that had entered its third year.

I promise to go to Korea!

After his inauguration, the bellicose Stalin died, and his successor Malenkov desired peace.

Let's end the Korean War at this point.

Sure. That's what we wanted too.

USSR

USA

On July 27, 1953, the two sides signed an armistice agreement that stopped gun shots on the Korean peninsula.

Cease-fire line

As a professional soldier, Ike was well aware of the unwieldiness and inefficiencies of traditional weapons.

Under the justification 'Atoms for Peace,' he sought to replace traditional weapons with nuclear weapons,

which led to a nuclear arms race between the U.S. and the Soviet Union. The world came to fear nuclear war amid the 'peace brought about by nuclear weapons.'

Ike also established SEATO, the South East Asia Treaty Organization, to stop the spread of communism in Asia.

1955	SEATO
· U.S. · Philippines	South
· Britain · Thailand	East
· France	Asia
· Pakistan	Treaty
· Australia	Organization

In 1956, Ike won the presidential election in a landslide victory.

Results of 1956 Election

Democratic Party	Republican Party
Adlai E. Stevenson	Dwight D. Eisenhower
26,022,752	35,590,472

Popular votes

73	457

Electoral votes

Meanwhile, throughout his term, the Cold War against the Soviet Union intensified.

*Ike with Khrushchev

On October 4, 1957, the Soviet Union successfully launched Sputnik, the first artificial satellite in history, which hurt U.S. prestige.

Sputnik
(meaning 'companion')
ø58cm
83.6kg

In 1958, the U.S. successfully launched its first artificial satellite, barely saving face.

From then on, the U.S. and the Soviet Union entered the space race era.

In 1960, a U-2 spy plane was shot down over Soviet air space,

For the past four years, I entered Soviet air space to spy on the USSR.

Press conference of captured American U-2 pilot

further aggravating relations with the Soviet Union.

We can't forgive this American provocation that disrupts world peace!

Nikita Khrushchev, First Secretary of the Soviet Communist Party, arbitrarily cancelled a scheduled summit meeting with Ike.

Suspend spy flights, investigate the facts, apologize and punish the persons in charge!

Soviet Delegate

Cuba further drove Ike into a difficult position.

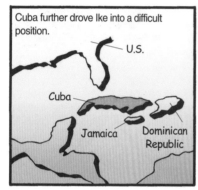

U.S.

Cuba

Jamaica

Dominican Republic

Fidel Castro drove out the pro-U.S. government in a revolution and established a communist regime.

Cuba

He severed diplomatic relations with the U.S. and expropriated its assets in Cuba.

Yankee, Go home!

Making matters worse, Castro joined hands with the Soviet Union, effectively aiming a gun in the face of America

*Fidel Castro with Khrushchev (1960)

on behalf of the communist bloc. The Soviet influence over Cuba led America to take the extreme measure of blockading Cuba during the Kennedy era.

Nuclear Cuba

Ike's eight-year term can be characterized as an era focused on confrontation with communism, a period during which the Cold War intensified.

Let's go all the way!

Meanwhile, the most significant domestic issue in America during the Ike era was racial segregation in schools.

School

Until then, due to racial segregation in America, black children could not attend schools attended by white students.

School

NO

WHITE ONLY

Ike passed laws that desegregated schools. There was fierce white resistance against this movement.

American citizens are equal and shall not be discriminated based on race!

We still cannot accept desegregated classrooms!

In particular, to block black students from attending an all-white public high school* in Little Rock, Arkansas,

I can't follow that order even if it's from the President.

Block the black students with the national guard!

Governor

*Little Rock Central High School

Governor Oval Faubus mobilized the Arkansas National Guard.

NO BLACKS ALLOWED

Hearing this, Ike immediately sent in federal Army troops to enable the nine black students to attend the school.

Rumble~

It was a dizzying moment in which U.S. Army and National Guard troops almost collided with each other.

U.S. Army

National Guard

USA

N. Guard

This incident set the fire on the issue of racial equality,

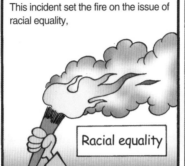

Racial equality

and the Eisenhower era is recorded in history as having opened a new chapter in racial relations.

In 1961, as he handed over the presidency to Kennedy, he turned down a request from Congress to serve as General of the Army,

Please serve your country a little more...

That's enough!

and returned to his farm in Gettysburg where he led a quiet life.

When he died on March 8, 1969, his death was mourned all over America.

*Charles de Gaulle paying his respects to Eisenhower

The image of the old President with his warm smile will probably stay in the hearts of Americans forever.

IKE

Ike had a cute grandson named David.

Grandpa

'Camp David,' the presidential retreat, is named after Ike's grandson David.

CAMP DAVID

John F. Kennedy 1961~1963

The Camelot Myth: Image More than Achievements

John Fitzgerald Kennedy

Democratic Party, 1917.5.29~1963.11.22

Birth Place   Brookline, Massachusetts

Wife   Jacqueline Lee Bouvier Kennedy
         1929~1994

Children   Caroline, John Jr., Patrick

Vice President   Lyndon B. Johnson

John Fitzgerald Kennedy is remembered for his exciting image that thrilled the world, much more so than for his achievements.

As the first U.S. President born in the 20th century,

| 32nd FDR 1882 |
| 33rd Truman 1884 |
| 34th Ike 1890 |
| 35th JFK 1917 |

Kennedy was also the first Catholic President in U.S. history.

Not only was he the youngest elected President, but his wife was also refined and beautiful.

All of this, coupled with his tragic premature death,

turned him into a romantic figure of mythic proportions, the stuff of legends and fairy tales.

Kennedy, an ambitious man, became President on his own terms without waiting in line for anyone.

Stop!

Presidency

He had to overcome various disadvantages, such as his young age, Roman Catholic religion and Irish heritage.

Prerequisites for U.S. Presidents

W A S P

└─┬─┘ └─ Protestant ✗ Catholic

└─ Anglo-Saxon ✗ Irish

└─ White OK

To overcome these disadvantages, he went on a charm campaign

JFK

Disadvantages

and didn't hesitate to exaggerate his experience. He also unsparingly spent his rich family's money.

Experience

$

He would grandiloquently remark that his election to the presidency was the will of the people.

The American public wants me!

In short, Kennedy was power-hungry and would do anything to reach the presidency.

All in!

Whatever the means, they are justified if they help me become President!

Money

Collusion

Money Trickery

Even though most leaders are severely criticized during their term,

He's indecisive!

And un-presidential!

He's stubborn in his ways and disregards the will of the people!

they tend to be praised after they leave office.

Better the devil you know than the devil you don't know.

He still acted on his conviction.

Clap clap clap

He left a great legacy.

On the other hand, although during his term Kennedy was praised throughout the world,

The guy's powerful and charming!

He symbolizes a youthful and strong America!

♥ROAR ROAR

He displayed consummate leadership that subdued the USSR!

he has received severe criticism after his departure from office.

Sure, he was popular but he was also an unskilled politician rough on the edges!

He resorted to reckless power politics backed by America's strength!

JFK ✝

JFK, who continues to charm people despite not having achieved much during his presidency,

JFK

JFK

JFK

is representative of the 'image politician' driven by personal charm, not political ability.

John F. Kennedy was born as the second of four sons of Joseph Kennedy, a wealthy Irish-American in Massachusetts.

*John F. Kennedy (center) with the Kennedy clan

His father, a ruthlessly ambitious man and former U.S. Ambassador to Britain, vowed to make one of his sons President.

This family must produce a President.

So his sons were groomed for high public office and raised in a competitive environment.

John   Robert   Edward

A book JFK wrote in 1940 when he graduated from Harvard University became a bestseller.

Why England Slept
J. F. Kennedy
1940

During his service as a naval officer in World War II, a boat under his command was sunk by the Japanese Navy.

He became a hero for rescuing his crew, but suffered for the rest of his life from back injuries sustained at that time.

What's the big deal? His boat was sunk by the Japanese!

In 1947, Kennedy entered politics as a U.S. Representative, but underwent operations due to the aggravated conditions of his back.

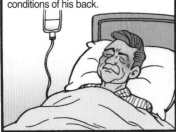

While recuperating, he wrote a book that was awarded the Pulitzer Prize* in 1957.

Pulitzer Prize in 1957

Profiles of Courage
J. F. Kennedy

In 1956, this ambitious young politician boldly sought out the nomination as the vice-presidential candidate, which he failed to obtain.

Candidate for Vice-President

*An American award regarded as the highest honor in newspaper journalism, literary achievements and musical composition

But four years later he went for the presidency instead,

Presidential candidate nomination

and received the Democratic Party's presidential nomination after defeating his bitter rival Lyndon B. Johnson.

Become my vice-presidential candidate instead.

I just lost to this guy who's younger than me.

During one of the closest elections ever held, JFK defeated the Republican Party's Nixon and was elected as the thirty-fifth President.

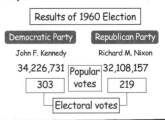

Results of 1960 Election	
Democratic Party	Republican Party
John F. Kennedy	Richard M. Nixon
34,226,731	32,108,157

Popular votes

| 303 | 219 |

Electoral votes

As soon as he assumed office, in April 1961, Kennedy carried out an invasion of Cuba, which had been under secret preparation since Ike's presidency.

Let's topple the Castro regime and install a pro-U.S. government!

This operation failed horribly, and Kennedy became the laughing stock of the world.

The Soviet Union, which took Kennedy for granted, started building a missile site in Cuba capable of launching attacks on the United States.

In October 1962, risking a breakout of World War III, Kennedy carried out a blockade of Cuba.

If the Soviet ships carrying missiles cross this line,

we won't hesitate to go to World War III!

In response, the Soviet Union removed the missiles on the condition that the United States wouldn't invade Cuba.

In exchange, you better not mess with Cuba!

This incident greatly boosted his prestige, and his approval rating shot through the roof.

At the height of his popularity, Kennedy was assassinated by gunshots from Oswald* in Dallas, Texas on November 22, 1963.

*Lee Harvey Oswald

Domestically, Kennedy proclaimed his 'New Frontier' policies

Expansion of medical care for the elderly

Tuition support

Expansion of space plan

Strengthening of civil rights

and ambitiously pushed forward his plans. However, he barely achieved anything due to opposition from Congress.

He just plagiarized FDR's New Deal!

Why are the Democrats so eager to increase tax expenditures?

We reject the budget fund request!

It was Kennedy's successor Lyndon B. Johnson who realized a significant portion of his policies.

GREAT SOCIETY
⬆
New Frontier

Kennedy actively involved the U.S. in Southeast Asian affairs to display American power to the world.

We need to show American power to prevent communist aggression!

During his term, the number of U.S. military advisors in Vietnam, a country on the brink of war, greatly increased from a few hundred to 17,000.

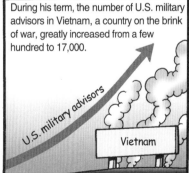

In fact, essentially, this started America's intervention in the Vietnam War.

Thus, Kennedy was the very person who turned the Vietnam War into an 'American War.'

He drove the Americans into the Vietnam War, a 'dirty war' that lasted 10 years.

Meanwhile, Americans love to compare Lincoln and Kennedy because of their mysterious resemblances.

Their resemblances are so remarkable to just call them a coincidence. So what are those similarities that have become a favorite topic of gossipers?

Lincoln and Kennedy both...

They were elected as U.S. Representatives in the same year.

L (Lincoln) — 1846

K (Kennedy) — 1946

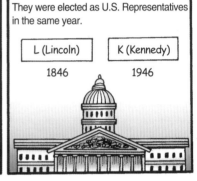

They were elected as President in the same year.

L 1860 — K 1960

Inauguration 1861 — *I shall abide by the Constitution...* — Inauguration 1961

They were married to women aged 24 years and fluent in French.

L Mary Todd — K Jacqueline Bouvier

Bonjour!

They were assassinated on the same day (Friday) next to their wives.

OH, NO! BANG

Their successors had the same name

L↓ Andrew Johnson — K↓ Lyndon B. Johnson

and were born in the same year.

Andrew Johnson 1808 — Lyndon B. Johnson 1908

The assassins of both Presidents were killed before they could be put on trial.

Lincoln's assassin → Shot in a gunfight while on the run.

Kennedy's assassin → Shot by another assassin.

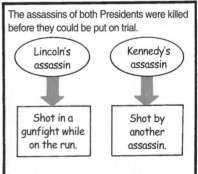

Lincoln was assassinated in the Ford Theatre, while Kennedy was assassinated in a Ford Lincoln Continental.

Ford Theatre	Ford Automobile

Lincoln Continental

They had kinsfolk named Robert and Edward.

Lincoln's sons

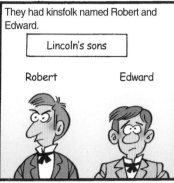

Robert   Edward

Kennedy's younger brothers

Robert   Edward

Their wives lost a child in the White House.

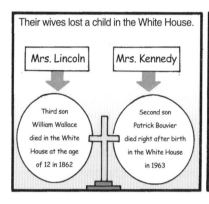

Mrs. Lincoln	Mrs. Kennedy

Third son William Wallace died in the White House at the age of 12 in 1862

Second son Patrick Bouvier died right after birth in the White House in 1963

If we were to look carefully, stories like these abound. Nevertheless, all of these similarities in this case are very mysterious, aren't they?

The tragedy of the Kennedy family didn't end with John. A few years later, his younger brother Attorney General Robert Kennedy was also shot to death like his older brother.*

*Robert Kennedy shot at the Los Angeles Ambassador Hotel in 1968

His youngest brother Edward was involved in a scandalous affair that dashed his dream of becoming President.

He was involved in the death of his female secretary.

With a scandal like that, no chance he can become President.

His widow Jacqueline, with fans all over the world, made a global sensation by marrying the Greek shipping tycoon Onassis.

Jacky to marry shipping tycoon Onassis!

His son John Jr. died in a plane crash in 1999, much to the sadness of the world.

All of these events have become imprinted in the minds of ordinary Americans as if they happened in a television drama or fairy tale.

Vision   Ambition   Beautiful wife   Onassis
Youth
Death
Wealth
Power
Tragedy
JFK

Apart from his presidency, his successes and his failed policies, the name John F. Kennedy

lives on in the memories of Americans as the symbol of an elegant gentleman with overlapping images of youthfulness and pain.

Lyndon B. Johnson 1963~1969

Man of Contradictions: Leader of the Great Society, Commander of the Dirty War

Lyndon Baines Johnson

Democratic Party, 1908.8.27~1973.1.22

Birth Place   Stonewall, Texas

Wife   Claudia Alta Taylor Johnson 1912~

Children   Linda Bird, Luci Baines

Vice President   H. H. Humphrey

As the twentieth century dawned, the President of the United States was called upon to oversee not only domestic but also global issues.

Whether desired or not, as America emerged as a world power, global order became a pressing concern for the nation.

After World War II, in particular from the Truman era, the President of the United States has taken control over state affairs of the United States while also steering the direction of global affairs.

There are diametrically opposing views of Lyndon B. Johnson.

His welfare policies dubbed the 'Great Society' were innovative programs that provided great benefits to the underprivileged in American society, but

he caused America to suffer a humiliating defeat for the first time in its history through the Vietnam War, otherwise known as a 'dirty war,' which he escalated in earnest.

A 'cowboy' born in Stonewall, Texas, Johnson also died there.

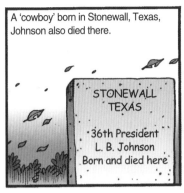

STONEWALL
TEXAS

36th President
L. B. Johnson
Born and died here

In his early twenties, he worked as a school teacher,

*Johnson during his school teacher days (1929, center)

but he joined the Democratic Party and participated in New Deal projects in Texas as Roosevelt started implementing New Deal policies in the 1930s.

NEW DEAL
TEXAS

Recognized by the Democratic Party, in 1937, he became a U.S. Representative but led a largely undistinguished career in the U.S. House of Representatives.

So he's a former cowboy, eh?

However, with the help of the influential Texas Democrat Sam Rayburn, Johnson won election to the U.S. Senate in 1948.

For that contribution, Johnson later on appointed Rayburn as White House Spokesperson.

U.S. Senate

This Senate election was so close that Johnson barely won by an 87-vote margin among the millions of votes that were cast.

Thought I might lose there...

Whew~

After he became a Senator, Johnson rapidly rose through the ranks by showing his political talent,

*Johnson's ranch in Texas (LBJ Ranch)

and emerged as a strong potential presidential candidate in the late 1950s with his advocacy for expansion of civil rights and welfare.

Expand civil rights and welfare benefits LBJ

Sunshine policy for underprivileged LBJ

But he lost the presidential candidate nomination to Kennedy, a rising star in the Democratic Party,

Ting

New Frontier

and eventually ran for and was elected as Vice President in the 1960 presidential election.

JFK
Presidential candidate

LBJ
Vice-presidential candidate

Sniff

Kennedy, however, was assassinated 1,000 days after Johnson's inauguration as Vice President,

*JFK shot to death on Nov. 22, 1963

and Johnson was sworn in as President in the Air Force One plane carrying Kennedy's body back to Washington D.C.

Under the 'Great Society' slogan, Johnson implemented bold welfare policies.

These policies were originally devised under the 'New Frontier' slogan by Kennedy, but had been blocked by Congress. Johnson, however, pushed forward with those policies.

Welfare policies

LBJ

Congressional opposition

He also expanded medical benefits, educational opportunities and benefits for the poor.

Focus of U.S. political parties	
Republicans	Democrats
Overseas issues	Domestic issues
Wealthy Industrialists	Middle class Ordinary people
Corporations Economy	Welfare Civil rights

In particular, ever since the Civil War, the Johnson era saw the greatest improvement in civil rights issues, such as those relating to African-Americans.

*Caricature of Johnson's strong performance in domestic issues and weak performance in foreign affairs (1964)

For his consideration of the underprivileged, Johnson won a landslide victory in the 1964 presidential election.

Results of 1964 Election	
Democratic Party	Republican Party
Lyndon B. Johnson	Barry M. Goldwater
43,129,566	Popular votes	27,178,188
486		52
	Electoral votes	

Yet, Johnson was hampered by the Vietnam War, which had become a nightmare for him, throughout his second term.

Vietnam War

In August 1964, when U.S. vessels were attacked by the North Vietnamese,

What?!

How dare those little bastards attack U.S. vessels?!

Johnson ordered a massive airstrike on the Tonking Bay, which started a nightmare.

Hanoi

Hainan Dao

Tongking Bay

South China Sea

Vietnam

Perceiving the communists as an evil no different from the Nazis that had to be eradicated at the root, he took the situation for granted.

We need to kill them the first time off

so they won't ever challenge America again...

He couldn't even imagine that America, which had never lost a war in its history, would lose against Vietnam, a 'worthless' country in his view.

Lose to Vietnam? Even a dog would laugh!

Ha ha ha ha ha

But that was the start of an unjustified and tiresome war without any merit, which ended in a humiliating defeat for America.

Ha ha ha ha

Vietnam

How embarrassing...

As a result, his illustrious 'Great Society' welfare policies completely lost their luster.

GREAT SOCIETY

Ever since Kennedy increased the number of U.S. military advisors from a few hundred to 17,000, thereby starting direct U.S. involvement in the Vietnam War,

Since the U.S. has initiative over world affairs,

let's improve our prestige by taking care of Vietnam, which France had to give up!

Johnson introduced 500,000 U.S. troops into this war during his four-year term. By doing so, he escalated it into a 'U.S. war.'

Number of U.S. troops at its height: 549,500

Number of Korean troops at its height: 60,000

Number of North Vietnamese troops: 1,180,000

U.S. troops killed in action: 58,000

Most destructive war ever in terms of bombs dropped, etc.

Several countries, including Korea, sent troops to Vietnam to assist America in the fight against communist troops in the jungles.

Blue Dragon Unit | Fierce Tiger Unit | White Tiger Unit | Pigeon Unit

---

It should be noted that the Vietnam War was not escalated by Johnson alone.

A war is not waged by the President alone~

Sniff

On August 7, 1964, Congress gave Johnson unlimited power to use military force in Vietnam.

We feel bad!

How dare Vietnam oppose America, the foremost world power? It's unacceptable!

We'll give the President all the power he needs so go crush the communists who challenge America!

However, there was persistent communist resistance,

Take this and that!

I'll never surrender! Never!

---

which, with Soviet and Chinese assistance, endlessly tormented U.S. troops in a war without any defined battleground. Johnson was forced to

---

continue increasing the number of troops to 100,000 and then 200,000 and so on.

U.S. troops are on the defensive!

This is crazy, really!

At the same time, he refused to listen to voices opposing the Vietnam War and his policies.

We oppose sending more troops!

Get out of Vietnam!

Last time they said they fully supported me...

He even hid the truth to the American public as he continued to more deeply push the nation into the Vietnam War.

Don't go any further!

Of course, not! I'm just standing still!

This was the result of his panic over the totally unexpected turn of events, and also a matter of American pride and obstinacy that made it difficult to give up on the war.

I'll never become the first President to lose a war!

In July 1965, he announced the additional dispatch of 50,000 troops when he was actually sending in 100,000 troops.

Even worse, the announcement wasn't made publicly through broadcast television but only passingly during his nomination of the Chief Justice of the United States.

By the way, I sent 50,000 more troops.

In 1966, he sent an additional 12,000 troops but covered it up.

I hear you're sending more U.S. troops to Vietnam?

I've got no such plan.

Due to Johnson's shady conduct and the numerous U.S. soldiers killed in action and returning home in body bags,

anti-war public opinion spread uncontrollably throughout America.

Pull out U.S. troops from Vietnam!

This war is a 'Dirty War!'

Roar Roar Roar

From college campuses, anti-war demonstrations spread throughout the nation.

*American college students protesting the war

The entire nation became restless over the Vietnam War.

NO WAR!

End the war!

PEACE

Roar Roar

Naturally, Johnson's approval rating plunged.

President Johnson's approval rating

In March 1968, he announced that he wouldn't run for re-election.

4 yrs   4 yrs   4 yrs

1st term   2nd term

If the predecessor served more than 1/2 of his term, his term is not counted toward the term of his successor.

Since Kennedy served more than 2 years, it was possible for Johnson to serve 8 more years after completing Kennedy's term.

As his successor, Johnson designated Hubert Humphrey to run as the Democratic presidential candidate.

*Humphrey (left) and Johnson

During the campaign for Humphrey, Johnson justified the Vietnam War and argued for the need to continue the war to achieve victory.

We must win victory in Vietnam!

These statements caused votes destined for Humphrey to go en masse to the Republican candidate Nixon who had pledged to end the war.

I support Humphrey

but am going to vote for Nixon to end the war...

Humphrey   Nixon

Toward the end of his term, 1968 was indeed a nightmare year for him. Anti-war demonstrations spread throughout the nation like a wild fire.

Anti-war

and Dr. Martin Luther King Jr.*, the respected black leader, was assassinated by a racist.

*African-American civil rights movement leader (center)

The assassination further intensified racial conflict.

ROAR ROAR ROAR

Meanwhile Robert Kennedy, a supporter of Israel, was assassinated by an angry Jordanese immigrant.

Bang
Bang
Bang

Rarely was American society so restless as back in 1968.

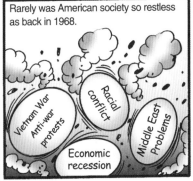

Vietnam War Anti-war protests

Racial conflict

Middle East Problems

Economic recession

Against such a backdrop, Johnson left the White House without any pomp.

Bye, bye. I'm leaving now

You won't be missed!

Historians view him as a leader with a far-reaching view who was also short-sighted,

⇨ World Peace

and a man who was lenient but cowardly, wise yet foolish.

He was a man of contradictions, both a successful and failed President.

The most puzzling person among all U.S. Presidents...

LBJ

*In 1964, Johnson was criticized over this photo showing him pulling on the ears of a dog (ASPCA magazine cover).

Successes of the 'Great Society' and failures of the 'Dirty War.'

GREAT SOCIETY

VIETNAM

He boldly implemented successful welfare policies but also ended up as the first President to lose a war in U.S. history.

Welfare President

1st President to lose a war

Unlike other Presidents, Lyndon B. Johnson surely won't be forgotten.

Richard M. Nixon 1969~1974

Diplomatic Genius Overshadowed by Watergate

Richard Milhous Nixon

Republican Party, 1913.1.9~1994.4.22

Wife   Thelma 'Patricia' Catherine Ryan
Nixon 1922~1993

Children   Patricia, Julie

Vice Presidents   S. T. Agnew 1969
Gerald R. Ford 1973

Richard M. Nixon is the only President in U.S. history to resign from office.

Nicknamed 'Tricky Dick,' he possessed savvy political skills.

Nixon eased the tensions of the Cold War by opening the era of 'détente'

---

and also greatly contributed to world peace by improving relations with China.

Although his presidency ended in disgrace and he was forced to resign over the Watergate scandal caused by his endless ambition,

when he died at the age of 81 in 1994, he was mourned by Americans who they considered as a source of pride.

Our great 37th President.

Nixon was a Westerner born in Yorba Linda, California.

*Baby Nixon

In 1937, he graduated from Duke University School of Law in Durham, North Carolina.

DUKE UNIV.
Founded in 1838 as Brown's Schoolhouse. In 1924, changed name to 'Duke University' with receipt of trust funds from Duke Endowment.

During World War II, he served as a naval officer in the South Pacific.

*Lieutenant Commander Richard M. Nixon

After the war, he worked for a while as a lawyer and then joined the Republican Party. In 1946, he ran for a seat in the U.S. House of Representatives.

Republicans

He won the election by attacking his opponent based on an unconfirmed allegation that his opponent was supported by the Communist Party.

You've got Commie supporters!

Stop that malicious propaganda!

Once he entered Congress, Nixon stood out for his active anti-communism activities.

Anti-communism

The Communists are evil!

As the Cold War intensified, Congress created the 'House Committee on Un-American Activities (HUAC).'

Un-American Activities Committee

In charge of investigating acts benefiting the enemy and traitorous and harmful to America

Under the justification that it was catching persons harmful to America, in essence, HUAC drove out communists from all facets of society.

You're a Commie, aren't you?

Anyone targeted by HUAC lost his job and everything else and was essentially 'buried.'

Company

You're fired!

Its very name sent chills down a person's spine. It was like the 'Grim Reaper' had come knocking on one's door.

The H... HUAC... has come for me?!

Nixon, a politician on the far right, was a core member of HUAC. He stood at the forefront of tracking down communists.

*Nixon at the HUAC

For such 'contributions,' Nixon gained national recognition and ran for election for a seat in the U.S. Senate in 1950.

Nixon, the Commie basher!

ROAR ROAR

R. NIXON

In this election, Nixon attacked his strong Democratic opponent Helen Gahagan Douglas, a female candidate,

Republican — R. NIXON
Democrat — H. G. Douglas

with allegations that she was a pro-communist 'Pink lady' and won the election.

Commie!

Another smear campaign?

In 1952, Eisenhower nominated this 39-year old man of ambition Nixon as his vice presidential candidate.

*Nixon as candidate for Vice President

During the campaign, Nixon was charged with engaging in illegal campaign activities,

A charge's been made!

Court

but he went on television and skillfully proved his innocence with success.

If there's anyone in U.S. politics with as much integrity as I have, please step forward!

From then on, he became known as 'Tricky Dick.'

He got away like a fox.

There ain't no one as tricky as Nixon!

As Vice President, Nixon displayed great political skill.

He's a politician with both a conservative

and internationalist bent, and he also has an open mind!

In 1960, he was finally nominated as presidential candidate.

Democratic Party
John F. Kennedy

Republican Party
R. M. Nixon

However, he narrowly lost to John F. Kennedy, after which his popularity plunged.

Nixon popularity

In 1962, he faced further humiliation by losing the election for the California governorship.

Nixon's political life is over.

To the surprise of many, however, he succeeded in making a comeback.

Get up!

In the 1968 presidential election, he defeated the Democratic candidate Humbert Humphrey and was elected as the thirty-seventh President.

Results of 1968 Election		
Republican Party		Democratic Party
Richard M. Nixon		Humbert H. Humphrey
31,785,480	Popular votes	31,275,166
301	Electoral votes	191

Nixon was elected based on his pledge to end the Vietnam War. At the time of his inauguration in early 1969, anti-war sentiments in America had reached their height.

Americans were suffering from the nightmare that the Vietnam War had become, the longest war ever in U.S. history.

The 'Johnson war' started by Kennedy

had become the 'Nixon war'...

College students throughout the nation continued their protests for the immediate end of the 'Dirty War.'

End the Dirty War right now!

Stop the further killing of young American lives!

NO WAR!

Amid such circumstances, in April 1970, when four students at Kent State University were shot to death by the police during a protest,

the anti-war movement in America climaxed.

PEACE! ROAR NO MORE VIETNAM WAR
ANTI-WAR ROAR ROAR
USA

Nixon sensed that it was necessary to obtain Soviet and Chinese cooperation for America to 'honorably' withdraw from the Vietnam War.

Well, we have to keep our pride.

We can't just withdraw as if we're being chased out...

He opened the détente era with the Soviet Union with which the U.S. signed arms control treaties,

Arms control

DÉTENTE

and opened the firmly closed door to China by extending a gesture of peace through 'Ping Pong Diplomacy.'

U.S.-Chinese exchange of table tennis teams

In 1972, he made a visit to China and opened the way for diplomatic relations.

*Nixon meeting with Chinese Party Chairman Mao Zedong

Boosted by intense anti-war sentiments, the diplomacy with the Soviet Union and China to end the Vietnam War was greatly supported by the American public.

As a result, Nixon won the 1972 presidential election in the largest ever landslide victory in history.

Results of 1972 Election	
Republican Party	Democratic Party
Richard M. Nixon	George S. McGovern
47,169,911	29,170,383
520	17

Popular votes

Electoral votes

Unfortunately, this shining victory ended in disgrace due to the Watergate scandal.

Diplomatic achievements

Water gate

Having won re-election in a landslide, Nixon signed a peace treaty with Vietnam in 1973.

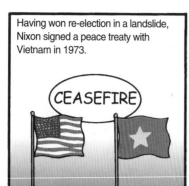

With this treaty, for the time being, the 10-year old Vietnam War was brought to an end.

Vietnam War peace treaty signed!

But there was no way that the Communists would honor a peace treaty for a war that the U.S. had given up on.

The U.S. signed the peace treaty to run away from Vietnam.

Why should we honor it when the U.S. is quickly withdrawing from Vietnam?

U.S. troops hastily continued withdrawing as the Communist attacks intensified.

Let's run!

Vietnam

Finally, Vietnam was unified as a communist nation after the last U.S. troops left Vietnam in April 1975.

*Last U.S. helicopter leaving Saigon

The U.S. had recorded its first humiliating war defeat in history.

How could the U.S. lose... The strongest nation in the world lost to a small Asian country...

Nixon's misfortunes started in the 1972 presidential election campaign—with the so-called 'Watergate scandal.'

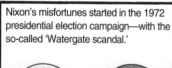

NIXON '72

Republican badge worn by Nixon supporters

Democratic badge worn by McGovern supporters

Some Cubans and ex-CIA operatives broke into the Democratic National Committee headquarters at the Watergate complex,

*Watergate apartment and hotel complex

where they were caught in their attempts to wiretap election strategy meetings of the Democratic Party.

Nixon knew in advance about the break-in but strongly denied the existence of any conspiracy until the summer of 1974.

I know nothing about it.

I'm not involved in any way.

NO!

But on June 23, 1973, tape-recorded statements made by him in his office were disclosed.

The Watergate break-in is a matter of national security,

so don't let the FBI* get involved!

*Federal Bureau of Investigation

Thus, he made the mistake of acknowledging the 'Watergate break-in.'

*The tape recorder that recorded the statement in question

This tape was soon disclosed to the press, and the recorded conversation became known as the 'Smoking Gun.'

A gun still smoking after having shot Nixon

The American public was shocked and enraged. Their President Nixon was a liar.

WHAT...!

What's worse than the wiretapping at Watergate

is that the President was lying.

Congress prepared to impeach the President.

A lying President can't be tolerated!

You're not fit to be President!

Impeach him!

IMPEACHMENT

Nixon was left with two choices.

My options are to honorably resign,

or get kicked out after being impeached...

In August 1974, Richard M. Nixon resigned from the presidency,

*Nixon announcing his resignation

and Gerald R. Ford succeeded him as the thirty-eighth President.

One month after his inauguration, Ford granted Nixon with a special pardon,

He shall be pardoned, with no criminal action to be pursued against him!

which was a big political risk to take back then when there was so much antagonism against Nixon. Eventually, the pardon became a factor in Ford's failure to win re-election.

Re-election? Are you kidding?

With great ability and skill, Nixon opened the era of détente for world peace through brilliant diplomacy.

After resigning, he spent much of his time trying to restore his reputation,

I assert my innocence. I'm truly clean!

I was wrongly accused!

and as time passed by, his reputation indeed started shining again.

Despite Watergate,

he was, after all, a capable President!

R.M.Nixon

Gerald R. Ford 1974~1977

Restorer of Ethics to the Presidency

Gerald R. Ford

Gerald Rudolph Ford

Republican Party, 1913.7.14~2006.12.26

Birth Place   Omaha, Nebraska

Wife   Elizabeth 'Betty' Bloomer Warren Ford
1918~

Children   Michael, John, Steven, Susan

Vice President   Nelson A. Rockefeller

Gerald Rudolph Ford was the first President ever to succeed a resigning President.

Succeeding the first President ever to leave office alive...

He was known for his integrity and honesty,

I can offer...

and America remembers him as the man who restored the image of an 'honest President.'

*President Nixon with Vice President Ford

But during his term, the American economy suffered from its worst recession ever since the Great Depression in the 1930s.

Even though Ford wasn't able to rehabilitate the American economy that had fallen into a bottomless pit,

aside from the economy, he's largely credited for restoring ethics and trust in the presidency.

Born in Omaha, Nebraska, Ford attended the University of Michigan, where he worked various odd jobs such as dishwashing to support himself.

He also played football during college.

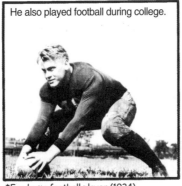

*Ford as a football player (1934)

After graduating from the University of Michigan, while working on the side as a football coach, he graduated at the top 25% of his class at Yale Law School.

Mr. Ford, do you major in physical education?

Shut up!

He was a gifted football player, and was even given offers by professional teams.

How about going pro?

Not interested.

After a stint as a lawyer, he joined the Navy during World War II.

Kennedy, Nixon and Ford,

They were all naval officers...

U.S. Presidents

His life in politics started with his election to the U.S. House of Representatives in 1948.

HOUSE OF REPS

Other than being known for his sincerity and integrity, Ford didn't stand out much as a congressman.

The guy's like a bear...

But when the then-incumbent Vice President Spiro Agnew resigned after being implicated in a bribery scandal,

Resignation

Bribe

Ford ascended to the vice presidency when Nixon nominated him to replace Agnew.

This is pretty odd...

Vice President

Then on August 9, 1974, Nixon resigned from the Office of President.

I'm resigning as President as of today...

Ford bid his farewells to the Nixons, the 'former' First Couple, who left on a helicopter,

*Ford bidding his farewells to the Nixons

and returned to the White House where he took the inaugural oath and was sworn in as the thirty-eighth President of the United States.

Exactly 30 days later, Ford granted a pardon to Nixon and made a plea to the American public.

My fellow Americans, our prolonged national nightmare is now over!*

*Watergate scandal

We must now open an era of forgiveness, brotherliness and reconciliation!

Even though his words rang a bell with the American public, it was still too early for them to forgive Nixon.

A pardon after only one month?

That's nonsense! Ford's just looking after him!

Ford's philosophy in life was honesty and integrity.

*Ford the dog-lover

President Ford possessed a warm heart toward the underprivileged and persecuted, based on his Christian faith.

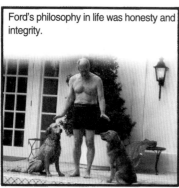

Immediately after his inauguration, on September 12, 1974, as a measure against racial discrimination,

White

Black

he outlawed racial segregation on school buses.

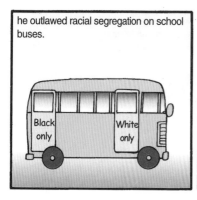

Black only

White only

Disgruntled white parents refused to send their children to school and even rioted,

We can't sit together with blacks!

Segregate blacks from whites!

ROAR

ROAR

in response to which Ford mobilized the army to protect black students on school buses.

There were many disgruntled white people who were unhappy about Ford's racial policies.

Ford's just siding with the blacks.

White interests are being infringed upon.

The blacks are going to run the world!

On September 5, 1975 in Sacramento, California,

BANG

and on September 22 the same year in San Francisco, there were assassination attempts on Ford.

*Ford with his bodyguards after a failed assassination attempt on him

The economy, after all, was the most pressing issue confronting the Ford administration.

Even though the Vietnam War had ended in April 1975,

Communist unification of Vietnam

the American economy was on the brink of bankruptcy due to the reckless Vietnam War expenditures.

For a non-war period, the U.S. recorded its worst inflation in history.

$ 10.99
$ 12.99

Prices rose while consumption dropped and the unemployment rate shot up.

Prices

Unemployment rate

Consumption

Vicious stagflation continued, and the U.S. suffered from its worst economic stagnation ever since the 1930s.

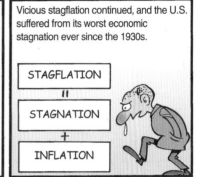

STAGFLATION
=
STAGNATION
+
INFLATION

Like all other Presidents, Ford too didn't acknowledge the economic difficulties facing the nation.

Our economic fundamentals are strong.

This is just an unusual slump caused by temporary illiquidity.

It doesn't make sense that cash-rich and very profitable large corporations are talking about a bad economy!

Ford's unprecedented good relations with Congress and the press

significantly deteriorated due to the continuing economic difficulties and Ford's obstinacy.

The President, wrapped up in his own self-righteousness,

is just blaming everything on the press!

Despite the stinging criticism of the press, Ford had no intention of changing his economic policies.

I... can't... hear... you...

The government needs to immediately deal with unemployment and inflation, but the President won't budge out of his stubbornness!

His policy was to cut taxes to control the inflation,

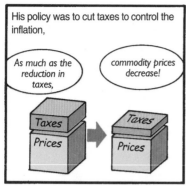

As much as the reduction in taxes,

commodity prices decrease!

but in 1975 when New York City was on the verge of bankruptcy due to the mountain of debt it had accumulated,

Ford was forced to authorize an increase in taxes to pay off New York City's debt.

In response to the press's question on whether Ford had changed his policies, his press secretary Ron Nessen cleverly replied:

Has he made a 180-degree turn in his policies?

Nope, Ford has only changed 179 degrees.

With his stubborn attitude, Ford clashed with Congress.

When oil prices skyrocketed due to the first oil shock in 1973 and 1974,

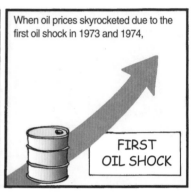

FIRST OIL SHOCK

Ford tried to raise oil prices to reduce oil consumption.

Boy, better reduce oil consumption...

Oil price increase

Congress, however, interfered with Ford's policies by reducing oil prices. Such conflict continued throughout Ford's term.

What...!

Oil price reduction

Consumer protection

Whereas Nixon only vetoed 42 spending bills during his five-and-a-half years in office, Ford vetoed as many as 66.

Amid the bogged-down economy and his inflexible policies,

I told you not to go that way!

U.S. economy

coupled with the public's critical view of the Nixon pardon, Ford ran in the 1976 presidential election.

Election

For the Republican presidential candidate nomination, he went against Ronald Reagan and won the nomination, with 1,187 delegates over Reagan's 1,070.

1976 Republican Presidential Primaries

G. R. Ford

R. Reagan

But the American public, desiring change and reform, chose political newcomer Jimmy Carter of the Democratic Party.

Change J. Carter

Honesty Integrity

Even though he served a short term as President that lasted only two-and-a-half years,

like Harry Truman, Ford opened the presidential era of the honest and good ordinary man.

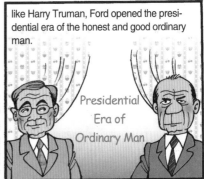

Presidential Era of Ordinary Man

His wife Betty Ford, the First Lady, was greatly loved by Americans.

*Ford taking the inaugural oath next to his wife Betty

She worked on the issues of abortion and improvement of women's rights.

Help alcoholic women

Pro-choice on abortion

Improvement of women's rights

In 1974, she surprised the world with her announcement that she had breast cancer.

*Betty on her sickbed

The Betty Ford Center established in 1982

is a leading social service organization that aids drug and alcohol addicts.

Ford's philosophy in life was simple.

Every person has more good sides than bad sides.

If we were to believe in and trust people, we can get along much better with all.

As much as he was simple, Ford was a man of integrity, a guileless yet inflexible man. Shall we hear what other people had to say about him?

G. Ford

The remarks of one newspaper editor:

This was a President with a warm heart,

but without the smarts.

Lyndon B. Johnson's view on Ford:

That Gerald Ford.

He's the only person I know who can't fart and chew gum at the same time!

Chomp chomp

Poop

James Earl (Jimmy) Carter 1977~1981

Unsuccessful Morality Politician, Reborn as Apostle of Peace

PEACE

Morality Politics

Re-

form

Reality

James Earl (Jimmy) Carter

Democratic Party, 1924.10.1~

Birth Place   Plains, Georgia

Wife   Eleanor Rosalynn Smith Carter 1927~

Children   John, James Earl, III, Jeffrey, Amy

Vice President   W. F. Mondale

'Jimmy!' A friendly childhood nickname for 'James.'

James... It's too formal!

Jimmy! How cute...

The use of this informal, open and chummy nickname

JIMMY Jimmy! Jimmy!

JIMMY

---

was indeed a new way to approach voters.

Wow, we can call the President like we call a friend...

Just like our next door neighbor!

Jimmy!

He was so new to politics that perplexed voters were asking who this Jimmy was.

Jimmy who?

Carter, who?

The first country-bred President from the South who narrowly defeated an incumbent President.

That man was Jimmy Carter, a peanut farm owner from Georgia.

James Earl Carter is a Southerner who was born in 1924 in Plains, Georgia. His father was a farmer and his mother a nurse.

*Carter in 1937

He entered the U.S. Naval Academy and graduated 59th out of his class of 820. After serving as an officer,

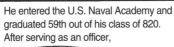

Second Lieutenant Carter, I see you got good grades.

he resigned his commission and returned to Georgia when his father died in 1953. He started managing a peanut farm that became successful.

*Carter married Rosalynn in 1946, the year he graduated from the Naval Academy.

Carter was open minded, especially toward racial issues.

An American citizen must not be discriminated based on color and race.

My momma taught me that.

After joining the Democratic Party, Carter served twice as a Georgia Senator since 1962.

Governor-ship

One, two

State Senator

After suffering a defeat in the 1966 gubernatorial election, he was elected the next time.

1966   1970

After his term as governor, Carter went for the presidency. The atmosphere back then was very favorable to him.

Truth   Morality   Trans-parency

After Watergate, America desired clean and moral politics,

Clean politics!   *Recovery of morality!*   *Ethics in politics!*

Roar   Roar

and the floored economy and disorderly society demanded change and reform.

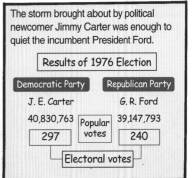

American society's wish for a truthful and open government

Not any more like this!   *America needs to change!*   *Change and reform!*

USA

found a fresh alternative in Jimmy Carter, whose catchphrase was morality, reform and human rights.

Morality Reform Human rights

The storm brought about by political newcomer Jimmy Carter was enough to quiet the incumbent President Ford.

Results of 1976 Election		
Democratic Party		Republican Party
J. E. Carter		G. R. Ford
40,830,763	Popular votes	39,147,793
297		240
	Electoral votes	

During his days as governor, Carter promised great reform.

State agency reform

Opening of public offices to blacks too!

Appointment of persons with diverse backgrounds

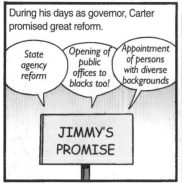

JIMMY'S PROMISE

Although these reform efforts partially succeeded, the public gradually began to disapprove of the excessively reform-based policies.

Stop the blabber about reforms and pay attention to the people's livelihood!

Re-form

This problem recurred after he took over the White House.

We're sick of this... Is he going to reform this country by himself?

Reform, reform

Despite having won by only a slim margin, Carter still implemented his ambitious plans after his inauguration.

Reform issues

White House

His approval rating soared to heights one year later, showing the great expectations of the people in him.

Carter ♥
Roar
Carter
Best!

Carter pardoned Vietnam War draft evaders,

The war's over. Let bygones be bygones!

Pardon

Thanks~

and created a cabinet-level Department of Energy, upgrading his energy policy chief to a cabinet-level position.

Cabinet-level

Dept. of Energy

After the oil crisis, the importance of energy can never be overstated!

Meanwhile, he aligned U.S. diplomacy principles with 'human rights,'

Human rights

and opened the era of the so-called American 'morality diplomacy.'

Since when did the U.S. become such a nation of virtue?

Human rights

He transferred the disputed Panama Canal to the Panama government,

Panama Canal

and commenced full diplomatic relations with China,

while concluding the SALT II Treaty with the Soviet Union in an effort to establish world peace.

Strategic
Arms
Limitations
Talks

SALT

USA

*Signing of 1980 diplomatic treaty with China

However, Congress rejected the SALT II Treaty and his energy policy.

Contrary to his promises, inflation worsened and the jobless increased day by day.

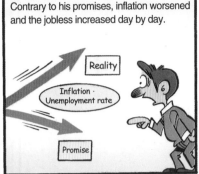

The American public, once enthralled by Carter, started to become skeptical of him.

Moreover, his promise to make personnel appointments from a diverse pool of talent didn't materialize in the

use of specialists within the party. Instead, he made appointments from among home town and personal friends, among others, based on personal connections.

No wonder he increasingly came into disfavor with the Democratic Party.

Then in 1978, Carter succeeded in creating a miracle by achieving the impossible.

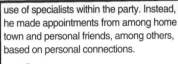

Carter brought over Egyptian President Saddat and Israeli Prime Minister Begin to Camp David.

Under Carter's mediation, they signed a peace treaty that greatly contributed to peace in the Middle East.

*President Saddat (left) with Prime Minister Begin (right)

Even with such a great diplomatic achievement, the American public still remained skeptical about Carter.

Against this background, when Iranian militants seized the American Embassy in Tehran on November 4, 1979,

the helpless American reaction to the Iranian challenge revealed Carter's incompetence.

To make matters worse, in December 1979, the Soviet army invaded Afghanistan, which caused an abrupt disruption in U.S.-Soviet relations.

*Afghanistan resistance

By subsequently boycotting the Moscow Olympics in 1980, Carter was criticized for tying sports with politics.

Boycott

1980

What does sports have to do with politics...

He also stopped the negotiations for SALT II, casting a dark cloud over world peace.

SALT II Suspension

His diplomacy is so emotional!

Jimmy Carter's problem was that he wouldn't listen to public opinion.

Face reality!

Too idealistic!

Open your ears to public opinion!

He's so intransigent!

Even though he insisted on unrealistic reforms based on his own morality,

I'm right!

What have I done wrong?

Reforms must continue!

he was incompetent and resourceless in his dealings in domestic and overseas problems.

The problem of the Carter administration is that they're just a bunch of political novices who assert their moral superiority!

They tenaciously pursue reforms without realizing how incompetent they are!

In the end, Carter was eventually abandoned by Americans in the 1980 election.

You're more fit for a peanut farm than the White House!

White House

In 1981, simultaneously with Reagan's inauguration as the fortieth President, Iran suddenly released the American hostages.

American hostages

People tend to misinterpret this event as the capitulation of Khomeini out of fear of the hardline Reagan,

So you were afraid Reagan would beat you up?

but in fact the hostages were let go due to Carter's decision to release billions of dollars of frozen Iranian assets in the U.S.

Exchange

American hostages

Iranian $ assets in U.S.

Thus, ultimately, it was Carter who resolved the Iran hostage crisis.

Even though the economy and the Iran hostage crisis held me back...

Despite all of this, the forsaken Jimmy Carter was reborn as an apostle of peace after he left the White House.

After his retirement, Carter greatly contributed to the promotion of peace, fair elections and human rights issues.

He is also greatly respected for his involvement in the Habitat for Humanity movement.

Greatly interested in peace on the Korean peninsula,

Carter visited North Korea in June 1994

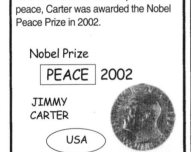

and delivered President Kim Young Sam's personal letter to President Kim Il Sung.

He reached an agreement for the dismantling of the North Korean nuclear program, among other things, thereby helping establish peace on the Korean peninsula.

For his various activities to promote peace, Carter was awarded the Nobel Peace Prize in 2002.

With his morality politics and poorly prepared reforms, Carter failed in real politics,

and left the White House after he lost the support of Americans.

But with his kindness, passion and warmth,

Jimmy Carter emerged in the world as a most virtuous model of the American politician.

He is a noteworthy figure who has won the respect of the world after leaving office.

Ronald W. Reagan 1981~1989

Conqueror of Communism

Ronald Wilson Reagan

Republican Party, 1911.2.6~2004.6.5

Birth Place   Tampico, Illinois

Wives 1. Jane Wyman Reagan 1914~2007
       2. Nancy Davis Reagan 1923~

Children   Maureen, Michael, Patricia, Ronald

Vice President   George H. W. Bush

Among all U.S. Presidents, Ronald Wilson Reason is noteworthy in several respects.

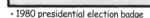

· 1980 presidential election badge

He was a former actor,

Cut!

---

and the oldest person ever to enter the White House.

You're too old to do that!

Reagan became President when he was 70!

He was also the first divorced President.

Even though there was a separated President...

A divorce was still seen as taboo back then...

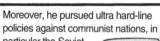

Moreover, he pursued ultra hard-line policies against communist nations, in particular the Soviet Union,

Commu-
nist
Coun-
tries

---

and, by doing so, played a decisive role in bringing down communism and ending the era of ideological conflict.

Commu-
nist
Coun-
tries

Reagan was born as the son of Jack Reagan, an alcoholic shoe salesman, in Tampico, Illinois.

* Ron: Nickname of Ronald

After college, he started out as a radio announcer in Des Moines,

* Reagan during his days as an announcer in Des Moines

and in 1937 was picked up by a Hollywood movie studio after which he appeared in 52 movies including 'King of the B's.'

However, he appeared in only 'B films' without ever playing a leading role.

* Reagan the Actor

After he joined the Democratic Party in the 1940s, he displayed more talent in politics than in acting,

and in 1947 he served as president of the Screen Actors Guild.

When the conservative and anti-communist wave hit Hollywood in the 1950s,

he reported on the ideologies of actors to the Federal Bureau of Investigation (FBI).

Reagan divorced Jane Wyman in 1949 and married Nancy Davis in 1952.

Until he died in 2004, Ronald and Nancy Reagan led a happy marriage life for 50 years.

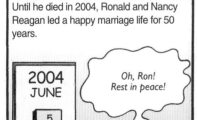

But he wasn't on such good terms with his children, with whom he rarely interacted.

After switching from a Democrat to a Republican, Reagan started attracting attention when he drafted a speech for presidential candidate Barry Goldwater in 1964.

With the support of the Republican Party, Reagan was elected as California Governor in 1966 and kindled his ambition for the presidency.

Next stop is the White House!

REAGAN GOVERNOR

CALIFORNIA

In 1968 and 1976, he sought out the Republican presidential nomination, but lost to Nixon and Ford, respectively.

Nixon   Ford

He finally won the nomination on his third try in 1980.

I never gave up!

Hup!

In 1980, American society suffered from a severe malaise.

Americans were greatly frustrated with U.S. diplomacy in the prolonged Iran hostage crisis,

How could we be so insulted by Iran...

ROAR

ROAR

---

and the domestic economy was undergoing a long-term stagflation, with a large increase in the unemployment rate.

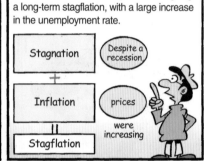

Stagnation — Despite a recession

+

Inflation — prices

=

Stagflation — were increasing

It was at that time that candidate Reagan, the former star, appeared before the languishing Carter era with a blue print for a 'strong America.'

USA

He promised to revamp the U.S. government.

Large, inefficient gov't → Small, efficient gov't

With his plan to reduce individual and corporate income taxes and promote investments and consumption,

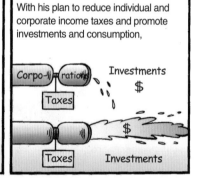

Corporations   Investments $

Taxes

$

Taxes   Investments

---

and improve productivity, Reagan introduced his 'Reaganomics' policies.

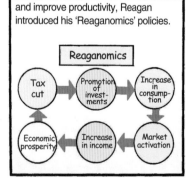

Reaganomics

Tax cut → Promotion of investments → Increase in consumption → Market activation → Increase in income → Economic prosperity

---

He argued for 'diplomacy with strength' to Americans upset by the bewildered Carter who had emphasized morality in politics.

Morality politics

Diplomacy with strength

Reagan eventually won the presidential election by an overwhelming margin over the incumbent Carter and was elected the fortieth President.

Results of 1980 Election		
Democratic Party		Republican Party
James E. Carter		Ronald W. Reagan
35,483,883	Popular votes	43,904,153
49	Electoral votes	489

'Reaganomics,' Reagan's economic policies, sounded pretty impressive first off, but it was impossible to implement substantial parts of those policies.

During the initial stages of its implementation, the government seemed to control inflation and reduce unemployment,

This painkiller will do for the time being...

Reaganomics

U.S. Economy

The middle and upper class, more than those living in poverty, primarily reaped the benefits of the tax cuts that formed the crux of Reaganomics.

Tax cut benefits

Tax cut benefits $

For this reason, during Reagan's tenure, his policies actually reduced the benefits available to the poor people, greatly increasing the people at the lowest poverty line.

Gap between rich and poor

Economic scissors

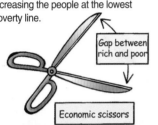

After the tax cuts were made, since there was no other source from which to increase national revenue,

No rain...

Tax cuts

$

the national debt snowballed in size.

Our last resort...

Debt (Bond issuances)

$

Expenditures greatly exceeded revenue,

MADE IN USA

Exports

Imports | Trade deficit

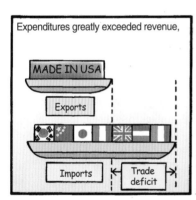

and with the twin deficit in the fiscal and current account balances, the U.S. economy fell into a deep quagmire.

Fiscal balance deficit

Current account balance deficit

Resulted from going into debt to compensate for shortage in tax funds

Resulted from imports exceeding exports

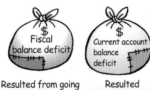
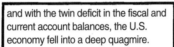

Still, because the world economy somewhat recovered since 1983,

World economy

1983

even though the U.S. national debt astronomically increased from US$900 million to US$2.7 trillion during the Reagan era,

$ 2,700,000,000,000

National debt

$900 mil.

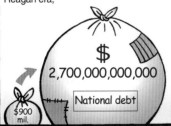

the economy seemed to have significantly recovered by the time Reagan's term ended in 1989, compared to when he started his term in 1981.

Unemployment rate: 7% 1981 / 5.3% 1989

Inflation: 13% 1981 / 4.7% 1989

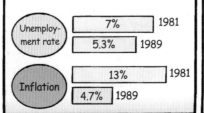

Reagan's approval rating surged, as a result of which he won re-election in the 1984 presidential election by winning the most electoral votes ever in history.

Results of 1984 Election		
Democratic Party	Popular/Electoral	Republican Party
Walter F. Mondale		Ronald W. Reagan
37,577,185	Popular votes	54,455,075
13	Electoral votes	525

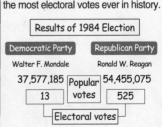

Reagan's diplomacy wholeheartedly took a hard-line approach against communism.

He harshly criticized the Soviet Union as the 'Evil Empire,'

You guys are the Evil Empire!

and opened the space war era with his announcement of plans for the Strategic Defense Initiative (missile defense system), otherwise known as 'Star Wars.'

With the U.S. deployment of the Pershing II missiles in West Germany and other U.S. measures, the world became concerned over a potential clash between the U.S. and the Soviet Union.

So you want to go all the way?

West Germany | Communist Bloc

However, when Mikhail Gorbachev rose to power as the General Secretary of the Communist Party of the Soviet Union in 1985, his *perestroika* and *glasnost* policies

Perestroika
Restructuring
Glasnost
Openness

marked a dramatic turning point in U.S.-Soviet relations.

Gorby, you're cool!

Ron, my friend!

From 1985 to 1988, the two leaders met as many as five times and made epochal progress on arms reduction matters.

In particular, the signing of the Intermediate-Range Nuclear Forces Treaty (INF) greatly surprised the world.

This is amazing!

WOW

U.S.-USSR agree to eliminate intermediate-range missiles

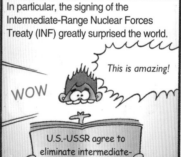

Reagan's hard-line style is well exemplified in how he handled a strike of federal air traffic controllers that took place immediately after his inauguration.

STRIKE

He just went ahead and mercilessly fired 12,000 pilots and air traffic controllers who participated in the strike.

You're all fired!

Meanwhile, Reagan is well known for leaving many amusing anecdotes. On March 30, 1981, he was almost assassinated by a would-be assassin's bullet.

On the way to the hospital in an ambulance, he didn't forget to crack a joke to the doctor treating him.

I hope you're Republican.

Reagan is known to have been a complicated and difficult to understand person.

Occasionally, he would embarrass those around him with his extreme ignorance.

Afghanistan?

Is that an African dance?

Mr. President!

He rarely wrote anything longer than a paragraph. In fact, he hardly read or wrote anything as President.

I just read what my aides wrote for me.

I haven't read or written anything for decades...

He also showed absolutely no interest in the policy discussions he attended,

and became the target of gossip for often dozing off during meetings, just like President Coolidge did.

Perhaps because of his old age, he frequently took off for vacation,

and made many outrageous mistakes during public speeches, which made his aides squirm.

In January 1989, the old President, aged 78, returned to California.

Washington

In 1994, his wife Nancy formally announced that Reagan was fighting Alzheimer's disease. Americans became heartbroken over the news.

How could Ron...!

On, no!

On June 5, 2004, Ronald Reagan passed away at the age of 93. His death was deeply mourned by Americans.

His policies—characterized by low taxes, a strong military and the weakening of communism—created a stronger America.

He will be remembered as the President who ended the persistent East-West conflict that stained the twentieth century and led the efforts to bring communism to its knees.

George H. W. Bush 1989~1993

Pioneer of New World Order

Iraq

Gulf War

NEW WORLD

SOCIALISM

George Herbert Walker Bush

Republican Party, 1924.6.12~

Birth Place   Milton, Massachusetts

Wife   Barbara Pierce Bush 1925~

Children   George, Robin, John, Neal, Marvin, Dorothy

Vice President   Dan Quayle

Since Martin Van Buren (8th President, 1837~1841), George Herbert Walker Bush

George Herbert Walker Bush

---

became the first serving Vice President to become elected President.

First time in 150 years!

Election

Vice President

President

As for the other Vice Presidents, the presidency was transferred to them or they were elected to the presidency after first suffering a defeat (like Nixon).

Succession

10th Tyler
13th Fillmore
17th A. Johnson
21st Arthur
26th T. Roosevelt
30th Coolidge
33rd Truman
36th L. Johnson
38th Ford

Many people were surprised by Bush's election as President

Hey... Bush got elected?

BUSH PRESIDENT!

---

because although his predecessor Reagan was popular, it looked like power would transfer to the Democrats due to the twin deficit and drug and environmental pollution problems.

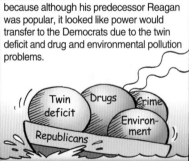

Twin deficit

Drugs

Crime

Environment

Republicans

Contrary to these expectations, Bush easily won the 1988 presidential election.

Results of 1988 Election	
Republican Party	Democratic Party
George H. W. Bush	Michael S. Dukakis
48,886,097	41,809,074
Popular votes	
426	111
Electoral votes	

A descendant of King William of England*, Bush is from a prominent New England family.

Historic family!

King William	
Samuel Bush (Grandfather)	Steel executive
Prescott Bush (Father)	Connecticut State Senator
George H. W. Bush	41st U.S. President

* Burke's Peerage

His grandfather was the wealthy steel executive Samuel Bush and father the Connecticut State Senator and banker Prescott Bush.

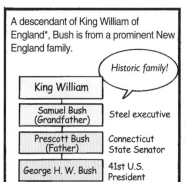

* Bush, aged 6, in 1930

Furthermore, he attended the well-known preparatory school Phillips Andover Academy,

Attended by only children of the upper class.

Phillips Andover Academy (Graduated in 1942)

and in 1945 married Barbara Pierce, daughter of the wealthy publisher of McCalls Magazine.

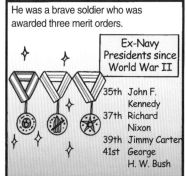

In sum, he was a lucky man who had it all, including family background, wealth, educational pedigree and personal connections.

Perfect!

Wealth $

Family

Education

Personal connections

During World War II, Bush joined the U.S. Navy and flew 58 combat missions as a naval aviator.

He was a brave soldier who was awarded three merit orders.

Ex-Navy Presidents since World War II

35th	John F. Kennedy
37th	Richard Nixon
39th	Jimmy Carter
41st	George H. W. Bush

After the war, he returned to school and graduated from Yale University in 1948 with a degree in economics

Has produced many U.S. Presidents

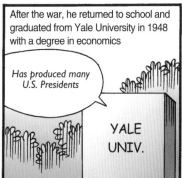

YALE UNIV.

and then took part in the oil development boom by venturing into the oil business in Texas.

After succeeding in business, he set up his own oil company in the early 1950s and accumulated much wealth.

* Texas Man Bush

With family, wealth, background, educational pedigree and personal connections, among other things, perfectly in place, Bush entered politics in 1960.

The last thing I need to secure is 'power.'

Washington D.C.

He aimed for a U.S. Senate seat in 1964 but lost the election.

Bush then left the oil business and concentrated on politics, winning election to the U.S. House of Representatives in 1966.

Elected 1966

Re-elected 1968

Recognized for his abilities by the Nixon and Ford administrations, Bush served in various key posts.

Ambassador to UN → Chief of Liaison Office to China → Director of CIA

* Nixon and Bush

Although he lost the 1980 Republican presidential candidate nomination to Reagan,

he accepted Reagan's offer to become his running mate and was twice elected Vice President in 1980 and 1984.

Become my Vice President.

In the 1988 election, he unexpectedly won election as President.

Democratic candidate
Dukakis

The American people were apprehensive of what kind of President he was.

He sort of has a wimpy image, doesn't he?

Somehow, I don't feel confident about him.

His first test came with Panama President Manuela Noriega's challenge to the United States in December 1989.

PANAMA

Noriega, who was into drug trafficking, had killed a U.S. serviceman dispatched to Panama to stop the drug trade. This was an open challenge to the U.S.

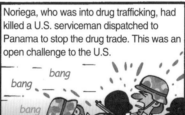

bang
bang
bang
bang
bang

In response, Bush resolutely ordered the U.S. military to invade Panama.

Within 48 hours, U.S. forces occupied Panama. On January 3, 1990, Noriega was arrested and sent to the United States where he was put on trial.

Despite international criticism that the U.S. had invaded a sovereign nation and arrested its national leader,

How could you just kidnap and arrest the leader of a sovereign nation? That's too heavy-handed!

ROAR
ROAR

Bush still clearly showed his resoluteness to Americans and the world.

We'll never forgive anyone who supplies drugs to Americans and kills American soldiers seeking to prevent that!

However, Bush's biggest test came with Iraq's invasion of Kuwait in August 1990.

Kuwait

Vrrrrrr

President Saddam Hussein, seeking to secure oil resources and initiative in the Middle East, had occupied Kuwait by force.

This is our land!

Kuwait

In response, Bush organized a coalition force under 'Operation Desert Shield.'

Multinational coalition force organized under U.S. initiative!

Uh oh... Bush's response is stronger than I expected it would be....

On January 17, 1991, the Gulf War started with 'Operation Desert Storm' under which coalition forces conducted large-scale attacks on Iraq.

KABOOM

This war unsparingly displayed the superiority and power of modern weaponry.

The Gulf War, which crushed Saddam Hussein's ambitions, ended in a one-sided victory for the U.S. and coalition forces.

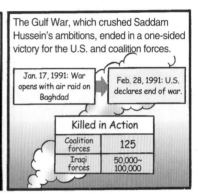

Jan. 17, 1991: War opens with air raid on Baghdad → Feb. 28, 1991: U.S. declares end of war.

Killed in Action	
Coalition forces	125
Iraqi forces	50,000~ 100,000

There are views that Bush's diplomatic successes and war victory are not attributable to his abilities

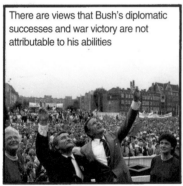

* Bush on visit in Poland

but to the disorder that prevailed in the Soviet Union, the only power that could check the U.S.,

I won't let you run wild all by yourself!

during the disintegration of the Eastern Bloc.

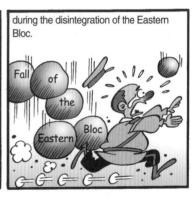

Fall of the Eastern Bloc

The world underwent enormous changes during Bush's term.

BABAM

Starting with Hungary, Eastern Bloc communist nations fell one by one,

Hungary Czecho-slovakia Poland East Germany

CRASH

and, with the fall of the Berlin Wall in November 1989, communism came to its miserable end.

Although the Eastern Bloc showed signs of collapse during the Reagan era,

it was Bush who was the driving force behind that phenomenon. Indeed, he was the victor in the war of ideologies.

BYE!

BYE!

THUD.

Bush, however, held back his joy.

Imagine if I danced and expressed my joy.

It would've provoked the Soviet military and put fire on what oil they had left!

←Facial expression control in progress

On October 3, 1990, Germany achieved dramatic unification.

To the museum...

Meanwhile, as for the Tiananmen Square Massacre in China in which the government rolled over the people's request for reform with tanks in June 1989,

Freedom! Democracy!

Bush kept his eyes closed and was indifferent to the incident for which he received fierce criticism from international society.

What happened to the 'human rights' that the U.S. always invoked?

To preserve its interests, the U.S. has maintained silence toward China that rejects democratization!

mumble

grumble

As the end of his term approached, Bush found himself in an increasingly difficult situation.

Uh...

Oh...

Uh...

With the victory in the Gulf War, his approval rating once shot up to an overwhelming 89%,

Approval rating

89%

but a dark cloud loomed over his re-election when the economy, including inflation and unemployment, didn't improve at all.

Inflation

Jobless

problems

Economic

Re-election

Due to the $2.7 trillion debt that Reagan left with him,

I'm counting on you.

$2,700,000,000,000 National debt

Bush had to break Reagan's promise not to increase taxes because the U.S. just couldn't handle that enormous debt.

Reaganomics

Tax cuts

Absolutely no tax increases

The increase in taxes dampened Bush's approval rating.

I'm sorry.

Tax Increases

Even though he had led the nation to victory in the Gulf War, the economy tripped him,

and he was defeated by former Arkansas Governor Bill Clinton.

Bill Clinton attracted great attention by focusing on the economy during the election.

It's the economy, stupid!

Instead of the 'new world order' emphasized by Bush, the American people living in an era with no Cold War

End of Cold War!

Creation of new world order led by the U.S.

Collapse of Eastern Bloc

selected a fat wallet.

We're not familiar with that kind of grand and lofty ideal.

What's more important is putting a lot of food on the table.

After leaving office, Bush has been enjoying a quiet and happy life with his family.

* The Bushes with their grandchildren

Even after his defeat to Clinton, a Gallup Poll showed that Bush and his wife Barbara are among the 'most admired people.'

It shows that they had earned the good will of Americans.

George! ROAR ROAR Barbara!

Barbara, especially, is a beloved model mother figure who has endeared herself to people all over America.

George W. Bush's election as the forty-third President and his re-election in 2004

was strongly backed by the unseen force of his mother Barbara Bush, who has been one of the factors of his success.

Barbara!

The 'great strength of the mother' resulted in the second father-son presidency, and the first son presidency to win re-election, in U.S. history.

William Jefferson (Bill) Clinton 1993~2001
Leader of Times of Unprecedented Economic Prosperity

Bill Clinton

IT Industry

IMPEACH-MENT

S E X SCAN DAL

ECONOMIC PROSPERITY

WHITEWATER SCANDAL

William Jefferson (Bill) Clinton

Democratic Party, 1946.8.19~

Birth Place Hope, Arkansas

Wife Hillary Rodham 1947~

Child Chelsea

Vice President Al Gore

Bill Clinton, born William Jefferson Bythe III, was the first Baby Boomer President.

The Baby Boomer generation

is the first generation born after World War II.

Birth rate

1945 (year in which WWII ended)

He opened a political era characterized by a new style that reflected the values and tastes of baby boomers.

Clinton presided over the most prosperous period in U.S. history.

* Clinton visiting Bosnia (1996)

He will be recorded as the leader of an era in which America emerged as the world's only superpower.

Also, despite the various scandals that continued to plague him,

Monica Lewinsky scandal

Whitewater scandal

Paula Jones incident

Scandal

---

he had the good fortune to lead America during its most economically prosperous period.

New York Stock Exchange Sets Record
Index shoots past 15,000

Acceleration of Silicon Valley-based Digital Revolution

Skyrocketing of IT Industry Stock Prices

Bill Clinton was born in Hope, Arkansas as the son of Virginia Cassidy Blythe.

His father died two months before he was born in an automobile accident, so he didn't even have a chance to see his father.

How could you just leave us like that...

Four years later, his mother remarried Roger Clinton, an alcoholic car salesman. Clinton followed his step-father's name.

You're last name is now Clinton. Did you get that boy?

* Clinton (left) at age 14 with his mother (1960)

He spent his childhood in unfortunate circumstances in Hot Springs, which was a hotbed of sex and crime.

The hamburgers and fast food that he ate during his poor childhood remain as his favorite food to this day.

Since his high school days, Clinton showed a deep interest in politics.

* Clinton meeting with Kennedy (1963)

Upon graduation from Georgetown University in Washington D.C.,

Country boy from Arkansas, has made his triumphal entry into the capital...

Georgetown University Washington D.C.

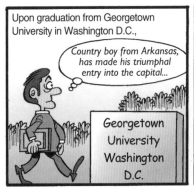

he won a Rhodes Scholarship to study at Oxford University in Britain for two years (1968~1970).

Oxford

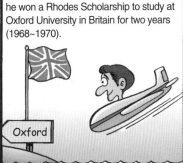

Controversy that he evaded military service during the Vietnam War due to his overseas study continued to plague him in the future.

Others were dying in Vietnam...

while you were evading the draft by studying abroad...

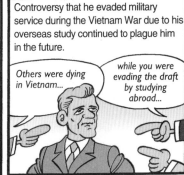

After returning from Britain, Clinton entered Yale Law School, from which he graduated in 1973 with a juris doctor degree.

Georgetown University

Oxford University (Rhodes Scholar)

Yale University (Law School)

Juris Doctor

He met his wife Hillary Rodham at Yale and married her in 1975.

After returning to Arkansas, he became a university professor and then Attorney General of Arkansas.

Attorney General at 30! Pretty fast, eh?

Attorney General Bill Clinton

In 1978, at the age of 32, Clinton was elected as Governor of Arkansas, making him the youngest governor in America.

32-year old Governor

All-time U.S. record

Although he lost the gubernatorial election in 1980, he was again elected governor and served from 1982 to 1992.

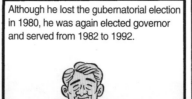

Governor of Arkansas

| 1982 | 1984 | 1986 | 1990 |

In the 1992 presidential election, he challenged President George Bush as the Democratic candidate.

* Clinton on the campaign trail

Despite Bush's high approval rating of 89%, independent Ross Perot took 19% of Bush's votes,

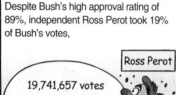

Ross Perot

19,741,657 votes Republican supporters

Crunch Crunch

as a result of which Clinton was able to defeat the incumbent Bush and become elected President with just 43% of the votes.

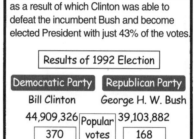

Results of 1992 Election

Democratic Party	Republican Party
Bill Clinton	George H. W. Bush
44,909,326	39,103,882
370	168

Popular votes

Electoral votes

Even though he had 'barely' won the presidency, Clinton was a really lucky guy.

Election!

As the digital revolution progressed, the U.S. economy prospered, with the information and technology (IT) industries propelling stock prices to new heights.

U.S. economy

DIGITAL REVOLUTION

After its bubble burst, Japan, which once rivaled America, entered a long recession.

Gasp

USA

The U.S. clearly emerged as a world-leading nation politically, economically, culturally and in all other aspects.

1

USA

However, during the 1996 mid-term election, the victorious Republicans took control of Congress.

Republicans

Congress

Democrats

From that time, Clinton's private life came under incessant attacks from Congress,

and he suffered from a real estate scandal known as Whitewater.

* Newspaper caricature of the Whitewater scandal

In the 1996 presidential election, despite a very low voter turnout rate of 49%,

Clinton easily won re-election due to the economic prosperity.

Results of 1996 Election	
Democratic Party	Republican Party
William J. Clinton	Robert J. Dole
47,402,357	39,198,755
379	159

Popular votes

Electoral votes

Since Franklin D. Roosevelt, Clinton became the first Democratic President to win re-election.

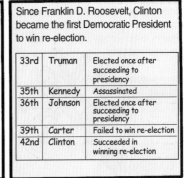

33rd	Truman	Elected once after succeeding to presidency
35th	Kennedy	Assassinated
36th	Johnson	Elected once after succeeding to presidency
39th	Carter	Failed to win re-election
42nd	Clinton	Succeeded in winning re-election

After he became President, the IT industries experienced explosive growth.

The economy prospered, while the crime rate went down.

American welfare improved, while unemployment dropped.

One reason Clinton easily won re-election was that he didn't involve America in any global war throughout his first term.

Meanwhile, in late 1995, when Congress didn't pass the government's 1996 budget,

in an unprecedented move, the federal government shut itself down in protest.

Even though Clinton had his successes, the Monica Lewinsky sex scandal that broke out in 1998, coupled with the Paula Jones scandal,

and the tenacious investigation of his affairs by Independent Counsel Kenneth Starr, drove him into a corner.

When it was eventually revealed that he had lied, he faced impeachment.

In February 1999, Clinton was at risk of becoming the first President in U.S. history to be removed from office in an impeachment trial.

He barely escaped removal from office as the Senate voted to acquit him.

We can't leave a precedent in U.S. history of kicking out a President.

Acquittal!

Whew~

There's probably no other President in U.S. history than Clinton who was so tormented by issues in his private life.

That was really mean to dig into my private life like that...

Despite these scandals, during the Clinton era, the American economy expanded while the national debt decreased.

U.S. economy

Nat'l

debt

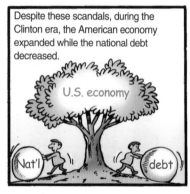

The U.S. also concluded the North American Free Trade Agreement.

NAFTA

North American Free Trade Agreement

Canada — U.S. — Mexico

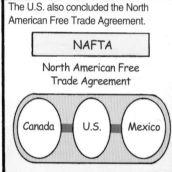

Also, family laws were improved to further protect the rights of women.

Family laws

And the nation promoted environmental protection. In short, America truly shined during this period.

America's brilliant era

The 'neo-capitalism' of the global era emphasized during Clinton's presidency

Free market economy

GLOBALISM

crossed borders and opened a period of freer capitalism.

Services   Culture   Information   Capital

Border

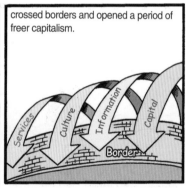

This neo-capitalism combined and struck a balance with the expanded welfare system in Europe

Neo-capitalism   Welfare system

Europe

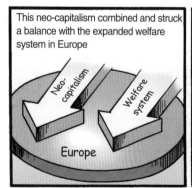

to open a European-style free and open market economy system known as the 'Third Way.'

Neo-capitalism   Welfare system

Third Way

Europe

All of this accelerated globalization all over the world at a furious pace.

Globalization

The Clinton era was a 'great period' during which America freed itself from the chronic frustration that had plagued the nation.

Society became more sensitive as political correctness became established in society.

High-level positions also opened up to women.

America solidly established itself as the world's only superpower.

Clinton will also be remembered as the first President to recognize the political potential of Asian-Americans

and the President who led America into the twenty-first century.

He was assisted by capable advisors such as Robert Rubin and Alan Greenspan

* Alan Greenspan

and was very knowledgeable about the information society and the economy.

It also helped a lot that he was a great saxophone player, skills that he used to his advantage during election campaigns.

When Clinton, appearing on a TV talk show, skillfully played an Elvis Presley piece,

he enthralled young Americans and made headlines in national newspapers.

Bill Clinton was indeed a 'skillful and charming bad boy' who opened America's twenty-first century.

George W. Bush 2001~

Self-righteous Warrior against Terror

George Walker Bush

Republican Party, 1946. 7. 6.~

Birth Place New Haven, Connecticut

Wife Laura Welch Bush 1946~

Children Barbara, Jenna

Vice President Dick B. Cheney

With the election of George Walker Bush as the forty-third President, father and son Bush became the second father-and-son Presidents in U.S. history.

Bush Sr.

Bush Jr.

2nd
John Adams

6th
John Quincy Adams

With his re-election, son Bush also became the first son President to win re-election in U.S. history.

2004 Victory

But George W. Bush became President through the most controversial and suspicious election in U.S. election history.

Gore won more votes!

Let's do a recount!

Grumble

Mumble

2000 Election

Suspicions of a rigged election!

Moreover, due to his unilateral diplomacy focused on the 'War on Terror,'

---

and ultra-conservative right-wing 'neocon' policies,

Neo-Cons = New Conservatives

CAWK

NEO CONS

Bush has been the target of fierce resistance and criticism from allied nations, more than any other President in U.S. history.

Don't you think you're going too far?

ANTI-BUSH

ANTI-AMERICA

ROAR

George W. Bush was born into a traditional, elite family in New Haven, Connecticut.

*Bush Jr. at age 11 with his father (1957)

He also attended Phillips Andover Academy, the privileged private school that his father attended.

Father and son...

Phillips Andover Academy

He then took the prototypical elitist path by attending Yale University and obtaining an MBA degree from Harvard Business School.

Phillips Andover	Yale Univ.	Harvard Univ.
Privileged private school	Ivy League Elite East Coast school	Business School

---

Although he was a member of a secret society* whose members came from prestigious families,

*Skulls and Bones

he wasn't the studious type and received C grades on average.

He scored higher in sociology than in his major.

Lecture hall

He was more of a 'frat boy' who was into drinking, dating and sports.

After finishing school, he is said to have served in the National Guard, but due to his lack of combat service, his military background has always been the subject of controversy in elections.

There are records indicating that he served in the military!

There are suspicions that he evaded service in the Vietnam War!

In 1975, Bush started an oil business in Texas. At that time he met Laura Welch, a librarian, who he married within three months.

*The Bush family (1987)

He entered politics in 1979 and ran for a House of Representatives seat but lost the election. He then returned to the oil business.

I guess it's not for everyone...

Congress

In 1988, when Bush Sr. ran for President, Bush Jr. served as his campaign advisor.

To win this election...

G. BUSH 1988

Bush also served as an advisor in 1992 as he did in 1988, even though his father lost the second time.

Sorry, Dad...

George! You've got to get revenge for me.

Sniff

In 1988, with other investors, he purchased a share in the professional baseball team the Texas Rangers for $600,000, which he later on sold at a whopping $15 million.

With this deal, Bush attracted much attention for his business savvy.

So he made it big by selling a ball club?

Like his father, he's good in business.

With this momentum, Bush ran for and was elected to the Texas governorship in 1994.

1994 | Elected
1998 | Elected

TEXAS

After he won re-election in 1998, from 1999, he naturally surfaced as a future presidential candidate using his father's network of connections.

To the White House!

Bush Network

In the 2000 Republican primary, Bush defeated Senator John McCain from Arizona, a strong opponent, and was nominated as the Republican presidential candidate.

BUSH CHENEY

After a fierce fight, even though he lost the popular vote to the Democratic Party's Al Gore, he barely won the election by winning the electoral vote with a margin of just five votes.

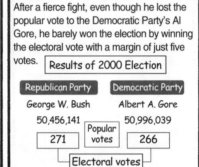

Results of 2000 Election	
Republican Party	Democratic Party
George W. Bush	Albert A. Gore
50,456,141	50,996,039
271	266

Popular votes

Electoral votes

This election was so close that it brought the entire world's attention to the vote counting.

Uh oh... Does this mean I might lose...?

Razor-thin margin!

Close match!

Bush's election victory based on the electoral vote, despite his loss of the popular vote,

I was the choice of the Americans.

I got elected thanks to the Constitution.

cast a spotlight on the winner-take-all U.S. election system. Its problems had been forgotten for 110 years since it had last become an issue in 1888. The winner-take-all system was written in the Constitution and studied in school,

Election victories won despite loss of popular vote

X	Andrew Jackson 151,271 votes	John Quincy Adams 113,122 votes	O
X	Samuel Tilden 4,288,546	Rutherford Hayes 4,034,311	O
X	Grover Cleveland 5,534,488	Benjamin Harrison 5,443,892	O
X	Albert Gore	George W. Bush	O

but Bush's victory still made Americans seriously rethink the problems of the electoral college system in U.S. elections.

How could we have such an undemocratic Constitution

in America, where democracy originated?

Eventually, when a winner wasn't declared even after a recount in Florida,

If we were to check each vote to see whether it's valid or not,

we won't be able to decide the winner even after the end of Clinton's term!

the U.S. Supreme Court, with a Republican Party-leaning disposition, declared Bush as the winner 36 days after the election.

Bush won!

U.S. Supreme Court

This decision ended the nerve-wracking 2000 election with Bush's victory, which was ridiculed by the world.

Whew

Ha ha
Hee hee
Ho ho

Even after his inauguration, Bush suffered from the after-effects of the election.

Is he really President?

In fact, he lost to Gore...

The Supreme Court elected him!

He agonized under the shadows of the 'shining Clinton era.'

We really miss the Clinton days...

Will the weak Bush perform well?

But the September 11, 2001 terrorist attacks gave Bush an opportunity to turn the tide.

With the 9/11 attack that killed 2,973 Americans, Bush was reborn as the leader of the 'War on Terror.'

He went to war against Afghanistan for supporting terrorist organizations,

Sponsor of terror!

Taliban Regime

Afghanistan

and then went after Iraq by commencing a protracted war against it.

You've got weapons of mass destruction, right?

I told you, no!

Even though Iraq was occupied and Saddam Hussein arrested,

How can you treat a head of state like this?

Bush was put in a difficult position when the U.S. couldn't find any weapons of mass destruction, which was his very justification for going to war against Iraq.

Beats me~~!

Then why did you start the war?

Due to this fiasco, in his bid for re-election in the 2004 election, Bush had to go through a tough fight with John Kerry in a very close election.

You sacrificed American money and lives for an unjustified war...!

But rather than the economic recovery espoused by Kerry,

It's the economy, stupid!

Economic Recovery

!

the Americans, in fear of threats of terror, chose the 'safe America' espoused by Bush.

You think you're Clinton?

A Safe America

!

Even though it was by a slim margin, Bush succeeded in winning re-election.

Results of 2004 Election	
Republican Party	Democratic Party
George W. Bush	John Kerry
58,535,827 Popular votes	54,994,460
274	252
Electoral votes	

Where does Bush's staying power come from?

It starts with his faith as a devout Christian and his family.

Around 1985, Bush was nothing but a drunkard; there was nothing extraordinary about him.

He has said that he quit drinking and was born again after meeting with Reverend Billy Graham.

Why do you live your life as you do? I will pray for you...

SNIFF

His faith shows up in the way he executes his policies without regard to how he may be perceived.

VROOM

Policies

Despite the worsening fiscal deficit, he reduced taxes on two occasions,

If you cut taxes now, that will reduce government revenues...

Just make the cut!

and despite critical international opinion, he has insisted on maintaining a policy line focused on America's self-interest.

USA

For such stances, his unilateral diplomacy has been the target of worldwide criticism

FOLLOW ME

He always has to have his own way!

and has provoked anti-American sentiments throughout the world.

ROAR
ROAR
YAN-KEE, GO HOME!

This has caused a global overflow of waves of anti-Americanism and anti-Bushism. There probably was no other

ROAR   ROAR

BUSH NO   USA NO   WAR NO

administration in U.S. history that arbitrarily pushed forward U.S.-centered policies as much as the Bush administration did,

The U.S. is mighty! Might is right!

We act because we're right!

nor would there be any other such administration in future U.S. history to be so scorned by the world.

We hate America and Bush!

Talk all you want. I'm going to do as I please!

Even though he possesses an elitist and dignified family background, with prestigious academic degrees and wealth,

| Prestigious Connecticut family |
| Ivy League degrees |
| Wealth |
| Great connections |

Bush himself is famous for his coarse and boorish side.

Ha ha ha ha

Ho ho ho ho

People who met him have consistently said that he has a charming side, a touch of humanity.

I didn't like Al Gore's perfectionist style. He seemed to be so cold.

Bush is free and easy, like makgeolli*

Didn't know there was makgeolli in America.

*Unrefined Korean rice wine

Still, there are several mountains that he needs to climb.

Although he has espoused 'compassionate conservatism,'

No child shall be disadvantaged!

NO CHILD LEFT BEHIND

he must handle the imminent task of reconciling the American people,

U S

Democrats

Republicans

who were bipolarized during the 2000 and 2004 elections.

Also, he needs to deal with the Iraqi War, which may turn out to be a second Vietnam War,

the War on Terror, an unseen war that may destroy the security of Americans at any time,

BOOM

the North Korean nuclear problem, which has attracted the world's attention as a hot potato for over a decade,

Give up the nukes first!

Guarantee the preservation of our regime first!

USA

N. Korea

and the challenges from China, which is emerging as a global economic superpower.

With all of these problems to solve, would it be an exaggeration to say Bush's second term looks like an unpredictable mine field…?

2005~2009

List of U.S. Presidents

No.	Name	Life-time	Years in Office	Former Occupation	No. of Terms	Party	Home State	Education
1	George Washington	1732~1799	1789~1797	Soldier	2	–	Virginia	Elementary school level (~15)
2	John Adams	1735~1826	1797~1801	Lawyer	1	Federalist	Massachusetts	Harvard University
3	Thomas Jefferson	1743~1826	1801~1809	Lawyer, etc.	2	Dem-Rep	Virginia	College of William and Mary
4	James Madison	1751~1836	1809~1817	Lawyer	2	Dem-Rep	Virginia	College of New Jersey
5	James Monroe	1758~1831	1817~1825	Lawyer	2	Dem-Rep	Virginia	College of William and Mary
6	John Quincy Adams	1767~1848	1825~1829	Lawyer, etc.	1	Dem-Rep	Massachusetts	Harvard University
7	Andrew Jackson	1767~1845	1829~1837	Lawyer	2	Democratic	South Carolina	Self-studied
8	Martin Van Buren	1782~1862	1837~1841	Lawyer	1	Democratic	New York	Self-studied
9	William Harrison	1773~1841	1841~1841	Soldier	1	Whig	Virginia	Hampden-Sydney College
10	John Tyler	1790~1862	1841~1845	Lawyer	1	Whig	Virginia	College of William and Mary
11	James K. Polk	1795~1849	1845~1849	Lawyer	1	Democratic	North Carolina	University of North Carolina
12	Zachary Taylor	1784~1850	1849~1850	Soldier	1	Whig	Virginia	Self-studied
13	Millard Fillmore	1800~1874	1850~1853	Lawyer	1	Whig	New York	Self-studied
14	Franklin Pierce	1804~1869	1853~1857	Lawyer	1	Democratic	New Hampshire	Bowdoin College
15	James Buchanan	1791~1868	1857~1861	Lawyer	1	Democratic	Pennsylvania	Dickinson College
16	Abraham Lincoln	1809~1865	1861~1865	Lawyer	2	Republican	Kentucky	Self-studied
17	Andrew Johnson	1808~1875	1865~1869	Tailor	1	Democratic	North Carolina	Self-studied
18	Ulysses S. Grant	1822~1885	1869~1877	Soldier	2	Republican	Ohio	U.S. Military Academy
19	Rutherford B. Hayes	1822~1893	1877~1881	Lawyer	1	Republican	Ohio	Kenyon College
20	James A. Garfield	1831~1881	1881~1881	Scholar, etc.	1	Republican	Ohio	Williams College
21	Chester A. Arthur	1829~1886	1881~1885	Lawyer	1	Republican	Vermont	Union College
22	Grover Cleveland	1837~1908	1885~1889	Lawyer	1	Democratic	New Jersey	Self-studied
23	Benjamin Harrison	1833~1901	1889~1893	Lawyer	1	Republican	Ohio	Miami University
24	Grover Cleveland	1837~1908	1893~1897	Lawyer	1	Democratic	New Jersey	Self-studied
25	William McKinley	1843~1901	1897~1901	Lawyer	1	Republican	Ohio	Allegheny College
26	Theodore Roosevelt	1858~1919	1901~1909	Scholar, etc.	2	Republican	New York	Harvard University
27	William Howard Taft	1857~1930	1909~1913	Bureaucrat	1	Republican	Ohio	Yale University
28	Woodrow Wilson	1856~1924	1913~1921	Scholar, etc	2	Democratic	Virginia	Princeton University
29	Warren Harding	1865~1923	1921~1923	Newspaper publisher	1	Republican	Ohio	Ohio Central College
30	Calvin Coolidge	1872~1933	1923~1929	Lawyer	2	Republican	Vermont	Amherst College
31	Herbert Hoover	1874~1964	1929~1933	Mining engineer	1	Republican	Iowa	Stanford University
32	Franklin D. Roosevelt	1882~1945	1933~1945	Lawyer	4	Democratic	New York	Harvard University
33	Harry S. Truman	1884~1972	1945~1953	Judge	2	Democratic	Missouri	Kansas City Law School
34	Dwight D. Eisenhower	1890~1969	1953~1961	Soldier	2	Republican	Texas	U.S. Military Academy
35	John F. Kennedy	1917~1963	1961~1963	Politician	1	Democratic	Massachusetts	Harvard University
36	Lyndon B. Johnson	1908~1973	1963~1969	Teacher, etc.	2	Democratic	Texas	Texas State University
37	Richard Nixon	1913~1994	1969~1974	Lawyer	2	Republican	California	Duke University
38	Gerald Ford	1913~2006	1974~1977	Lawyer	1	Republican	Nebraska	University of Michigan
39	Jimmy Carter	1924~	1977~1981	Farm owner	1	Democratic	Georgia	U.S. Naval Academy
40	Ronald Reagan	1911~2004	1981~1989	Actor	2	Republican	Illinois	Eureka College
41	George H. W. Bush	1924~	1989~1993	Businessman	1	Republican	Massachusetts	Yale University
42	Bill Clinton	1946~	1993~2001	Lawyer	2	Democratic	Arkansas	Yale University
43	George W. Bush	1946~	2001~	Businessman	2	Republican	Connecticut	Yale University

Died in office　Assassinated in office　Resigned from office　Succeeded to presidency

abandon VERB

If you abandon a place, thing, or person, you leave the place, thing, or person permanently or for a long time.

EX However, the public was disgusted with the corruption of the Grant administration, and voters had abandoned the Republican Party. (122)

abide by PHRASAL VERB

If you abide by a law, agreement, or decision, you do what it says you should do.

EX I will abide by the Constitution. (182)

abolish VERB

If someone in authority abolishes a system or practice, he formally puts an end to it.

EX Such an inhumane system should be abolished right away! (92)

accountable ADJ

If you are accountable to someone for something that you do, you are responsible for it and must be prepared to justify your actions to that person.

EX In these difficult times, cabinet members placed all the responsibilities on the President for matters for which they may be held accountable. (117)

accumulate VERB

When you accumulate things or when they accumulate, they collect or are gathered over a period of time.

EX During the Civil War, he also accumulated military experience by volunteering for service in the army. (128)

acquisition N-COUNT

If you make an acquisition, you buy or obtain something, often to add to things that you already have.

EX But his greatest achievement was the acquisition of Florida and the Pacific Northwest from Spain. (44)

addictive ADJ

If something is addictive, you cannot stop taking or doing it.

EX They say politics is addictive like drugs…Once you get a taste of it, there's no way out! (91)

administration N-UNCOUNT

Administration is the range of activities connected with organizing and supervising the way that an organization or institution functions.

EX The Johnson administration confronted very difficult problems, problems that really needed to be resolved. (110)

affiliation N-VAR

If one group has an affiliation with another group, it has a close or official connection with it.

EX Party affiliation doesn't matter! (187)

ailment N-COUNT

An ailment is an illness, especially one that is not very serious.

EX When he was a child, he suffered from a host of health problems such as nearsightedness and asthma, so he came to enjoy sports, nature and history to overcome his ailments. (157)

annex VERB

If a country annexes another country or an area of land, it seizes it and takes control of it.

EX First, America would annex the huge territory of Texas. (74)

annihilate VERB

To annihilate something means to destroy it completely.

EX He was overshadowed by the general who became an American hero for annihilating the

British forces at the Battle of New Orleans in January 1815. (32)

apathetic ADJ
An apathetic person does not seem to be interested in or enthusiastic about doing anything.

EX Pouring oil on fire, Harriet Beecher Stow published a novel entitled 'Uncle Tom's Cabin,' prompting even Northerners who had been apathetic to slavery to actively oppose it. (92)

appropriate ADJ
Something that is appropriate is suitable or acceptable for a particular situation.

EX Ultimately, he's seen as a leader who was competent but not appropriate for times of crisis. (191)

ardent ADJ
Ardent is used to describe someone who has extremely strong feelings about something or someone.

EX This was because Jefferson was a central leader of the Anti-federalist camp, whereas Adams was an ardent Federalist. (20)

assert VERB
If someone asserts a fact or belief, they state it firmly.

EX Thus, peace (and democracy) that he so vigorously asserted to the world... (172)

authorize VERB
If someone in a position of authority authorizes something, he gives his official permission for it to happen.

EX Ford was forced to authorize an increase in taxes to pay off New York City's debt. (232)

bachelor N-COUNT
A bachelor is a man who is not married.

EX By the time he became President, Jefferson had been a bachelor for nearly 20 years. (29)

be prone to ADJ
To be prone to something, usually something bad, means to have a tendency to be affected by it or to do it.

EX According to Reeves, Arthur was sentimental and romantic and prone to tears. (136)

bewildered ADJ
A bewildered person is completely puzzled or confused.

EX He argued for 'diplomacy with strength' to Americans upset by the bewildered Carter who had emphasized morality in politics. (241)

biased ADJ
If someone is biased, they prefer one group of people to another, and behave unfairly as a result. You can also say that a process or system is biased.

EX Thus, resistance arose in the Democratic Party, not to mention fierce opposition in the North due to Buchanan's biased support of the Southern position. (98)

bid N-COUNT
A bid for something or a bid to do something is an attempt to obtain it or do it.

EX Polk failed in his bid to obtain nomination as the presidential candidate for the Democratic Party. (77)

blossom VERB
If someone or something blossoms, they develop good, attractive, or successful qualities.

EX Thereafter, his political career blossomed. (194)

bureaucrats N-COUNT

Bureaucrats are officials who work in a large administrative system. You can refer to officials as bureaucrats especially if you disapprove of them because they seem to follow rules and procedures too strictly.

EX Why argue all the time with bureaucrats who are outnumbered by my slaves? (14)

calamity N-VAR

A calamity is an event that causes a great deal of damage, destruction, or personal distress.

EX It was the then-largest calamity that ever occurred to humankind. (170)

candidate N-COUNT

A candidate is someone who is being considered for a position like, for example, someone who is running in an election or applying for a job.

EX This decision threw the Republican Party into a panic because the party hadn't sought out another candidate. (184)

capable ADJ

If a person is capable of doing something, he has the ability to do it.

EX Regardless of nationality, the people wish to have a heroic leader capable of wisely leading the nation in times of crisis. (103)

clique N-COUNT

If you describe a group of people as a clique, you mean that they spend a lot of time together and seem unfriendly towards people who are not in the group.

EX Jackson, however, left a disturbing legacy in the form of 'clique politics,' which became deeply rooted in American politics. (51)

coffin N-COUNT

A coffin is a box in which a dead body is buried or cremated.

EX On the train ride back to his hometown, Wilson all along sat next to his wife's coffin. (173)

coincidence N-VAR

A coincidence is when two or more similar or related events occur at the same time by chance and without any planning.

EX Their resemblances are so remarkable to just call them a coincidence. So what are those similarities that have become a favorite topic of gossipers? (214)

colleague N-COUNT

Your colleagues are the people you work with, especially in a professional job.

EX When he returned, his colleagues referred to him as the Vice President. (67)

companion N-COUNT

A companion is someone who you spend time with or who you are travelling with.

EX Although Pierce was a kind and good person, and a skilled orator and pleasant drinking companion, history records him as an incompetent President who was incapable of stopping the massive wave striking in the direction of the Civil War. (90)

competitive ADJ

Competitive is used to describe situations or activities in which people or firms compete with each other.

EX So his sons were groomed for high public office and raised in a competitive environment. (211)

compromise N-VAR

A compromise is a situation in which people accept something slightly different from what they really want, because of circumstances or because they are considering the wishes of other people.

EX It became clear that the problems between the North and the South could not be resolved by dialogue and compromise. (106)

concede VERB
If you concede something, you admit, often unwillingly, that it is true or correct.

EX I'm never going to concede the candidacy! (176)

conceive VERB
If you conceive a plan or idea, you think of it and work out how it can be done.

EX The basic principle of checks and balances between these three branches was conceived by James Madison. (31)

confront VERB
If you confront a difficult situation or issue, you accept the fact that it exists and try to deal with it.

EX After the election was over, Harrison confronted a serious problem. (64)

consecutive ADJ
Consecutive periods of time or events happen one after the other without interruption.

EX He was the last President from among the four Presidents from Virginia who served two consecutive terms. (36)

consequence N-COUNT
The consequences of something are the results or effects of it.

EX He left a message to the future generation on what are the consequences of taking pains to distort reality and failing to accurately assess the situation. (186)

conservative ADJ
Someone who is conservative tends to preserve established traditions or oppose any changes to them.

EX Jackson was criticized over this matter again

and again from the then conservative American society. (49)

considerable ADJ
Considerable means great in amount or degree.

EX His father was a Presbyterian minister with considerable oratorical skills. (168)

consolation prize N-COUNT
A consolation prize is a small prize which is given to a person who fails to win a competition.

EX In the past, the vice presidency was usually the consolation prize awarded to the faction that lost the fight for supremacy in the party. (132)

controversial ADJ
If you describe something or someone as controversial, that thing or person is the subject of intense public argument, disagreement, or disapproval.

EX Franklin Delano Roosevelt (FDR) is the most controversial President among all U.S. Presidents. (192)

corrupt ADJ
Someone who is corrupt behaves in a way that is morally wrong, especially by doing dishonest or illegal things in return for money or power.

EX Not to mention that he also runs a corrupt administration that installed a billiards table in the White House with public funds! (47)

crude ADJ
A crude person lacks culture, refinement, tact, etc.

EX True to his countryside log cabin origin, Lincoln was very crude in appearance and manner. (107)

D

dedicate VERB
If you dedicate yourself to something, you commit yourself to a particular course of thought or action.

EX After leaving the presidency, he worked for a philanthropic organization dedicated to the improvement of education of blacks and whites...(125)

defeat VERB
If you defeat someone, you win a victory over that person in a battle, game, or contest.

EX FDR defeated the extremely unpopular Hoover and was elected as the thirty-second President. He easily won re-election four years later. (195)

descendant N-COUNT
Someone's descendants are the people in later generations who are related to him.

EX As you can tell by his name, he was the descendant of a Dutch immigrant. (55)

devote VERB
If you devote yourself, your time, or your energy to something, you spend all or most of your time or energy on it.

EX I will devote all my efforts to the resolution of the issue of slavery and mediate North-South conflicts and disputes. (96)

diametrically ADV
If you say that two things are diametrically opposed, you are emphasizing that they are completely different from each other.

EX The two men held diametrically opposite political ideologies. (20)

dignity N-UNCOUNT
If someone behaves or moves with dignity, he is calm, controlled, and admirable.

EX He was one of the most well educated Presidents in U.S. history, who sought dignity as an intellectual, not popularity with the people. (42)

diplomat N-COUNT
A diplomat is a senior official who discusses affairs with another country on behalf of his own country, usually working as a member of an embassy.

EX He was a plantation owner and lawyer, diplomat and architect and scientist and philosopher. (25)

discard VERB
If you discard something, you get rid of it because you no longer want it or need it.

EX He changed his name to Woodrow Wilson by discarding the name 'Thomas' after graduating from Princeton University. (168)

discharge VERB
When someone is discharged from the hospital, prison, or one of the armed services, he is officially allowed to leave, or told that he must leave.

EX This led to heavy drinking and alcoholism, which caused him to become dishonorably discharged in 1854. (115)

disclose VERB
If you disclose new or secret information, you tell people about it.

EX But on June 23, 1973, tape-recorded statements made by him in his office were disclosed. (226)

discord N-UNCOUNT
Discord is disagreement and argument between people.

EX Due to the discord and conflict between Taft and Teddy that fractured the Republican Party, Wilson, almost a newcomer to politics, easily won election to the presidency. (169)

dismal ADJ
Something that is dismal is bad in a sad or depressing way.

EX His inauguration day is said to have been a very cold and dismal day in late winter, with even rain pouring on. (65)

display   VERB
If you display something that you want people to see, you put it in a particular place, so that people can see it easily. It also means to disclose or reveal.

EX There were no significant events that required him to display his leadership skills. (46)

disposition   N-COUNT
Someone's disposition is the way that he tends to behave or feel.

EX Pierce's pro-Southern disposition and policies designed to appease the South turned out to be like pouring oil on fire. (95)

distinguished   ADJ
If you describe a person or his work as distinguished, you mean that he has been very successful in his career and has a good reputation.

EX Second, he was one of the most distinguished soldiers in U.S. history. (60)

divorce   VERB
Divorce means the legal and formal dissolution of a marriage.

EX He was also the first divorced President. (240)

doctorate   N-COUNT
A doctorate is the highest degree awarded by a university.

EX In contrast, when Andrew Jackson received an honorary doctorate from Harvard University, it is said that he shouted out the few Latin words he had memorized. (89)

dominate   VERB
To dominate a situation means to be the most powerful or important person or thing in it.

EX In the early 1920s when he served as Governor, America was dominated by violent labor movements with strikes occurring incessantly. (181)

draft   N-COUNT
Someone who evades the draft avoids compulsory military service.

EX Even though he didn't violate the law, it was a serious moral flaw for a presidential candidate to have evaded the draft. (140)

dutiful   ADJ
If you say that someone is dutiful, you mean that he does everything that he is expected to do.

EX As a dutiful and courageous soldier, Taylor served with great distinction during the War of 1812 against Britain. (80)

embarrass   VERB
If something or someone embarrasses you, you feel shy or ashamed.

EX What most disconcerted the people around him was the outrageous jokes he would make that didn't suit the occasion and would embarrass those around him. (107)

emerge   VERB
If someone or something emerges as a particular thing, they become recognized as that thing.

EX Andrew Jackson, who had emerged as a national hero from the war with Britain, also had ambitions to become President. (45)

emigrate   VERB
If you emigrate, you leave your own country to live in another country.

EX Eisenhower was one of the seven sons of a German-Swiss protestant family that emigrated to America in escape from warring Europe.

(205)

emissary N-COUNT
An emissary is a representative sent by one government or leader to another.

EX So Adams sent three emissaries to France, which was at war with Britain. (21)

encounter VERB
If you encounter problems or difficulties, you experience them.

EX From the very start, the Harding administration encountered difficulties over personnel problems. (178)

end up PHRASAL VERB
If you end up doing something or end up in a particular state, you do that thing or get into that state even though you did not originally intend to.

EX Garfield ended up compromising with these persons. (129)

engulf VERB
If one thing engulfs another, it completely covers or hides it, often in a sudden and unexpected way.

EX Nationalism engulfed the Americans, who had completely freed themselves from British influence. (35)

enormous ADJ
Something that is enormous is extremely large in size or amount.

EX The entire country fell into chaos over the enormous losses from the war. (32)

entrust VERB
If you entrust something important to someone, you give over that thing to another for care, protection, or performance.

EX Within just a month, the American public, who had received the oldest President, entrusted the government into the hands of the youngest

President. (69)

equilibrium N-VAR
Equilibrium is a balance between several different influences or aspects of a situation.

EX This was because back in the Monroe era, slave states and free states were maintaining a 50:50 equilibrium in Congress. (40)

eventually ADV
Eventually means in the end, especially after a lot of delays, problems, or arguments.

EX Eventually, the war turned out to be Lincoln's most significant achievement. (106)

extraordinary ADJ
If you describe something or someone as extraordinary, you mean that it or he has some extremely good or special quality.

EX Around 1985, Bush was nothing but a drunkard; there was nothing extraordinary about him. (262)

fatal ADJ
A fatal accident or illness causes someone's death.

EX Hayes'diary remains to this day, including the diary entries he kept when he was almost fatally wounded at the Battle of South Mountain in 1862. (125)

fierce ADJ
A fierce animal or person is very aggressive or angry.

EX This kind of one-sided pro-Southern disposition brought about fierce Northern resistance and caused Buchanan to lose the presidential nomination for re-election. (99)

flexible ADJ
Something or someone that is flexible is able

to change easily and adapt to different conditions and circumstances as they occur.

EX If Wilson had seen the world from a more flexible perspective and compromised with Congress and joined the League of Nations, Congress will agree to U.S. entry into the League of Nations! (173)

fluent ADJ

Someone who is fluent in a particular language, can speak the language easily and correctly. You can also say that someone speaks fluent French, Chinese, or some other language.

EX He was also fluent in Chinese so that he spoke in Mandarin with his wife to prevent eavesdroppers from listening into their discussions on sensitive matters. (187)

fugitive ADJ

Trying to avoid being caught by the police. Also, a fugitive is a person who flees or has fled from danger, justice, etc.

EX As soon as he became President, Fillmore accepted the Compromise of 1850, which made it very easy for Southerners to capture fugitive slaves. (87)

fulfill VERB

If you fulfill something such as a promise, dream, or hope, you do what you said or hoped you would do.

EX Hoover promised to fulfill their expectations with 'affluence.' (188)

fuss N-SING

Fuss is anxious or excited behaviour which serves no useful purpose.

EX Its no big deal, so don't make such a big fuss! (189)

governor N-COUNT

In some systems of government, a governor is a person who is in charge of the political administration of a region or state.

EX In 1928,... FDR was elected as Governor of New York. (195)

guarantee VERB

If one thing guarantees another, the first is certain to cause the second thing to happen. It also means a pledge or assurance.

EX Under Jefferson's leadership, the Bill of Rights, which guaranteed state freedom and rights, was added as amendments to the Constitution. (26)

hesitate VERB

If you hesitate, you do not speak or act for a short time, usually because you are uncertain, embarrassed, or worried about what you are going to say or do.

EX If the Soviet ships carrying missiles cross this line, we won't hesitate to go to World War III! (213)

humble ADJ

A humble person is low in condition, rank or position.

EX Unlike most other U.S. Presidents, Fillmore came from poor and humble origins. (85)

ignorance N-UNCOUNT

Ignorance of something is lack of knowledge about it.

EX But as President, Coolidge's big weakness was his ignorance about the economy. (183)

imminent ADJ

If you say that something is imminent, especially something unpleasant, you mean it is almost certain to happen very soon.

EX Over slavery, division and war between the North and the South became imminent. (71)

impeach VERB

If a court or a group in authority impeaches a president or other senior official, it charges them with committing a crime which makes them unfit for office.

EX Congress prepared to impeach the President. (227)

improvement N-VAR

If there is an improvement in something, it becomes better. If you make improvements to something, you make it better.

EX In particular, ever since the Civil War, the Johnson era saw the greatest improvement in civil rights issues, such as those relating to African-Americans. (217)

inauguration NOUN

The action of inaugurating; formal induction, institution, or ushering in, with auspicious ceremonies.

EX He didn't even attend Jefferson's inauguration. (22)

incumbent N-COUNT

An incumbent is someone who holds an official post at a particular time.

EX Fall became the first incumbent cabinet officer to become arrested for abuse of authority. (182)

indecisive ADJ

If you say that someone is indecisive, you mean that they find it very difficult to make decisions.

EX The indecisive and wait-and-see attitude of the Van Buren government caused its approval rating to plunge to rock bottom. (58)

inform VERB

If you inform someone of something, you tell them about it.

EX Coolidge's father woke his son up to inform him that he had become President. (182)

infringement N-VAR

An infringement of a law or rule is the act of breaking it or disobeying it.

EX This is clearly an infringement of state rights, and we shall consider secession from the Union! (82)

inherit VERB

If you inherit something such as a property, task, problem, or attitude, you get it from the people who used to have it.

EX Washington returned to the Mount Vernon plantation he had inherited from his parents. (13)

insignificant ADJ

Something that is insignificant is unimportant, especially because it is very small.

EX As a newborn nation, America was insignificant and weak. (20)

instigate VERB

Someone who instigates, urges or incites people to some action.

EX I will not instigate the people with shallow populism. (47)

intervene VERB

If you intervene in a situation, you become involved in it and try to change it.

EX More than any other President in U.S. history, Wilson frequently utilized military force to intervene in the affairs of other countries. (172)

irrelevant ADJ

If you describe something such as a fact or remark as irrelevant, you mean that it is not connected with what you are discussing or dealing with.

EX From Adams, we discover that political failures are irrelevant when evaluating a true leader. (23)

irritate VERB

If something irritates you, it keeps annoying you.

EX I'm irritated and bored by doing the same things every day! (194)

justifiable ADJ

An action, situation, emotion, or idea that is justifiable is acceptable or correct because there is a good reason for it.

EX "If it is deemed that Spanish ownership of the Cuban island constitutes a threat to U.S. peace and independence, it shall be justifiable for the U.S. to take Cuba by force!" (94)

lack VERB

If you say that someone or something lacks a particular quality or that a particular quality is lacking in them, you mean that they do not have any or enough of it.

EX With seven children, he was a powerful politician who lacked the financial means. (128)

ladder N-COUNT

A ladder is a piece of equipment used for climbing up something or down from something. It also figuratively means anything by means of which a person climbs or rises.

EX Helped by his family background, Pierce made his debut in Washington society and rapidly ascended the political ladder. (91)

lament VERB

If you lament something, you express your sadness, regret, or disappointment about it.

EX Later on, General Ulysses S. Grant, the Civil War hero, is also said to have lamented what America did to Mexico. (76)

landslide N-COUNT

A landslide is a victory in an election in which a person or political party gets far more votes or seats than their opponents.

EX And surprisingly, he won in a landslide. (176)

launch VERB

To launch a rocket, missile, or satellite means to send it into the air or into space.

EX On October 4, 1957, the Soviet Union successfully launched Sputnik, the first artificial satellite in history, which hurt U.S. prestige. (207)

legacy N-COUNT

A legacy of an event or period of history is something which is a direct result of it and which continues to exist after it is over.

EX Thus, Lincoln's greatest legacies are the preservation of the Union and the abolishment of slavery. (104)

literacy N-UNCOUNT

Literacy is the ability to read and write.

EX Johnson opened his eyes to the world after his wife Eliza tutored him to improve his literacy and imparted much knowledge to him. (109)

loyalty N-UNCOUNT

Loyalty is the quality of staying firm in your friendship or support for someone or something.

EX The party highly regarded his undying loyalty to the party. (92)

negotiate VERB

If people negotiate with each other or negotiate an agreement, they talk about a problem or a situation such as a business arrangement in order to solve the problem or complete the arrangement.

EX He refused to negotiate with the enemy unless the enemy immediately and unconditionally surrendered. (116)

neutral ADJ

If a person or country adopts a neutral position or remains neutral, they do not support anyone in a disagreement, war, or contest.

EX He was not the type of impartial and neutral leader that America needed in the chaotic 1850s. (101)

nevertheless ADV

You use nevertheless when saying something that contrasts with what has just been said.

EX He failed just like his father! Nevertheless, JQA was a 'prepared President' and the recipient of a 'presidential education' from his childhood days. (42)

nominate VERB

If someone is nominated for a job or position, his name is formally suggested as a candidate for it.

EX In 1816, Monroe was finally nominated as the presidential candidate to succeed Madison. (38)

obsolete ADJ

Something that is obsolete is no longer needed because something better has been invented.

EX Another achievement of the Coolidge era was the enactment of a law that prohibited the use of war as a national policy tool... But this law

became obsolete. (184)

obtain VERB

To obtain something means to get it or achieve it.

EX Buchanan bribed the judge, among others, in his hometown Pennsylvania to obtain a favorable judgment for the South. (99)

odd ADJ

If you describe someone or something as odd, you think that he or it is strange or unusual.

EX This resulted in an odd situation where the incumbent President was without any party affiliation. (70)

ominous ADJ

If you describe something as ominous, you mean that it worries you because it makes you think that something unpleasant is going to happen.

EX But immediately after his inauguration, ominous signs showed up. (92)

opportunity N-VAR

An opportunity is a situation in which it is possible for you to do something that you want to do.

EX As a realist in economic affairs, he also viewed the war as an opportunity for economic development. (154)

overcome VERB

If you overcome a problem or a feeling, you successfully deal with it and control it.

EX Garfield tried to overcome poverty by leaving home at the age of 16 and working as a crew on a small boat that sailed up and down a canal, a job he held for six weeks. (127)

overweight ADJ

Someone who is overweight weighs more than is considered healthy or attractive.

EX Being overweight, Arthur suffered from a number of diet-related diseases. (135)

patriotic ADJ

Someone who is patriotic loves his country and feels very loyal towards it.

EX At that time, whether or not it was on his own volition, a politician must have served in the war to be considered as a 'patriotic' politician. (140)

pave VERB

If a road or an area of ground has been paved, it has been covered with flat blocks of stone or concrete, so that it is suitable for walking or driving on. It also means to prepare the way for or facilitate the introduction of something.

EX His honest and diligent personality and thorough sense of responsibility eventually paved the way for his election as a U.S. Senator in 1934. (199)

peculiar ADJ

If you describe someone or something as peculiar, you think that they are strange or unusual, sometimes in an unpleasant way. Peculiar also refers to something that is unique.

EX Martin Van Buren is peculiar in that his political skills and the political significance of his work command more weight than his political achievements. (54)

perpetual ADJ

A perpetual feeling, state, or quality is one that never ends or changes.

EX Lincoln surpasses these three men in the rankings because he managed to preserve the Union that was on the brink of perpetual division by waging a war that required enormous sacrifice. (103)

persecute VERB

If you say that someone is persecuting you, you mean that they are deliberately making your life difficult.

EX He also persecuted Indians. (29)

personality N-VAR

Your personality is your whole character and nature.

EX She had a complicated personality and wasn't very generous to her husband. (105)

pioneer VERB

Someone who pioneers a new activity, invention, or process is one of the first people to do it.

EX That we can't do! It goes against the American spirit to pioneer every aspect of one's own life! (191)

pledge N-COUNT

When someone makes a pledge, they make a serious promise that they will do something.

EX Going along with the times, Polk got elected by making a campaign pledge for 'territorial expansion' based on 'Manifest Destiny.' (73)

portray VERB

When a writer or artist portrays something, he or she writes a description or produces a painting of it.

EX Arthur was always negatively portrayed as an incompetent President. (136)

predecessor N-COUNT

Your predecessor is the person who had your job before you.

EX As with his predecessors, James Monroe was born as the son of a wealthy plantation owner in Westmoreland County, Virginia. (37)

predict VERB

If you predict an event, you say that it will happen.

EX Amazingly, Jefferson accurately predicted that a civil war would break out over slavery. (25)

pretext N-COUNT

A pretext is a reason which you pretend has caused you to do something.

EX The pretext of this statute was to prevent instigation, espionage and traitorous acts. (21)

principle N-VAR
A principle is a general belief that you have about the way you should behave, which influences your behaviour.

EX It's difficult to find another President who so thoroughly prepared himself in public office with such strong principles before entering the White House. (96)

proclaim VERB
If people proclaim something, they formally make it known to the public.

EX Domestically, Kennedy proclaimed his 'New Frontier' policies. (213)

progressive ADJ
Someone who is progressive or has progressive ideas has modern ideas about how things should be done, rather than traditional ones.

EX His progressive thinking was fiercely attacked by Christians. (28)

prominent ADJ
Something that is prominent is very noticeable or is an important part of something else.

EX He was a great leader who could inspire people with his clear judgment and prominent leadership. (13)

prosperous ADJ
Prosperous people, places, and economies are rich and successful.

EX Truman built a safer, more stable and more prosperous America. (198)

provoke VERB
If you provoke someone, you deliberately annoy them and try to make them behave aggressively.

EX If you keep provoking us, it's gonna get ugly!

(170)

reconcile VERB
If you reconcile with someone, you restore friendship or harmony.

EX Toward the end of his life, Adams reconciled with Jefferson, his long-time comrade and enemy. (23)

remarkable ADJ
Someone or something that is remarkable is unusual or special in a way that makes people notice them and be surprised or impressed.

EX But Hoover showed that remarkable ability could mean nothing if a leader blossomed in the wrong times. (186)

repeal VERB
If the government repeals a law, it officially ends it, so that it is no longer valid.

EX In particular, Jefferson worked very hard to repeal the Alien and Sedition Act, which contained unconstitutional elements. (26)

reputation N-COUNT
To have a reputation for something means to be known or remembered for it.

EX Even though he avoided conviction, Johnson not only suffered politically, but he also sustained a major blow to his reputation. (113)

resolute ADJ
If you describe someone as resolute, that person is very determined not to change his mind or not to give up a course of action.

EX Taylor won wars based on his resolute judgement and conviction, rather than strategy. (79)

resolve VERB
To resolve a problem, argument, or difficulty means to find a solution to it.

EX They lived in times during which no man could distinguish himself without resolving the North-South conflict, which could be resolved only by an extreme measure like war. (90)

responsibility   N-UNCOUNT
If you have responsibility for something or someone, or if they are your responsibility, it is your job or duty to deal with them and to make decisions relating to them.

EX Less then a year after he left office, the Great Depression engulfed the nation. For the moment, he was able to avoid responsibility. (185)

retire   VERB
When one retires, he leaves his job and usually stops working completely.

EX Franklin, I beg you to retire from politics. (91)

rhetoric   N-UNCOUNT
If you refer to speech or writing as rhetoric, you disapprove of it because it is intended to convince and impress people but may not be sincere or honest.

EX Despite all such rhetoric, America frequently invaded other countries in South America to uphold its interests. (172)

ridicule   VERB
If you ridicule someone or ridicule the ideas or beliefs of others, you make fun of them in an unkind way.

EX The people turned their backs on him and ridiculed him by punning his name. (58)

sacred   ADJ
You can describe something as sacred when it is regarded as too important to be changed or interfered with.

EX As he left the presidency, Washington issued

his famous Farewell Address, which lives on to this day as a sacred historical statement of American values. (17)

sanctions   N-PLURAL
If you impose sanctions, you impose a penalty, especially by way of discipline.

EX However, just because he imposed sanctions on capitalism, that doesn't mean TR was an anti-capitalist. (159)

sarcastically   ADV
Saying things that are the opposite of what you mean, in order to make an unkind joke or to show that you are annoyed.

EX Opponents sarcastically referred to such clique politics as the 'kitchen cabinet.' (51)

scar   N-COUNT
A scar is a mark which is left after a wound has healed.

EX What America needs is not a hero but a healer of the scars of the war! (176)

shrewd   ADJ
A shrewd person is able to understand and judge a situation quickly and to use this understanding to his own advantage.

EX The shrewd Harrison selected John Tyler, a Southerner, as his running mate and Vice Presidential candidate. (62)

significant   ADJ
A significant amount or effect is large enough to be important or affect a situation to a noticeable degree.

EX Madison and Jefferson shared the perspective that Britain was the most significant threat to America. (33)

splendid   ADJ
Something splendid is gorgeous, magnificent and sumptuous.

EX The people received him with splendid

welcoming ceremonies as if he were a king. (15)

status quo N-SING
The status quo is the state of affairs that exists at a particular time, especially in contrast to a different possible state of affairs.

EX Let's not further provoke each other. Let's just maintain the status quo. (93)

strengthen VERB
If a person or group strengthens his or its position, he or it becomes more powerful and secure, or more likely to succeed.

EX Strengthened by his high approval rating, Jackson constantly battled with Congress throughout his eight-year term. (52)

stubborn ADJ
Someone who is stubborn or who behaves in a stubborn way is determined to do what he wants and is very unwilling to change his mind.

EX He's stubborn in his ways and disregards the will of the people! (210)

suffocate VERB
If you say that you are suffocating or that something is suffocating you, you mean that you feel very uncomfortable because you are suppressed or stifled.

EX The Germans were on the verge of suffocating from excessive reparation payment obligations resulting from its defeat in World War I. (184)

suitable ADJ
Someone or something that is suitable for a particular purpose or occasion is right or acceptable for it.

EX Can't find a suitable job. (199)

summon VERB
If you summon someone, you order them to come to you.

EX Eventually, Monroe was summoned back to

America, and became estranged for good from Washington, Adams and other Federalists. (37)

symbolize VERB
If one thing symbolizes another, it is used or regarded as a symbol of it.

EX He symbolizes a youthful and strong America! (210)

sympathizer N-COUNT
The sympathizers of an organization or cause are the people who approve of it and support it.

EX 14th President Franklin Pierce 1853~1857: Northern Traitor, Southern Sympathizer (90)

synonymous ADJ
If you say that one thing is synonymous with another, you mean that the two things are very closely associated with each other so that one suggests the other or one cannot exist without the other.

EX He is synonymous with the progressive man of inquiry, contemplation and action. (29)

territory N-VAR
Territory is land which is controlled by a particular country or ruler.

EX As the size of U.S. territory continued to expand, the question of whether to maintain or repeal slavery became an increasingly serious problem. (40)

thorn in one's side PHRASE
If you describe someone or something as a thorn in your side or a thorn in your flesh, you mean that person is a continuous problem or annoyance to you.

EX Instead of assisting Adams during his four-year term, Jefferson became a thorn in his side by opposing his policies to the end. (20)

thorough ADJ
A thorough action or activity is one that is done very carefully and in a detailed way so that nothing is forgotten.
EX Naturally, Wilson received a thorough training in oratory from his father. (169)

tolerate VERB
If you tolerate a situation or person, you accept them although you do not particularly like them.
EX All of this reached a point that could no longer be tolerated by America. (20)

tragic ADJ
A tragic event or situation is extremely sad, usually because it involves death or suffering.
EX Contrary to the people's expectations and his ambition that he would become a 'great President,' Hoover became another tragic victim of the Great Depression. (187)

traitor N-COUNT
If you call someone a traitor, you mean that he has betrayed beliefs that he used to hold, or that his friends hold, by his words or actions.
EX 14th President Franklin Pierce 1853~1857: Northern Traitor, Southern Sympathizer (90)

troop N-PLURAL
Troops are soldiers, especially when they are in a large organized group doing a particular task.
EX Jefferson also sent U.S. troops to Tripoli to assist in the suppression of pirates there. (26)

tuition N-UNCOUNT
Tuition refers to the amount of money that you have to pay for being taught particular subjects, especially in a university, college, or private school.
EX Here's $17 that I saved. I want you to go to school and use this as your tuition. (127)

undertake VERB
When you undertake a task or job, you start doing it and accept responsibility for it.
EX Secretary Hoover successfully undertook relief efforts to aid Belgian refugees after World War I (187)

upright ADJ
If you are upright, you are righteous and honest.
EX He is remembered as a courageous, upright and responsible President. (139)

vast ADJ
Something that is vast is extremely large.
EX That vast plain···! America must go in the direction of a peaceful agrarian nation. (26)

versatile ADJ
If you say that a person is versatile, you approve of them because they have many different skills.
EX He's a trustworthy leader of versatile talents! (188)

veto N-UNCOUNT
Veto is the right that someone in authority has to forbid something.
EX There is probably no other President who so frequently exercised his veto power under the Constitution. (52)

wander VERB
If you wander in a place, you walk around there in a casual way, often without intending to go in any particular direction.
EX I enjoy wandering around here and there. (193)

영어로읽는 먼나라이웃나라 · **USA**